DATE DUE

OC 12 98			
NO 4 98			
DE 7 '98			
DE 6 '99			
MY 20 02			
DE 1 04			
JE 10 09			

DEMCO 38-296

FLASH POINT

FLASH POINT

The American Mass Murderer

Michael D. Kelleher

Westport, Connecticut
London

Library of Congress Cataloging-in-Publication Data

Kelleher, Michael D.
    Flash point : the American mass murderer / Michael D. Kelleher.
        p.   cm.
    Includes bibliographical references and index.
    ISBN 0–275–95925–2 (alk. paper)
    1. Mass murder—United States—Case studies.   2. Mass murderers—
    United States—Psychology—Case studies.   I. Title.
    HV6529.K45   1997
    365.15′23′0973—dc21   96–53936

British Library Cataloguing in Publication Data is available.

Library of Congress Catalog Card Number: 96–53936
ISBN: 0–275–95925–2

First published in 1997

Praeger Publishers, 88 Post Road West, Westport, CT 06881
An imprint of Greenwood Publishing Group, Inc.

Printed in the United States of America

The paper used in this book complies with the
Permanent Paper Standard issued by the National
Information Standards Organization (Z39.48–1984).

10 9 8 7 6 5 4 3 2 1

For Kerry and Katie

Contents

Illustrations

TABLES

x   Illustrations

Introduction

Politicians are perennially fond of reminding all who will listen that America has achieved a leadership position across an impressive array of human endeavors—that as a nation, we can claim preeminence in many things. What these politicians say about our national achievements is often true. Indeed, this country has attained greatness in many arenas of thought and endeavor since its inception, and particularly since the end of World War II. However, we have also plumbed the depths of our own dark nature in many other activities, such as homicide, serial killing, and mass murder. In these things, America has also attained preeminence.

We are a country that is committed to absolute freedom; as a nation, we loathe compromise. We regale in a fiercely independent citizenry; however, we are also quick to share our resources when fellow Americans are in need. We are ready to defend our values at any cost when we believe that our national security, principles, or pride are at stake. These are qualities by which Americans judge themselves and of which they can be justifiably proud. They are fundamental to our culture and remain unquestioned from generation to generation. These cultural characteristics are assets that have become indigenous to our national soul and psyche. However, despite these straightforward and unambiguous qualities, we are not a simple people with an elementary culture. We are many, we are complex, and we are often aggressive, brutal, and covert. We are a nation of composites and complexities—generally good, but with much that is hidden away and unexplored.

We are also a nation that is steeped in violence. Our citizens murder each other in alarming numbers, and often in particularly heinous and vicious ways. Sadly, violence has been the American companion to progress throughout our history, and it remains so today as we approach the new millennium. We often look toward the future with confusion and a disturbing composite of fear and optimism that is uniquely American in nature. In great measure, this is because we have attained a national level of violence that is both unprecedented and unsettling—a situation that does not bode well for the future. When we murder our own, we do not exempt the young or the old, the infirm or the innocent, the unwary or the unknowing. When we murder our own, we do so in accordance with another fundamental American tradition—we see the deed through to the end, regardless of the consequences. In this, the most heinous of human endeavors, we are leaders.

As citizens who benefit from the most technologically advanced nation in the world, we are acutely aware of our actions, accomplishments, and crimes to an extent previous generations could not have imagined possible. We are intrigued by incessant reports of our own dark exploits. With an unsurpassed knowledge and awareness of our own crimes, we often prey upon each other in diverse and brutal ways. We have attained much more than a passing knowledge of fear, mayhem, and murder. We are regularly dragged into an unthinking and pervasive distrust of our fellow citizens by media accounts of homicidal maniacs and serial killers who roam this country, slaying the innocent and unsuspecting in the most gruesome manner. In the last decade of the twentieth century, the cult of those who are fascinated by a single criminal—the serial killer—has attained the status of a national movement. In great measure, we can thank the media and the entertainment industry for perpetuating this macabre fascination. Embodied within the anxiety that must naturally accompany our awareness of the exploits of such a murderer, we also find intrigue and an uneasy sense of relief when we read of the horrors that have befallen the unacknowledged, the unlucky, or the unwary. We are simultaneously alarmed and captivated by these accounts. In the end, with the daily news relegated to the nightly trash, we accept what has happened and move routinely about our lives, fairly certain that the unspeakable horror that we have experienced in the media will not fundamentally touch our lives. We have learned to enthrone violence without understanding it. Hidden within the horror of violent crime, we find a sense of excitement and acceptability that does not demand comprehension. We have accepted violence on a national scale, and we have developed the skills to market it in a uniquely American way.

Often, we find the anticipation of the next report of a murder to be irresistible in its appeal, despite its inevitable and egregious outcome. We speculate about the nature of the perpetrator, his whereabouts, his motivation, and his next victim. We follow the frustrations of law enforcement personnel as they try to piece together the details surrounding the most inscrutable crimes of homicide. We wonder and speculate as we read accounts of forensic scientists, behaviorists, or profilers as they struggle to play catch-up with their prey. We fear for ourselves, our families, and our children. We secretly anticipate where and when the murderer will strike next and who will be his next victim. Our anticipation keeps the story alive in the media and the crime real in our minds.

From time to time, and more often today than ever before, we read reports of an exceptionally unsettling category of crime in which America has also cornered the market—mass murder. However, unlike the exploits of the serial killer, with this crime we experience no anticipation of the future and find little reason to speculate. With this felony, we experience only a brief moment of shock and horror; that is, if we learn about it at all. The crime of mass murder is merely a flash point on the pages and screens of the media. For a passing moment, the recollection of this crime may claim a brief headline; however, for the press, the story typically dies as quickly as did the victims it describes because it lacks the crucial element of anticipation. Today, mass murder has become merely a transitory moment of drama that is horrible in its consequences but fleeting in its impact to all except the victims and their loved ones. We can sit back with assurance when we read about these horrendous crimes, knowing that the danger has already passed even as we read of the gruesome details; we can take comfort in the knowledge that the crime is complete and the perpetrator has been apprehended or is dead.

This is the public nature of the crime of mass murder and the usual destiny of its perpetrator. It seems a simple thing—a fleeting crime. As reported in the media, the story of mass murder is devoid of that critical element of anticipation that is necessary to maintain anything but a momentary recognition of its true impact. For most of us, it holds little of the interest of a notorious serial killer; however, when he attacks, the mass murderer is sometimes a far more lethal and pernicious criminal. For most Americans, the flash point of mass murder passes abruptly and with no farewell; its details soon fade from the headlines and from our minds. We quickly lose the proper perspective on this crime because the media has deemed it unworthy of our continuing concern and abiding attention. It seems a simple thing; however, it is not.

The nature of this crime and how it is viewed by the American press lends a profoundly disturbing aspect to the subject. In recent years, mass murder has become a crime that is often too common to attract and retain the highly valued column-inch space of the national media unless it is of such gruesome and heinous proportions that it simply cannot be ignored. The media plays a numbers game when it deals with this crime; it is only validated in importance if the number of victims is significantly unsettling or the manner in which they died sufficiently disturbing to be unavoidable. How superficially we deal with the dark nature of our souls! How simple it has become to turn away from mass murder—a crime that has been unwittingly redefined as mere background noise in our own complex and busy lives.

The reality and the truth of mass murder are not as easily discarded as yesterday's newspaper; it is not as insignificant as a missed headline. This is a crime that plagues our nation from coast to coast and border to border. It grows increasingly virulent each year as its perpetrators feed ever more voraciously upon the innocent and the unsuspecting. Far too many of our fellow citizens die each year at the hands of the mass murderer. He strikes quickly and with explosive violence, yet like the serial killer, he, too, plans his crime and is often lethally methodical. This is a murderer who quietly moves for years along a path that must inevitably end in the death of the innocent. He moves easily among us and is seen by many; however, he is usually unrecognized until it is too late. He kills for revenge, because he hates, because he covets, or because he loves in a way that is unrecognizable and perverse. He may even kill for reasons that no one can understand or accept. He has a story to tell and a message that must be heard—a message that is always deadly and unforgiving. Unfortunately, the story of the mass murderer and his crimes is often ignored or given far too little attention by most Americans.

Crimes of mass murder are typically tales of unacceptable horror and mayhem that are repeated again and again in this country, the most successful experiment in democracy that the world has ever witnessed. However, for the majority of our citizens—those of us fortunate enough to be the mainstay of this experiment in freedom—the mass murderer is regularly dismissed as an anomaly; his crimes are usually considered freakish and exceptional. The explosive violence of the mass murderer is perceived as distant, impersonal, and unlikely to touch our lives in any meaningful way. Indeed, to many people, mass murder is a crime that is unworthy of abiding consideration or serious investigation. However, though the crime remains far from the national headlines, nothing could be further from the truth.

CHAPTER 1

The Crime and the Criminal

He threatens many that hath injured one.

Ben Jonson
Fall of Sejanus, act 2

The terms *mass murderer* and *serial killer* are often used interchangeably, and incorrectly, by Americans. These terms convey very different concepts to the criminologist or behavioral scientist, even though their distinctive characteristics are frequently lost in casual conversation. The act of mass murder describes a crime in which multiple individuals are slain by a perpetrator in the same incident, or closely related episodes of violence. On the other hand, serial killing defines a crime in which a number of individuals are slain over a protracted period of time which may range from a few months to many years. Each murder committed by the serial killer is a discrete criminal act which is followed at some later time by yet another discrete crime, even though the perpetrator's method of operation may remain constant.

The period of time during which the murderer is not criminally active is known as a *cooling-off* period. The serial killer will usually experience a cooling-off period that may last days, weeks, or even months, during which he fantasizes about his crime and plans for (or selects) his next victim. This period of quiescence is a primary element that differentiates the serial killer from other murderers who claim multiple victims.[1] On the other hand, the mass murderer typically commits his mayhem in a single incident or (rarely) in a cluster of closely related incidents in which multiple individuals are slain. If the murderer claims multiple victims at more than one location, the crime is usually referred to as a *murder spree*.

Examples of serial killers who have achieved wide notoriety for their crimes include historical characters such as Jack the Ripper, who brutally mutilated and murdered at least five women in London in the last century and contemporary killers such as John Wayne Gacy, an American who sadistically tortured and murdered dozens of boys and young men for sexual gratification. These men murdered their victims in a serial fashion, one after another, in which each killing was a discrete criminal act.[1] Notorious mass murderers, such as Charles Whitman, who shot passersby randomly from a university clock tower, and Timothy McVeigh, who, (with a coconspirator, it is alleged) murdered at least 168 adults and children by bombing a federal government building, typically slay their victims in a single incident—a discrete act or episode of sudden and extreme violence.

Although the crimes of serial murderers garner tremendous attention in the press and other media, mass murderers also account for a significant number of victims each year. Between 1976 and 1991, there were approximately 350 incidents of mass murder in the United States in which the number of victims exceeded three. These murderers claimed approximately 2,000 victims during that fifteen-year period.[2] Since 1991, the annual number of mass murders has increased, as has the number of victims slain in each incident. In recent years, there has been an average of two to three mass murders each month in this country. These crimes claim approximately 150 to 200 lives each year, excluding atrocities such as the terrorist bombing of the federal building in Oklahoma City in 1995.[3] In whatever form it takes, this heinous crime continues to plague our society, and judging by recent statistics, it will continue to do so in the coming years with even greater impact.

DEFINING MASS MURDER

The definition of when multiple homicides committed in the same incident or episode become categorized as a crime of mass murder has been debated over the years. A common definition of mass murder requires the intentional death of at least four individuals in a single incident. Another interpretation of the term reduces the number of slain victims to three for the crime to be considered mass murder. Both of these definitions are obviously arbitrary and focus exclusively on the number of victims killed. Many mass murderers injure far more victims than they kill; however, they must certainly be considered mass murderers by the obvious *intention* of their actions. For example, if an individual randomly attacks children in a school yard with an AK-47 assault rifle or indiscriminately assaults coworkers with a powerful handgun, yet only manages to kill two individuals while wounding dozens, is

---

I. See "Appendix 1: A Survey of Some Notorious American Serial Killers."

he less an intended mass murderer than the perpetrator whose aim was better or whose victims were less fortunate? Certainly he is not.

The crimes of Larry Wayne Shoemake provide an indisputable example of the meaning of the phrase, *mass murder by intention*. On April 12, 1996, this fifty-three-year-old white supremacist went to a crowded shopping center in Jackson, Mississippi, at the peak of its normal business hours. He entered a restaurant in the mall and began to indiscriminately shoot African-Americans. The panicked patrons ran from the restaurant and surrounding stores to seek shelter wherever they could, but not before one individual was killed and ten others were wounded. At the end of his shooting rampage, Shoemake set the restaurant on fire and subsequently died in the inferno (see Table 1.1). The gunman was carrying two AK-47 assault rifles, an MAC-11 assault weapon, a 12-gauge shotgun, an AR-15 assault rifle, two handguns, and hundreds of rounds of ammunition. With this incredible arsenal of weapons, he had fired off more than 100 rounds of ammunition; miraculously, he only managed to kill one victim.

Investigators later discovered that the perpetrator's home contained several handwritten notes proclaiming white supremacist views and threatening lethal violence against African-Americans. They also discovered a Nazi flag, a variety of white supremacist literature, and a copy of Adolph Hitler's *Mein Kampf*, along with over a dozen additional firearms and three, 80-pound boxes of ammunition.[4]

Table 1.1: Larry Wayne Shoemake

Perpetrator	A fifty-three-year-old white supremacist.
Incident date/location	April 12, 1996, at a shopping center in Jackson, Mississippi.
Incident category	Politics and hate.[II]
Weapons	Two AK-47 assault rifles, an MAC-11 assault rifle, a 12-gauge shotgun, an AR-15 assault rifle, two handguns, and over 100 rounds of ammunition.
Deaths/Injuries	Two killed, ten wounded.
Motivation	Racial hatred.
Disposition	Perpetrator died in an arson fire that he set at the crime scene.

By any formal categorization, this crime would not be considered mass murder because the number of victims was insufficient to warrant that designation. However, no one would doubt the intentions of this perpetrator in attacking African-Americans indiscriminately with an obvious motivation of

II. The various categories of mass murder that are used in this book are outlined later in this chapter, in the section entitled, "The Ways of Mass Murder."

pathological hatred. Clearly, this perpetrator *intended* to commit mass murder. It was only by virtue of luck and excellent emergency services in the area that the incident did not become another statistic in the number of mass murders that are recorded each year in America. The intentions of Larry Shoemake to commit mass murder were clear; his actions were both carefully planned and obviously focused.

On the other hand, some would-be murderers whose actions fail to meet the traditional criteria needed to categorize their crimes as mass murder exhibit more bizarre and unexplainable motives than those of Shoemake. Nonetheless, their intent to commit mass murder is equally obvious. For example, in 1993, Ricky Thorp proved to be an intended mass murderer whose motivations were inexplicable but whose purpose was quite clear (see Table 1.2).

Living in the small town of Bonney Lake, thirty-five miles southeast of Seattle, Thorp was known as a man who used drugs, loved guns, and could be unpredictably violent. On March 26, 1993, without any apparent motive, Thorp left his home and began to walk aimlessly down the main road in Bonney Lake. He was carrying his brother's .22-caliber semiautomatic rifle, which was loaded with a twenty-five-round clip. As he walked along the road, Thorp began to randomly shoot at every individual unlucky enough to cross his path. During his rampage, Thorp managed to fire off forty rounds, kill one person, and injure another seven individuals. He was finally stopped when he was seriously wounded by responding law enforcement officers. Thorp was never able to provide an explanation for his actions. None of his friends, neighbors, or family could shed any light on why he did what he did that day. It was simply a matter of good luck and excellent police response that denied Thorp his place in the history of categorical mass murderers.[5] However, it is clear that Ricky Thorp was a mass murderer by intent.

Table 1.2: Ricky Thorp

Perpetrator	A thirty-year-old man who used drugs and was fond of weapons.
Incident date/location	March 26, 1993, in Bonney Lake, Washington.
Incident category	Unexplained.
Weapons	A .22-caliber semiautomatic rifle with a 25-round clip.
Deaths/Injuries	One killed, seven injured.
Motivation	Unknown. It was only by luck and quick law enforcement response that Thorp did not become a mass murderer by the traditional definition of the crime.
Disposition	Thorp was seriously wounded by responding law enforcement personnel and taken into custody.

There can be no dispute that a rigid definition of the crime of mass murder is important for categorization or research purposes. However, if the goal is to understand the nature of this crime and its perpetrator, perhaps a less rigid rule would prove more helpful—a definition that embodies the *intention* of the perpetrator as being of equal importance to his accomplishment of that intention. Therefore, for the purposes of investigating the American mass murderer, a two-part definition of this crime will be used, which includes (1) the murder of at least three individuals, and (2) the demonstration of a clear intent to murder multiple individuals in a single incident or episode.

The intent to murder multiple individuals is an important element in understanding the motivations of the mass murderer, as well as an aid to defining the crime in a more meaningful way than merely counting victims. In fact, it is the intention of the perpetrator to kill others that defines the possibility of mass murder, even if the number of victims does not equate to any preordained expectation. Since our investigation into the American mass murderer tries to focus on an understanding of his actions and motivations, more emphasis will be given to the intentions of the perpetrator than to the number of victims that he claims. Without question, it can be argued that it is often quite difficult to determine the intention of an individual who resorts to murder. This is a valid argument for some incidents of mass murder, but not for the majority of them. In most incidents of mass murder, the perpetrator does make his intentions quite clear, and in some cases, he has done so for a significant period of time before he acts out his brooding, violent ideation.

THE EVOLUTION OF MASS MURDER

A disturbing aspect of the crime of mass murder is that it appears to be evolving over time. For example, in 1949, while in his twenties, Howard Unruh went on a shooting rampage in Camden, New Jersey. On the morning of September 6, 1949, Unruh walked the streets of East Camden and, in a period of twelve minutes, shot and killed thirteen individuals in what appeared to be a completely random act of violence. However, law enforcement personnel later determined that Unruh had planned his attack for more than a year before the rampage and had even compiled a detailed list of his intended victims. When he was apprehended, Unruh immediately confessed to the murders but was never prosecuted for his crimes because he was found unfit to stand trial. By the medical and legal standards of the time, Unruh was considered to be insane and therefore incapable of understanding the nature of his actions. As of today, he has been institutionalized for over forty years for his crime, suffering from a schizophrenic condition that apparently has not yielded to any form of treatment. In 1994, Howard Unruh once again claimed headlines after four decades of hospitalization. Still residing in the Trenton, New Jersey, Psychiatric Hospital, Unruh was finally allowed to have only a single attendant (rather than two attendants) accompany him on his daily walk around the hospital grounds because, at the age of seventy-three, he was no longer considered to be a significant threat to others (see Table 1.3).[6]

The case of Howard Unruh exemplifies the evolving nature of mass murder as it is understood by law enforcement personnel, the courts, and the public. Since 1949, the view of culpability for the crime of mass murder has changed significantly. It is far less likely that Howard Unruh would be found unfit to stand trial for his crimes if they occurred today than it was some fifty years ago. Today, mass murder is still a relatively rare event. However, in the 1940s, it was an even more unlikely occurrence. Five decades ago, it was the general consensus that an individual who committed any crime similar to that of Howard Unruh simply had to be insane. However, as we approach the new millennium, the American court system and juries hold a much different view of culpability because of the increasing number of mass murders that occur each year in this country. The modern mass murderer is usually not considered to be insane by today's legal standards. Rather, he is viewed as an individual whose motives are complex and whose crimes are often planned with care and precision. Such evidence of careful planning and clear motivation prompts juries to almost always reach the conclusion of sane and guilty when judging the contemporary perpetrator of mass murder.

Table 1.3: Howard Unruh

Perpetrator	A World War II veteran in his twenties at the time of the murders.
Incident date/location	September 6, 1949, in East Camden, New Jersey.
Incident category	Sane/insane. Unruh was declared unfit to stand trial for his crimes.
Weapons	Two handguns.
Deaths/Injuries	Thirteen killed.
Motivation	Unclear, but perhaps revenge. The perpetrator was considered to be insane at the time of the murders and is still confined in a psychiatric hospital.
Disposition	Unruh, suffering from schizophrenia, has been hospitalized since the crime.

Since 1986, a new perpetrator of mass murder has scarred our nation and its citizenry—the lethal employee. This criminal, who is typically a middle-age, middle-class male, has become the most common and prolific mass murderer in American history. Whereas the mass murderer of a few decades ago (like Howard Unruh) was considered to be either a deranged individual who would murder indiscriminately or a murderer of loved ones or family members who was seeking revenge, the mass murderer of the most recent decade is now recognized as a more complex and determined criminal who circulates among the American workforce. He may specifically target certain individuals for death, or he may attack those he hardly knows or does not know at all. In some incidents, he will do both. The contemporary mass murderer can be both precise and random in his actions; he may lash out against his victims with focused intent or direct his wrath in a symbolic gesture of outrage.

Acts of symbolic mass murder, such as those carried out for political motives or hate, are also evolving and often claim victims who are unrelated or unconnected to the perpetrator except in a pathologically disturbed and symbolic manner. To compound the changing nature of this crime, mass murder motivated by terrorism appears to have made significant inroads into American society—a situation that is both new and extremely foreboding to all citizens of this country.

Finally, the nature of the weapons involved in mass murder has also evolved significantly in recent years. Since their introduction in the 1980s, the availability of powerful automatic, semiautomatic, and paramilitary-style weapons has directly contributed to an increase in the number of fatalities per incident. In the past fifteen years, our nation has experienced seven of the ten worst mass murders in its history, due primarily to the use of these powerful, and sometimes illegal, weapons.[7]

PROFILING THE MASS MURDERER

Perpetrators of mass murder claim their victims for many and diverse reasons. Many murderers pursue long-standing, overwhelming desires for revenge and retribution, while others strike out against loved ones or family members in an act of distorted and perverted love. A few perpetrators are insane, and their actions are wholly beyond understanding, while a small number of crimes remain unexplained. Although most mass murderers are male adults who are typically over twenty-five years of age, in a few cases, they are adolescents, and, on rare occasions, female. The ranks and diversity of the perpetrators of this crime are increasing, as is the vehemence of their actions. Even though the crime of mass murder is generally a simple issue for law enforcement personnel because the evidence obtained at the crime scene is unambiguous and the perpetrator is known, the complex and dark motivations of the mass murderer have kept us from a satisfactory understanding of why this type of violence continues to plague our society.

A common myth surrounding the nature of the mass murderer is that he is usually insane—at least, in the common use of the term. This is an understandable belief and is based on the nature of the crime itself. The actions of a mass murderer appear to be explosive and random in nature; the killings are often incredibly brutal and grotesque, seeming to occur with little or no planning while typically ending in a final, abrupt act of extreme violence. The victims may appear to have been selected completely at random and can range in age from infants to the elderly. The crime is usually so disturbing as to leave the impression that it could only have been committed by an individual who was insane. However, most mass murderers are quite sane, at least in the legal sense, and their crimes are frequently planned in advance with considerable care and attention.

Without question, there are some incidents of mass murder that indicate the probable insanity of the perpetrator.[III] There are also incidents of mass murder that seem to yield no evidence of planning. However, truly random acts of mass murder undertaken by an individual who is legally insane are rare; they are the exception, not the rule.

The typical American mass murderer is a white male who is over the age of twenty-five years; in at least 40 percent of mass murders, the perpetrator will be in his thirties or forties.[8] He will often have no significant criminal record and may even be perceived as a caring husband and father who otherwise contributes to society in a positive, meaningful way. However, the murderer who does not fit this profile may alternatively exhibit strange or bizarre behavior to those who know him well yet still be perceived as generally innocuous and nonviolent to casual observers. In many ways, the mass murderer will usually not stand out in a crowd until he acts on the anger and hostility that are a major part of his psyche and motivation.

On occasion, the mass murderer will exhibit a long-standing behavioral history that indicates that he was an individual who was bent on violence in one form or another. James Edward Pough was just such a man. On June 18, 1990, Pough went to the General Motors Acceptance Corporation (GMAC) offices in Florida, where he had financed the purchase of a 1988 Pontiac Grand Am automobile two years earlier. In January 1990, GMAC had repossessed his car, and in March of the same year, the finance company had written to him, to demand payment of the residual balance on his loan. When Pough came to the GMAC offices three months later, he was armed with a clip-fed, .30-caliber semiautomatic rifle; a .38-caliber revolver; and a 9mm semiautomatic pistol. At the time when Pough arrived at the GMAC offices, the lobby was crowded with customers and staff; it was later estimated that there were eighty-six individuals in the office at the time of his arrival.

Immediately upon entering the offices, Pough began to randomly shoot employees and customers with his semiautomatic rifle. His targets tried to scurry for cover under desks and tables, in desperate efforts to avoid the random gunfire; however, Pough would not be deterred. He fired underneath the desks at anyone he could target, reloading his powerful weapon several times in an effort to annihilate everyone he could find. During the rampage, Pough murdered eight individuals and wounded another five before fatally shooting himself in the head. Several of his victims had been shot seven or eight times. The day before his rampage at GMAC, Pough had shot and killed two other individuals on a street near his home in Jacksonville, Florida—he had apparently been in a dispute with one of the victims about the services of a local prostitute (see Table 1.4).

III. The word *insanity* is used here in the common understanding of the term.

James Edward Pough was a man of violence throughout his adult life. He had a history of minor offenses—and of some that were not so minor. In 1968, Pough was arrested for dangerously displaying a weapon in public. In 1971, he was arrested on a charge of homicide but was never tried for the crime. Later that same year, he was found guilty of aggravated assault. Pough was known to be a man with a volatile temper who liked to settle issues with violence. He was an avid collector of powerful, paramilitary weapons; he was significantly socially isolated and hostile toward those around him. By the time he attacked the GMAC offices in 1990, Pough had a clear history of violence; however, for a variety of legal reasons, he was still able to legitimately purchase and own firearms. Those who knew Pough were not surprised that he had reacted violently, but only at the extreme nature of his crime.

Despite his egregious crimes and history of violence, James Pough was an exception to the general profile of the mass murderer. Few perpetrators of this crime exhibit such a clear and obvious history of criminal behavior. In fact, most mass murderers exhibit just the opposite behavioral history and have little or no record of violent behavior.

Table 1.4: James Edward Pough

Perpetrator	A forty-two-year-old man with a history of violence.
Incident date/location	June 18, 1990, in a commercial office in Jacksonville, Florida.
Incident category	Revenge.
Weapons	A semiautomatic rifle, a revolver, and a semiautomatic pistol.
Deaths/Injuries	Eight killed, five injured.
Motivation	Angered at the organization for repossessing his vehicle, Pough lashed out at employees and customers. He had murdered two other individuals the night before his rampage.
Disposition	Pough committed suicide at the crime scene.

Even though the vast majority of mass murderers are males who use guns, there are exceptions to this basic profile. For example, female mass murderers are rare, but they do exist. Whereas the typical male mass murderer will favor weaponry or explosives, his female counterpart may not use such traditional weapons. Instead, she may use poison, passive forms of asphyxiation (such as carbon monoxide poisoning), the administration of lethal chemicals or medications, or a mock accident (see Table 1.5).

However, even within the very small ranks of female mass murderers, there are exceptions to this general profile. The case of Sylvia Seegrist, who in 1985 randomly shot and murdered individuals in a shopping center and came to be known in the media as the "Female Rambo," demonstrates that the crime of mass murder is often replete with exceptions as to both the method of murder and the motivation of the perpetrator (see Table 1.6).

Table 1.5: Maureen Barbieri

Perpetrator	A thirty-seven-year-old mother of three young children who was under treatment for depression and had been arguing with her husband.
Incident date/location	September 19, 1996, in Hayward, California.
Incident category	Perverted love (family murder/suicide).
Weapons	The family automobile.
Deaths/Injuries	Four killed, three were children (ages eight, six, and two).
Motivation	Depressed and having argued with her husband about family issues, Barbieri put her children into the family automobile and drove it at high speed into an electrical transmission tower.
Disposition	Barbieri and her three children were killed in the ensuing crash.

Although legally sane, some mass murderers exhibit one or more psychological disorders which can range from mild to severely debilitating. Evidence of chronic or severe depression is common among perpetrators of mass murder. Individuals suffering from serious psychological deficits such as antisocial personality disorder (commonly known as *sociopaths*) and from other illnesses such as paranoid schizophrenia, are found among the ranks of mass murderers. Some mass murderers are found to be suffering from paranoia that is both extreme and debilitating. It is not unusual to find a high degree of social isolation in the background of a mass murderer, even if he or she resides with a family or other loved ones. Evidence of childhood trauma, family separation, and physical or sexual abuse is often discovered in their life histories.

It is a common misperception that mass murderers spontaneously erupt in a flash point of extreme violence that has no fundamental basis or history. On the contrary, the crime of killing multiple individuals is most often the culmination of a long period of developing frustrations, stresses, anger, and personal disappointments that ultimately become intolerable. Although a specific triggering event—an incident that prompts a culminating act of mass murder—may be apparent just before the crime is committed, the final, lethal actions of the mass murderer are typically the result of years (if not decades) of a growing inability to adequately cope with the challenges of life. Mass murderers do not spring into existence at the moment of their crime; their actions are not typically the result of a single event with which they cannot cope. The development of the mass murderer is most often a life long process that is both complex and often surprisingly covert; their life history is one that is typically filled to overflowing with anger, frustrations, unanswered challenges, and disappointments.

Table 1.6: Sylvia Seegrist

Perpetrator	A twenty-five-year-old woman with a long history of mental illness.
Incident date/location	October 30, 1985, at the Springfield Mall in Delaware County, Pennsylvania.
Incident category	Sane/insane.
Weapons	A .22-caliber semiautomatic rifle.
Deaths/Injuries	Three killed, seven injured.
Motivation	Unclear. Seegrist had a long history of severe mental illness and often vocalized threats against others.
Disposition	Sentenced to three consecutive life terms for the murders and a minimum of ten years for each of seven counts of attempted murder.

Kenneth Tornes provides an example of a mass murderer who had experienced years of chronic frustration and anger that led to extreme violence. Tornes was a thirty-two-year-old firefighter, separated from his wife, who became entangled in a long series of disputes with several battalion chiefs and supervisors over a variety of relatively insignificant job performance issues. So trivial were some of these complaints that Tornes had even been disciplined for making a typographical error on a written report that he had produced. For years, the firefighter fumed and complained about the harassment that he believed had been reserved especially for him by the battalion chiefs. One of his coworkers said of Tornes: "He was a perfect gentleman except when you got him talking about the chiefs."[9] Speaking of his supervisors, one of Tornes's coworkers said, "They put the pressure on this man. He is a victim too. When you brought up the administration [of the fire department], he would just blow up."[10] The local firefighters union president described Tornes as "a time bomb waiting to go off" because of the intense frustration and anger that he had experienced with his supervisors over so many years.[11] Tornes had also been arguing with his estranged wife for many months prior to his crime (see Table 1.7).

Early on the morning of April 25, 1996, at the family home, Tornes shot his wife through the head as she stood in the family carport. He then dragged her body inside, to the kitchen, and returned to the carport to clean up the crime scene. Tornes's neighbors called the police when they saw him washing blood away from the carport and surrounding areas. However, the police did not arrive in time to prevent Tornes from reaching his other intended victims— the battalion chiefs and supervisors whom he so deeply despised. Just before the police arrived at Tornes's home, he sped away in his car, heading for the main fire station in downtown Jackson, Mississippi.

When Tornes arrived at the fire station, he went directly to the second floor of the building that housed the offices of his supervisors. He was armed with a .45-caliber semiautomatic handgun; an MAC-11 assault rifle, and a TEC-9 automatic pistol. On his way to the battalion chiefs' offices, he passed a woman in the hallway, whom he recognized. Focusing exclusively on his intended targets, Tornes spared the woman, shouting at her, "Lady, get back, I am going to blow the place up."[12] He was very clear about who should die that morning.

Table 1.7: Kenneth Tornes

Perpetrator	A thirty-two-year-old firefighter with workplace and marital difficulties and a long history of frustration and anger on the job.
Incident date/location	April 25, 1996, at his place of work in Jackson, Mississippi.
Incident category	Revenge by a lethal employee.
Weapons	A .45-caliber semiautomatic handgun, an MAC-11 assault rifle, and a TEC-9 automatic pistol.
Deaths/Injuries	Four killed, two injured (at the crime scene); one policeman injured in a shoot-out with Tornes. The perpetrator had also murdered his wife prior to the rampage.
Motivation	Revenge against his supervisors and revenge against his estranged spouse.
Disposition	Wounded in a shoot-out with police and taken into custody.

Tornes found some of his targets in a meeting room and sought out the others in their private offices. During the ensuing rampage, Tornes encountered at least two other coworkers, whom he ordered out of the way so that their lives would be spared. Within a few moments, Kenneth Tornes had killed two captains, two district chiefs, and had critically wounded another captain and a third district chief. A deputy fire marshall at the crime scene said of Tornes: "He didn't shoot blue shirts [those who were not supervisors]. He didn't shoot the lower ranks. He picked his targets."[13]

Having finished his murderous rampage, Tornes sped off in his car, causing a number of vehicular accidents as he raced from the crime scene toward the outskirts of Jackson. After a ten-mile chase, he was forced from his automobile in a shoot-out with pursuing officers. Gunfire was exchanged and an officer was wounded, although not critically. Tornes was shot in the head, ending his morning of mayhem.

In many ways, Kenneth Tornes was the classic mass murderer, who had experienced years of anger, frustration, and disappointments that inevitably impelled him to the ultimate form of retribution. When asked why Tornes had murdered his wife and supervisors, one of his long time coworkers replied: "Apparently he was upset about his wife and he came here and did this. But he's been talking about this for years."[14]

THE WEAPONS

The weapon of choice for most mass murderers is a gun. Powerful, automatic handguns or military-style weapons capable of firing large rounds of ammunition rapidly are often used by mass murderers in an effort to inflict the maximum damage on their victims. These instruments of war, such as the .45-caliber handgun used by Tornes and assault rifles like the MAC-11, have become the weapon of choice for many mass murderers in the past decade. They are capable of causing massive and lethal wounds to their victims with a single shot. These weapons also interject an element of panic and fear in those at the crime scene—an aspect of this crime that is crucial to the mass murderer's need to demonstrate his absolute domination over his victims.

Explosives are also used by the mass murderer, although this is a relatively rare occurrence, which is often linked to terrorist or hate-group activities. These devices afford the perpetrator an opportunity for anonymity and escape from apprehension—behavior that is atypical of most mass murderers, who frequently give little or no thought to their apprehension or, at times, even their own survival. In this form of the crime, the use of explosives also permits a high degree of depersonalization of the victims, who may not be viewed as individuals but rather as symbolic representatives of groups targeted by the perpetrator for revenge. Also unusual (but not without precedent) is the use of a weapon that requires intimate contact with the victims, such as a stabbing or hacking weapon. Weapons that require intimate contact with the victim are sometimes linked to crimes of sexual homicide or family slayings in which multiple individuals are murdered.

Whereas the serial killer will typically slay his victims in a highly personal manner that requires intimate interaction with the victim (such as stabbing or strangulation), the mass murderer generally wishes to distance himself from his victims in their final moments of life—to depersonalize them, while simultaneously ensuring that he can still complete his heinous mission.[IV] Using a handgun or powerful military-style weapon allows the mass murderer to both exercise a high degree of control over his victims and to attack in a sudden, explosive manner that is designed to underscore the maximum impact of his actions to those at the scene.

IV. Exceptions to this are perpetrators who commit sexual homicide and (generally) those who murder family members. These individuals typically personalize their crimes to a significant extent.

PROFILING AND PREDICTION

It is virtually impossible to predict who will become a mass murderer, how they will attack their victims, when they will strike, or the weapons that they will employ. Reviewing the case histories of these criminals is revealing, but it can also be misleading if assumptions are drawn too readily from what is learned about the apparent motivations or behavior of a single mass murderer. It is a fairly simple process to analyze the actions of a mass murderer after he has committed his crime. The motivations and imperatives that drove him to lethal action are sometimes quite clear—in hindsight. However, the reality of this crime is that it represents a rare and extraordinary response to the same life challenges that confront millions of other Americans who never turn to violence or homicide. In this sense, despite the numbers of mass murderers and their victim count, we can be thankful that the overwhelming majority of Americans are able to cope with the complexities of the late twentieth century in a nonviolent, productive way.

The art of profiling criminals through forensics and the behavioral sciences has become fashionable in recent years. Without question, it is a valuable addition to the arsenal of law enforcement techniques. However, it is more art than science. Profiling cannot predict the future; it can only examine possibilities derived from an incident that has already occurred. Therefore, despite the fact that one can develop a general profile of the American mass murderer, it serves more as a point of learning and interest than a tool. We cannot predict mass murder today, and we will likely never be able to do so with any degree of meaningful success. The best that we can hope for is to better understand the crime, its perpetrator, and his motivations in an effort to develop strategies that may eventually prove to be the basis for positive intervention for those individuals with a high potential for turning to violence.

MOTIVATIONS AND IMPERATIVES

Even though the mass murderer typically strikes with a sudden viciousness that may appear spontaneous, he has usually tread the path that leads to homicide for years, or even decades. Most mass murderers have endured long and complex periods of many disappointments, feelings of inadequacy or loss of control, rejection, social isolation, and significant frustration. Years or decades of despair, hostility, and anger are sometimes apparent in the individual's behavior or speech long before the perpetrator finally commits himself to an act of lethal violence. These individuals find themselves unable to cope with the stressors of their lives and will engage (sometimes for years) in fantasy and ideation that is centered on themes of revenge and retribution. The mass murderer is often obsessed with what he perceives to be a continuing series of life failures and a lack of control that he typically attributes to others. Even when he clearly understands his own role in these failures, the individual will sometimes involve others in a twisted and symbolic fantasy of culpability that demands the ultimate revenge.

Unlike the common belief that a single, intolerable triggering event is the sole motivating factor for mass murder, the perpetrator of this crime has usually suffered a significant period, or many recurring periods, of frustration and disappointment which cumulatively impels him to murder. Even though a single triggering event may be the apparent final motivation for mass murder, a closer examination of the life experiences of the perpetrator will usually indicate a lengthy history of failing to cope with setbacks and disappointments.

Significantly, most mass murderers exhibit an obsession with issues of control. They are frequently overwhelmed by the need to control others, even if doing so is clearly unwise or impossible. Ultimately, they discover that their obsession to control is futile, and rather than reconsidering their pathological need for domination, perpetrators will focus on others, who they blame for this inadequacy. The path that leads to this violent crime is not often short or simple; it is typically complex, covert, and riddled with the murderer's sense of failure to achieve control over many aspects of his life.

A significant burden of disappointments and frustration, especially when experienced over an extended number of years or decades, causes the potential mass murderer to develop deep and abiding resentments upon which he will incessantly dwell. Even at an early stage in this evolutionary process, he will frequently engage in fantasies of retribution and ideation of revenge, which may include the preliminary planning for how he can make good on his growing passion for retribution. Over time, and with a continuing obsession about his frustrations and failures, these fantasies of revenge begin to take shape and become a feasible option to the potential murderer. Nonviolent alternatives eventually become unsatisfactory, and as the individual encounters further failures, violence takes on a more reasonable, and perhaps inevitable, veneer. At this point, many mass murderers have already formulated a relatively detailed plan of violence; in turn, this plan becomes an overwhelming obsession unto itself. Without intervention or a significant change in life circumstances, the potential murderer can now be suddenly impelled to act out his violent fantasies through the experience of an ultimate, intolerable triggering event.

It is important to recognize imperatives other than anger, frustration, and a sense of revenge that are also integral to the crimes of the American mass murderer. Many, if not most, of these individuals will have suffered some form of significant rejection in their lives—rejection or abandonment that often began at a young age. They will frequently have been confronted with a painful inability to achieve acceptance among their peers, associates, friends, or loved ones; in many instances, this sense of rejection will have been apparent in their lives since early childhood. In other cases, such as that of a spurned lover, an incident of rejection will have become so traumatizing and intolerable that the perpetrator lashes out in an explosion of violence in order to satisfy a compelling sense of revenge and retribution that was irresistible. In either scenario, it is not uncommon to discover a series of rejection experiences in the history of a mass murderer, with each experience becoming more intolerable.

The cumulative effect of these experiences can eventually lead to a violent or lethal reaction. Rejection and a sense of loss of control are intimately related to each other; and both are crucial elements in the evolutionary development of the mass murderer.

Another prevalent feature in the background of many mass murders is evidence of significant social isolation. Many perpetrators have experienced chronic social isolation for most of their lives, while others became traumatized by a more recent, but unexpected and intolerable, isolation from friends or loved ones. Whether the evidence of social isolation extends throughout an individual's life or the isolation was experienced as a series of events within a relatively short time preceding the crime, this is a contributing factor to lethal violence and is quite common in the background of a mass murderer. Even those individuals who are surrounded by family or loved ones are often socially isolated, at least in a psychological sense. In some instances, the potentially violent individual has experienced a deteriorating relationship with those close to him and is unable to enjoy a reliable and meaningful support network in times of distress. Mass murderers frequently exhibit histories that are quite poor in terms of meaningful companionship and devoid of an effective emotional support network when it was most needed.

Many perpetrators of violent crimes, including mass murderers, exhibit a troubled history in their childhood. There is often evidence of family violence, separation, rejection, social isolation, and in some cases, physical and sexual abuse. As children, many mass murderers had difficulty forming or maintaining close relationships with others and may have developed a propensity for resolving ordinary life challenges with aggression and violence. Even as children, these individuals were obsessed with issues of control and rejection; they may have demonstrated significant emotional difficulties throughout their childhood. In a few instances, there will be evidence of a mental illness or a significant psychological or neurological disorder. However, these latter cases represent a minority of those individuals who go on to commit mass murder as adults. Overall, however, it is common to discover that the mass murderer experienced a childhood history of trauma and discomfort that was persistent and significant.

It is important to recognize that the individual who commits mass murder does not predictably display any predetermined personality profile or invariable history of life experiences. Many individuals are socially isolated or face continuing and significant frustrations and disappointments throughout their lives; many adults have experienced a childhood filled with abuse, rejection, and trauma. However, the vast majority of individuals who face such adversity are able to meet their challenges and, in most instances, become all the stronger for their negative experiences. A significant percentage of the American citizenry can point to a troubled childhood in which they experienced separation, abuse, or violence, and yet as adults, they managed to find a sense of purpose and happiness, without any need for aggression or violence. The number of individuals who resort to mass murder is very small, while the number of Americans who face some or all of the challenges experienced by the mass murderer is quite large. Clearly, most individuals are capable of overcoming the difficulties of both childhood and adulthood without resorting to murder. However, for those few individuals who cannot cope with their life experiences and who eventually do resort to murder, there appear to be identifiable themes of behavior and history that are often associated with their crimes.

PLANNING

There are many myths surrounding the crimes of the American mass murderer. Two of the most persistent are (1) that he selects his victims at random, and (2) that he makes little or no effort to plan his murderous rampage. In fact, most mass murderers plan their crimes, at least to some extent, and many perpetrators target specific individuals for death as part of their planning process. Although there are cases of random mass murder, such as the crimes of James Huberty, who indiscriminately shot innocent children at a fast food restaurant; or Sylvia Seegrist, one of the few female mass murderers, who indiscriminately executed individuals at a shopping center, these incidents do not predominate the history of the crime. The mass murderer will frequently target one or more specific individuals for death, even though he may also be quite willing to slay at random once he has attacked his primary victims. Even if the perpetrator has not specifically identified certain individuals prior to his rampage, he will often have targeted them symbolically as representatives of a group or organization that he deems deserving of death or annihilation.

Gang Lu, a graduate student from China who was attending the University of Iowa in 1991, planned his crime of mass murder with great care, including the selection of his victims. Lu had earned a doctorate in physics from the university and was hopeful that his dissertation would gain him the nomination for the prestigious D.C. Spriestersbach Award, a postdoctoral fellowship that provided the continuing financial support for research and education that he desperately needed. When Lu learned that another graduate student, a rival from his homeland, had been nominated for the award, he was furious. He first filed a complaint with the Academic Affairs Office, and when no action was immediately taken, decided on a lethal course of his own. Lu removed all the personal effects from his apartment and then carefully prepared five letters. Four of these letters were written in English and one was prepared in his native language. Each letter complained bitterly about his perception of the unfair decision that had been made by the university administrators in bypassing him for the postdoctoral fellowship. Each letter also stated that he intended to murder those individuals whom he held responsible for his loss of the award, and it went on to specifically name them. The content of one of these letters made Lu's intentions quite clear: "Private guns make every person equal, no matter what/who he/she is. They also make it possible for an individual to fight against a conspired/incorporated organization such as [the]

Mafia or dirty university officials."[15] Lu gave these letters to his friends and addressed two of them to newspaper organizations; however, he did not mail these last two letters to prevent the details of his planned attack and the names of his intended victims from being publicly known.

On November 1, 1991, Lu brought a .38-caliber revolver and a .22-caliber handgun to a weekly seminar on the third floor of Van Allen Hall, the university building that housed the physics and astronomy departments. He knew that several of his predetermined targets would be in attendance at that regular meeting, including his dissertation advisor, an associate professor of physics and astronomy who had sat on the panel that reviewed his work, and the graduate student who had been nominated by them for the coveted award. After remaining seated against the wall in the meeting room throughout the initial part of the conference, Lu suddenly stood up and began firing the .38-caliber handgun, hitting each of his predetermined targets. Without waiting to determine the condition of his victims, Lu ran two blocks to Jessup Hall, the administration building for the university, pausing momentarily on the way to reload his .38-caliber revolver. When he arrived at the administration offices, Lu asked to see the associate vice president of academic affairs, with whom he had filed his complaint about the award nomination process. As she approached Lu to greet him, he shot the administrator and another staff member who was seated nearby. He then made his way to the second floor of the building, directly above the office of the president of the university, and fatally shot himself in the head (see Table 1.8).

Gang Lu had murdered three professors, an administrator, and his rival, and had seriously wounded another faculty member before he finally committed suicide. Each of his victims had been specifically named in the letters that Lu had prepared before his murderous rampage. The killings perpetrated by Lu were carefully planned in every detail and carried out in a brutal and methodical manner. In addition to the infamous letters, Lu had even mailed some of his personal effects back to China, in anticipation of his own death, once he had eliminated those against whom he held such a deep sense of revenge.

Table 1.8: Gang Lu

Perpetrator	A Chinese graduate student in physics who was attending the University of Iowa.
Incident date/location	November 1, 1991, on the campus of the University of Iowa.
Incident category	Revenge.
Weapons	A .38-caliber revolver and a .22-caliber handgun.
Deaths/Injuries	Five killed, one injured.
Motivation	Revenge against faculty and a fellow student for failure to obtain an academic award.
Disposition	Lu committed suicide at the crime scene.

Another perpetrator of mass murder who typically plans his crime carefully is the lethal employee. Fatal incidents involving employees or ex-employees frequently indicate that specific supervisors or coworkers were targeted for revenge. These incidents also often indicate that the crime itself was planned well in advance. However, in addition to targeting specific individuals for death, these frustrated and angry employees will sometimes target an entire organization in a symbolic manner. Under these circumstances, the perpetrator will sometimes be willing to murder his colleagues indiscriminately, in a symbolic effort to destroy the organization itself. The literature of the lethal employee abounds with just such cases, which have occurred with increasing frequency in the past decade.

Willie Woods is an example of a lethal employee who was precise and methodical in carrying out his crime of mass murder. He specifically targeted four supervisors against whom he held an abiding and lethal grudge. When the time came to act out his compulsion for violence, Woods was unwilling to injure his coworkers or the organization itself; his act of revenge proved to be highly focused and deadly in its precision.

Woods was a city electrician who worked at the C. Erwin Piper Technical Center in Los Angeles for twelve years. For ten of those years, he had a solid career with consistently good performance evaluations; he even earned a promotion at one point. However, in 1994, his performance began to deteriorate and Woods became the subject of concern by several of his supervisors. By mid-1995, Woods had received at least five written warnings about poor work performance, two substandard performance evaluations, and a notification of a formal hearing to determine if further disciplinary action should be taken against him. Each conversation with Woods became a matter of increasing concern for his supervisors. Whenever these supervisors tried to engage Woods in a conversation about his performance, he would react with growing anger, at one point even throwing furniture around the room in the course of a performance counseling session. The four supervisors tried to work together to bring Woods back to an acceptable level of performance; however, after a year of struggling with the issue, they had made little progress. Even though his supervisors had no formal plans to terminate him, Woods was convinced that the four men had conspired to end his long career at Piper Tech. Indeed, he believed that these men were getting very close to achieving their goal of ridding the organization of his services.

On July 19, 1995, Woods reported to work as usual. Shortly after his arrival, he became embroiled in a bitter argument with a coworker about his latest performance evaluation. Deeply angered, Woods left his work area to retrieve a weapon that he had previously hidden among his tools; it was a Glock semiautomatic pistol with a clip containing nineteen rounds of ammunition. Returning to the work area with his weapon, Woods began to search for the four supervisors whom he held responsible for his tenuous work situation.

The Piper Tech Center is a sprawling, four-story office building that houses some 300 Los Angeles city employees, many of whom are involved in services to law enforcement agencies. Any individual who roamed these halls with a weapon in his hand was bound to attract a good deal of attention. While searching out his victims, Woods passed numerous other employees in the hallways and corridors, many of whom saw the weapon in his hand and unsuccessfully tried to get help. He ignored all his coworkers and spoke not a word as he moved from area to area. Woods was determined to hunt down and kill only those supervisors who, he was convinced, were conspiring against him.

Woods found two of his victims working in their cubicles on the first floor of the office building. He shot and fatally wounded both men before they were able to move from their chairs. Woods then went to the lower level of the building, again silently bypassing any number of coworkers he met along the way, and sought out the other two supervisors who had counseled him previously. The third supervisor was shot and killed in a hallway connecting a row of offices; Woods's fourth victim died in his office, sitting behind his desk, having been shot fatally in the head and chest. Woods then quietly slipped away from Piper Tech using a rear exit, apparently trying to escape from the crime scene. However, too many of his coworkers had witnessed his brutal crime and were already scurrying to summon help.

Two law enforcement officers, who happened to be at Piper Tech that day on police business, heard the sound of gunfire as Woods attacked his victims. Directed by frightened office workers, the officers responded to where Woods had last been seen. They followed him from the offices into an open field in back of the Piper Tech building. Confronted by the two officers with their guns drawn, Woods quietly surrendered himself and relinquished his weapon. His later explanation to authorities for the murders was that he felt that the four slain supervisors had "picked on" him needlessly and that he feared losing his job (see Table 1.9).

Clearly, Willie Woods had been both methodical and precise in carrying out his vengeance—characteristics that are common to many lethal employees who commit mass murder. However, another lethal employee, Joseph Wesbecker, was anything but precise when it came to exacting his revenge.

Wesbecker, who was nicknamed "Rock," was a pressman for the Standard Gravure Corporation in Louisville, Kentucky, for twenty years. He was arguably the best pressman at Standard Gravure, and because of his long and loyal service, was often rewarded with the opportunity to work a good deal of overtime. This overtime work provided Wesbecker with significant discretionary income that he invested in the stock market. It was a source of pride and security for the hardworking pressman; however, the relentless overtime work also caused a good deal of stress in his life.

By 1987, Wesbecker was a man in deep emotional trouble. His marriage had failed, the incessant overtime had created significant stress in his life, and he was suffering from chronic depression. Realizing that he needed help,

Wesbecker approached the management of Standard Gravure with a request to place him in a less stressful position. His request was denied; in fact, the organization assigned him to work at an even more stressful, high-speed press which worsened his already deteriorating emotional condition. Wesbecker was outraged at how the company had rewarded his decades of loyal service. He filed a complaint with the Jefferson County Human Relations Commission, contending that the company was harassing him rather than helping him overcome his depression, which was well documented. After a year of languishing without a decision, Standard Gravure eventually agreed to place Wesbecker on a long-term disability leave at 60 percent of his normal pay and rehire him when he had recovered sufficiently to return to work.

Table 1.9: Willie Woods

Perpetrator	An electrician who was employed by the city of Los Angeles for twelve years. Despite a long history of satisfactory performance, Woods had experienced work difficulties for two years prior to his rampage.
Incident date/location	July 19, 1995, at the C. Erwin Piper Technical Center in Los Angeles, California.
Incident category	Revenge by a lethal employee.
Weapons	Glock semiautomatic pistol.
Deaths/Injuries	Four killed.
Motivation	Perpetrator was angry at supervisors and had been experiencing work performance difficulties for approximately two years before his crime.
Disposition	Woods was captured without incident after his shooting rampage.

By 1989, Wesbecker was chronically ill and pathologically furious at his employer. He had been placed on a drug regimen of Prozac to ease the symptoms of his depression, but it did not seem to help. Wesbecker was living alone, without a support network of any kind, and he was obsessed with the injustices that he had suffered at the hands of his employer. For more than a year, he made numerous threats against Standard Gravure and its management, often vocalizing his intention to murder those who had treated him so unfairly.

By September 13, 1989, Wesbecker had made his final plans for revenge. He had purchased an AK-47 assault rifle earlier that year and spent the evening cleaning and preparing the weapon. The next morning, he left his wallet and personal effects on the kitchen table of his home, where they would be easily found by anyone searching his residence. He then prepared a last will and testament, also leaving it in plain sight on the kitchen table. Finally, he filled a canvas bag with a variety of weapons and ammunition, including the AK-47, and drove to the Standard Gravure Corporation for the last time.

Wesbecker arrived at the company around 8:30 on the morning of September 14, 1989. When he reached the plant, he immediately took the elevator to the third floor, where the business offices were located. Without speaking a word, he indiscriminately shot at whoever crossed his path, working his way throughout the building and down to the lower floors. Using both the AK-47 and a semiautomatic pistol he had brought along, Wesbecker continued to shoot randomly at coworkers and supervisors. His rampage lasted for approximately twenty minutes, during which time he killed seven employees and wounded another fifteen, many seriously. In a final act of desperation, the "Rock" put a gun to his own head and pulled the trigger (see Table 1.10).

Table 1.10: Joseph Wesbecker

Perpetrator	A pressman who suffered from depression but who also had a solid performance record for over twenty years at the Standard Gravure Corporation.
Incident date/location	September 13, 1989, at his former workplace in Louisville, Kentucky.
Incident category	Revenge by a lethal employee.
Weapons	An AK-47 assault rifle and a semiautomatic pistol.
Deaths/Injuries	Seven killed, fifteen injured.
Motivation	Angered at his employer for what he perceived to be harassment and unfair treatment.
Disposition	Wesbecker committed suicide at the crime scene.

Unlike Willie Woods, who was precise and methodical in his crime, Joseph Wesbecker attacked his victims in a highly symbolic and indiscriminate manner. His mass murder was not a crime of precision based on revenge against specific supervisors or coworkers; rather, it was an attempt to annihilate the entire organization that he viewed as the singular source of his anger and frustrations.

Woods and Wesbecker provide opposing examples of the nature of mass murder that is committed by the lethal employee; however, in many ways, they share the same motivations and factors that impel many mass murderers to violence. It was in the way that they carried out their crimes that the most obvious differences are clearly seen. However, the reasons behind their crimes were shared and, in many ways, were typical of the workplace mass murderer, who has become a significant threat to the American work environment in the last decade. Even though Joseph Wesbecker's victims were apparently selected at random, his crime was planned and carefully considered—it was the object of a long period of brooding contemplation occurring before he committed himself to violence. This is also the typical pattern and process of the workplace mass murderer. Most often, he is an individual who plans his crime carefully, even when his ultimate target is purely symbolic and highly depersonalized.

In other workplace related homicides that are not committed by employees or ex-employees, such as the murders committed by Gian Luigi Ferri in 1993, in which he randomly killed employees and clients of a law firm against which he held a longstanding grudge, the organization itself is the primary target of revenge (see Table 1.11).

Table 1.11: Gian Luigi Ferri

Perpetrator	A fifty-five-year-old real estate investor who was facing financial and legal difficulties.
Incident date/location	July 1, 1993, in a high-rise office building in San Francisco, California.
Incident category	Revenge.
Weapons	Two 9mm semiautomatic pistols, a .45-caliber automatic handgun, and a briefcase filled with ammunition.
Deaths/Injuries	Eight killed, six injured.
Motivation	Revenge against a law firm related to the perpetrator's investment failures. Ferri also carried a list of over forty intended victims in his pocket, none of whom were injured or killed in his attack.
Disposition	Ferri committed suicide at the crime scene when surrounded by responding police personnel.

In this case, specific victims, even if they are precisely identified beforehand, are not an overriding concern when it comes time for the perpetrator to act. Even when specific victims are not predetermined and the murderer is not employed by the target organization, there is usually ample evidence that the crime itself was still the subject of significant planning and preparation. Regardless of whether the perpetrator had a specific victim in mind or was symbolically targeting an entire organization for annihilation, there is usually substantial evidence that the murderer had pondered his options for some time, fantasized about his crime, prepared the elements of his attack in some detail, and given consideration to his own fate.

Like many incidents of workplace murder, mass killings based on racial motivations or other aspects of hate also exhibit obvious symbolic characteristics in terms of victim selection; these crimes typically demonstrate a considerable degree of planning and preparation. Regardless of the apparent randomness of victim selection, a large percentage of mass murders are not spontaneous acts of violence. Rather, they are calculated and considered acts of brutal domination and annihilation, whether they occur in the workplace or elsewhere.

Most incidents of family slayings, political or hate murders, revenge murders, and incidents of employee retaliation usually indicate considerably more than a passing degree of preparation. In some instances, this preparation includes the recruitment of accomplices to the crime who join with the perpetrator in the planning phase and sometimes in the crime itself. The alleged crimes of Timothy McVeigh and Terry Nichols, involving the 1995 bombing of the federal building in Oklahoma City, Oklahoma, demonstrated a complex and sophisticated degree of planning and preparation that went on for many months preceding the incident (see Table 1.12).

Table 1.12: Oklahoma City Bombing

Perpetrator	Timothy J. McVeigh and Terry Nichols (alleged).
Incident date/location	April 19, 1995, at a federal office building in Oklahoma City, Oklahoma.
Incident category	Politics and hate.
Weapons	Explosives secreted in a rental truck that was parked in front of a federal building.
Deaths/Injuries	168 killed, over 400 injured. Nineteen of the victims were children.
Motivation	Domestic terrorism, possibly linked to the death of members of the Branch Davidian religious sect in Waco, Texas, two years earlier, during a government standoff.
Disposition	Perpetrators are awaiting trial.

Mass murders committed by employees or ex-employees, which have constituted a large percentage of this crime category in the past decade, tend to demonstrate sufficient preparation to enable the perpetrator to successfully gain entrance to an organization and attack specific supervisors or coworkers considered to be deserving of death. When analyzing incidents of mass murder in which revenge is obvious (this is the most common motivational factor), planning is usually evident, and sometimes surprisingly sophisticated. Such planning is almost always sufficiently detailed to allow the perpetrator to successfully target one or more predetermined individuals of his choosing. In the case of mass murder that is motivated by racial hatred or a political agenda, it is common for this planning to include a means for the perpetrator to flee from the crime scene and avoid apprehension by law enforcement authorities.

In rare incidents, such as the case of George Hennard, who in 1991 crashed his truck through the storefront of a cafeteria and began executing patrons indiscriminately, there appears to be no planning or predetermination of victims (see Table 1.13).

However, even in such seemingly random cases, we cannot be sure that planning was absent or that specific individuals were not singled out for death. In many incidents of mass murder, the perpetrator does not survive his crime; often he commits suicide at the end of his murderous rampage or is killed by law enforcement officials at the scene. When the perpetrator does not survive his crime, it is sometimes difficult or impossible to be sure of who or what was his intended target. However, when the perpetrator does survive, it is generally easy to determine the extent of his planning and who, if anyone, was his primary target of revenge. In some incidents of mass murder, such as a family slaying, even when the perpetrator takes his own life, the intended targets are obvious and the planning is usually apparent. However, like the murders perpetrated by George Hennard, there are a small, disconcerting number of incidents in which no planning was apparent and, because of the death of the mass murderer, for which we will never know or understand the path that lead to the violent outburst.

Table 1.13: George Hennard

Perpetrator	An unemployed merchant marine who had been discharged from his job for using marijuana.
Incident date/location	October 16, 1991, at Luby's Cafeteria in Killeen, Texas.
Incident category	Unexplained.
Weapons	Two semiautomatic pistols.
Deaths/Injuries	Twenty-three killed, twenty injured.
Motivation	Uncertain. Possibly an act of revenge with little or no evidence of planning. It has been speculated that Hennard held an abiding hatred for women and that this obsession may lie at the root of his crime. There is no hard evidence to support this, or any other precise motivation.
Disposition	After being wounded by responding law enforcement officers at the crime scene, Hennard committed suicide. He left no indication of his motive for the crime.

SUICIDE-BY-PROXY AND PUBLIC MURDER

Serial killers who are organized and methodical in their crimes typically take great pains to avoid detection and capture.[V] It is their intention to survive their actions in order to experience the perverse pleasure of killing again. These organized killers plan their crimes quite carefully and in such a way as to account for the possibility of detection or apprehension; they frequently develop patterns of behavior that make their identification by law enforcement personnel quite difficult. On the other hand, the mass murderer may give little or no consideration to detection or apprehension. In fact, judging by the large percentage of perpetrators of mass murder who commit suicide or induce suicide-by-proxy at the hands of others, these criminals seem to often welcome

---

V. Serial killers are usually considered to be either *organized* or *disorganized*. See "Appendix 2: Organized and Disorganized Serial Killers."

their obvious identification with the crime and may sometimes act as willing participants in their own apprehension or death.

Other than incidents involving the murder of family members, which usually occur in the privacy of the victims' homes, the mass murderer typically carries out his crime in a public or semipublic place and in full view of witnesses. Unlike the organized serial killer, who may go to extraordinary measures to remain unnamed and unidentified, the mass murderer will frequently plan and execute his crime in such a way that it has the maximum impact on all who are nearby. The mass murderer will often take steps to be sure that he is easily identified with his actions and overtly demonstrated to be the perpetrator of the mayhem that he brings to the crime scene. This drive to be recognized as the perpetrator is frequently a crucial element in the criminal behavior of the mass murderer, who wishes to give evidence, for all who see his actions, that he has attained complete mastery or control over those who are his victims. From a psychological point of view, it is as if the moment of fury that is imposed by the mass murderer upon his victims and any witnesses is thus transformed into an extraordinarily vicious symbolic gesture designed to reestablish control in a life that is otherwise completely out of control.

Many mass murderers do not survive their crimes, and for those who do not, this is frequently a conscious and predetermined decision that is integral to their homicidal planning and intentions. The perpetrator may commit suicide at the crime scene, or he may induce law enforcement officials to use lethal force to bring his actions to an end in an effort to minimize the number of potential victims. In some incidents of mass murder, such as those involving an attack against loved ones or family members, the perpetrator views the death of his victims as an extension of his own suicidal intentions. In these situations, the perpetrator will view the demise of his victims and his own death as intimately related and inevitable.

In approximately one-half of recorded incidents, the American mass murderer does not survive his crime. Unlike the organized serial killer, who places a high value on his own survival, the mass murderer will often *intend* to commit suicide, either directly or through the intervention of others at the crime scene. Wishing to die at the end of his rampage or being otherwise unconcerned about his own welfare, the mass murderer presents an obvious and enormous risk to anyone in his path at the moment when he acts out his murderous intentions.

TRIGGERING EVENTS

Acts of extreme violence, such as multiple homicides, are typically preceded by a triggering event that impels the perpetrator to violence. From an objective perspective, a triggering event can appear to be of major or minor consequence; however, from the viewpoint of the potential murderer, it is the final incident that motivates him to violence:

It is the proverbial straw that broke the camel's back, and like that straw, may often be perceived by others with far less significance than it is perceived by the perpetrator. Frustration, a sense of helplessness or abandonment, and a sense of loss of control frequently contribute to the continuum of experiences that chip away at an individual's ability to cope with even minor stressors.[16]

Individuals who are entrapped in this cycle of frustration, helplessness, and anger can be pushed to violence by any number of incidents that, under less stressful circumstances, could have been handled in a nonviolent way. When an incident pushes the potentially violent individual to actually act out his aggressions, it is known as a *triggering event*. The final triggering event is typically the culmination of a prolonged period of fantasy or ideation that is often violent in nature and content; it provides the impetus or excuse—the final motivation—for lethal aggression. The triggering event is frequently linked to issues of control that are critical to the perpetrator—involving a need that is often pathologically paramount in the mind of a potential mass murderer, while at the same time, perceived as absent and unattainable.

Some triggering events are classic and easy to comprehend, even though they provide the impetus for unacceptable and brutal behavior. The loss of a job, severe financial setbacks, significant legal difficulties, the loss of a loved one, or the breakup of a family structure are common triggering events for violence. Potentially violent or lethal individuals may be able to cope with a series of obvious and difficult incidents that would normally be considered triggering events and yet suddenly explode in response to a relatively minor incident. For example, Clifton McCree, who murdered six coworkers, committed himself to violence more than a year after he was fired from his job. For a while he was able to cope with the loss of his employment after twenty-four years, the illness of his wife, the loss of her job, and the low-paying, temporary work as a security guard, which was all he could find. However, when he was unable to pay the utility bill for his family, resulting in their inability to take a hot shower, he was forced to move his wife and children out of their home of many years. For McCree, this was the final triggering event which sent him looking for revenge at his former place of work (see Table 1.14).

When analyzing incidents of mass murder in which the perpetrator was aware of the implications of his actions, it is difficult to find a case in which there was not an apparent triggering event, or series of triggering events, that prompted the perpetrator to his final act of aggression. These triggering events can play an important role in understanding the motivations that drive an individual to mass murder. Regardless of how insignificant or nonsensical a final triggering event may appear in relation to the crime itself, it is sometimes possible to trace any number of precipitating events which together created a cycle of anger and frustration that drove the murderer to his final act. In fact, it is usual to discover a series of setbacks that, in retrospect, clearly set the stage for an ultimate, fatal triggering event which led to violence.

Table 1.14: Clifton McCree

Perpetrator	A forty-one-year-old African-American laborer who was terminated from his job after twenty-four years of service.
Incident date/location	February 9, 1996, at his former work site in Fort Lauderdale, Florida.
Incident category	Revenge by a lethal employee.
Weapons	A 9mm semiautomatic handgun and a .32-caliber revolver.
Deaths/Injuries	Six killed, one injured.
Motivation	Revenge against his employer one year after McCree was terminated from his job.
Disposition	McCree committed suicide at the crime scene.

The case of Clifton McCree also provides a stark example of the cumulative effect of a series of triggering events that led inevitably to mass murder. It would be absurd to close the case of McCree by considering only the final triggering event of his inability to provide a hot shower for his family as the sole motivation for his crime. McCree held his job for well over two decades. It was a career that allowed him to house his family in a comfortable, middle-class neighborhood and provide his children with a fulfilling life style. After failing a routine drug test for the use of marijuana, McCree lost his job because he reacted to the inevitable disciplinary action of a twenty-day work suspension with anger and threatening behavior. It was over a year after McCree lost his job that he returned to the work site with murder in mind. During that year, he was able to get another job as a security guard; however, it did not pay enough to sustain the lifestyle that he had attained for his family. This was an obvious financial and emotional setback which he blamed squarely on his former employer.

To worsen the situation, the McCree family was deprived of Mrs. McCree's income when she became ill. McCree was understandably concerned about his wife's illness and further frustrated by yet another financial setback. Eventually, McCree was fired from his job as a security guard. The family was then left without any income whatsoever. McCree was deeply angered, socially isolated, depressed, and devoid of any hope to regain what he had lost when he was fired from his job fourteen months earlier. Brooding and despondent, Clifton McCree became obsessed with his plight. In his mind, the year of brutalizing failures had been caused by a single act of rejection and abandonment—when his employer terminated him from a job that he was sure he would never be without. He had lost everything that he had spent his entire adult life working for, and *someone* was to blame. That someone was his former employer. When McCree experienced the ultimate triggering event of being unable to provide his family with the most fundamental housing necessities, he was pushed beyond his ability to cope. He became, in that moment, a man without options—a man focused completely on revenge for all the setbacks and frustrations he had experienced.

The specific frustrations and disappointments that were experienced by Clifton McCree were obviously unique to his own life. However, the pattern of such setbacks, and their compounding effect which served to heighten the frustrations and anger of a potentially violent individual beyond the breaking point, were not unique. This pattern of disappointments and frustrations is a common scenario in the life history of many mass murderers; it is often the genesis for a final act of murder by those individuals who are unable to deal with an ultimate, irresistible triggering event.

THE PROFILE OF VIOLENCE

Individuals who are prone to violence frequently exhibit behavioral characteristics that, to some extent, can be isolated and identified. However, these characteristics are not necessarily predictors of violence and certainly do not evidence the potential for murder or mass murder. Rather, they represent patterns of behavior, or psychological manifestations, that may demonstrate a higher probability of violent behavior than if they were not apparent in an individual. For example, the behavioral sciences have long recognized that an individual who has reacted violently in the past will be predisposed to do so again in the future. Therefore, a history of violent behavior may indicate an increased likelihood of future violent behavior. Other characteristics that are associated with potential violence are more subtle and not so apparent.

Certain psychological disorders are closely linked with violent behavior. For example, an individual suffering from antisocial personality disorder (commonly termed a *sociopath*) will often display a blatant disregard for the welfare of others, sudden and extreme outbursts of anger, and little or no remorse for his harmful actions. The disorder of paranoid schizophrenia, or other dysfunctions that may be accompanied by a psychotic or delusional mental state, are often associated with aggressive or violent behavior. Individuals suffering from these severe psychological deficits may be unable to process their experiences in an appropriate manner, and may even have little or no understanding of the ramifications of their actions. Paranoia, especially if it is severe or accompanied by delusional states, is also sometimes associated with violent behavior.

An individual who suffers from an addiction to alcohol or certain illicit drugs may be prompted to aggression or violence more readily than an individual who is not addicted. There are any number of drugs, both illegal and legal, that can cause sudden and significant changes in personality that may lead to violence. Given the pervasive problem of alcohol and drug abuse in America, it is not uncommon to associate these addictions with a wide variety of aggressive behavior.

A major depressive episode, or a period of chronic and severe depression may also lead to violence that is self-directed, directed at others, or both.

Individuals suffering from long periods of frustration or stress can react with sudden and extreme violence, as can individuals who are severely socially isolated and unable to benefit from a close support network when they are facing a life crisis. The background and history of many mass murderers demonstrates periods of severe depression and pervasive social isolation, which in some cases have plagued them since childhood.

Violent and lethal individuals may exhibit other identifiable characteristics, such as an obsession with weapons or an unnatural and overwhelming fascination with murder, mass murder, serial killing, homicides in the workplace, sex crimes, or sadism. A persistent and pathological blaming of others, particularly when it is accompanied by threatening or intimidating behavior, may presage a potentially violent or murderous outburst. Even such remote and rare occurrences as the accidental ingestion of foreign substances through the lungs or skin can result in a sudden and violent reaction in some individuals.

However, in general, most mass murderers are subject to long periods of frustration, disillusionment, anger, a perceived lack of control, rejection, and a growing sense of hostility which eventually becomes intolerable. They frequently view themselves as individuals who are without options and who are lacking the social support necessary to regain a rational perspective about their life situation. They are preoccupied with the wrongs that they perceive and consumed with fantasies of revenge and retribution. In a few cases, they are incapable of rational behavior or even a fundamental understanding of their criminal actions, despite the fact that they may later be judged legally sane and accountable for their crimes.

THE WAYS OF MASS MURDER

The question of categorizing incidents of mass murder is open to debate among criminologists, sociologists, and behaviorists. The typology of the mass murderer is also an issue that is subject to continuing discussion. The crime of mass murder is both simple and complex. It is simple, from the viewpoint of law enforcement personnel, in that it is typically understood who committed the crime and how it took place. There is rarely any question as to the perpetrator or the method of his crime. However, the complexity of the crime lies in the motivation of the perpetrator, his state of mind, his physical and psychological condition, and the imperatives (both personal and societal) that aided his drive toward homicide. Therefore, the nature of the mass murderer is often complex and covert. He will frequently not survive his crimes and will therefore allow no opportunity for further understanding of why he undertook such a heinous course of action. He is usually victimized by long periods of anger, frustration, and disappointment—elements that, in combination, form a complex series of motivations leading to murder.

It is sometimes possible to observe certain patterns and points of similarity across a range of mass murders, while other incidents of this crime are sometimes completely obscure and defy understanding. However, in general, this crime happens for reasons that can be comprehended. Although they are not always in completely clear focus, they offer tantalizing hints at patterns of behavior and activity that are repeated over and over again. These recognizable patterns can provide the basis for a better understanding of the motivations of the mass murderer.

However, despite these somewhat familiar patterns, much about the context and motivations for mass murder seems to shift and evolve over time, inevitably making any final effort at categorizing the crime difficult and uncertain. For example, prior to the past decade, the crime of occupational homicide committed by employees or ex-employees was a rare event. Today, the lethal employee has become the most common perpetrator of mass murder in America. He represents an evolution in this category of crime that was unknown and unforeseen just a few years ago.

In the 1950s and 1960s, it was a generally held opinion that mass murderers were, by definition, insane, in the common understanding of the term. However, it is now held that mass murderers are typically not demented individuals who slay for no reason. Rather, they are now considered to be generally sane individuals who, for a variety of reasons, commit an insane and unforgivable crime. The mass murderer of the late twentieth century has become more prolific and, at the same time, more complex. Today, his reasons for killing are more diverse and complicated than they were a few decades ago. There can be little doubt that the patterns that are now recognizable in the activities of the mass murderer will continue to evolve and become more complex in the future as the societal motivations for this crime become more complex and convoluted as well. The crime of mass murder is continuing to evolve because the murderer himself continues to evolve, along with the society of which he is a part.

SEVEN CATEGORIES OF MASS MURDER

This book will examine seven broad categories of mass murder. It must be recognized that this is a clear departure from the traditional categorization scheme of mass murder, in which only two forms of the crime are recognized: *family* and *traditional* slayings. The categories could have been two in number, or twelve; in the final analysis, it is a matter of perspective and preference. The categories used in this book evolved from an analysis of many incidents of mass murder in America; however, they are admittedly subjective. This effort at recategorizing mass murder is based on the nature of the crime itself, as evidenced by the activities and motivations of the perpetrator. These new categories attempt to account for two important aspects of the crime that are often overlooked: (1) the *intent* to commit mass murder is a crucial element in the crime itself because it speaks to the motivations of the perpetrator; (2) the crime of mass murder is evolving over time and becoming more complex as the perpetrator continues to evolve along with the society in which he carries out his crime.

In an absolute sense, these categories provide nothing more than an informal basis to aid in understanding the crime of mass murder. As with any other categorization scheme that deals with such an issue, these elements are clearly open to debate and change.

Perverted Love. Acts of perverted love are a particularly disturbing aspect of mass murder. They are exemplified by the father who murders his entire family or the mother who slays her children. However, the perpetrator may also be an enraged adolescent who strikes out against his loved ones or a spurned lover whose primary motivation is revenge but who decides to victimize other family members, or perhaps even strangers. For a variety of complex and psychologically unsettling reasons, this form of mass murder twists the concept of love into a grotesque perversion that demands the lives of innocent victims in an effort to spare them from the unacceptability of life which is obvious to the perpetrator. For example, in 1995, a husband and father murdered his family of three (and himself) in the family's vehicle by detonating a bomb that was hidden in the glove compartment. He was despondent about financial difficulties and could not allow his family to share in what he perceived to be a disastrous future. In 1989, an unemployed man murdered his entire family and his ex-boss—a total of seven victims—because he was unable to find work and could not face the embarrassment of his inability to support his family. Two men, both family murderers, killed twenty-four loved ones within months of each other in 1987. The first perpetrator murdered eight family members because of financial difficulties that he believed would ruin the family lifestyle that he had worked so hard to attain; the second man murdered his family of sixteen because his wife had threatened to file for divorce and he feared the imminent disintegration of his family. Although such cases are not prolific (and certainly not as common as mass murder carried out by a lethal employee), they occur with disturbing regularity. This category of mass murder is arguably the most disquieting form of the crime because it almost invariably victimizes the young and innocent in an extreme and brutal manner.

Politics and Hate. Crimes involving politics and hate that result in mass murder are as old as humanity itself. America is not exempt from this type of crime; in fact, it is one that seems to be gaining national momentum in the late twentieth century. Multiple homicides based on racial hatred—crimes targeting individuals completely unknown to the perpetrator, who are victimized solely as symbolic objects of his fury and disdain—are increasing across this nation.

For example, in 1989, Patrick Purdy shot randomly at Asian-American children in their Stockton, California, school yard; he managed to kill five youngsters, and wound many more, simply because he was angered at the increasing number of Asians who were emigrating to this country at that time (see Table 1.15). Purdy knew none of his victims—they were merely symbolic of his pathological racism and rage. Socially isolated and known to have expressed resentment against immigrants for several years prior to his murderous rampage, Purdy harbored a particularly vehement hatred for Southeast Asian families. He had often expressed the fear that they would find undeserved opportunities in America and therefore cheat him out of what he felt was his by birthright alone. In addition to his pathological hatred of Asian-Americans, Purdy was known to be a violent individual, with a criminal history in both Los Angeles and Woodland, California. In fact, Purdy had an extensive criminal record that extended back to 1977 (see "Appendix 3: Chronology of Patrick Purdy"). On January 17, 1989, Purdy attacked the young children in their schoolyard, randomly spraying them with powerful blasts from his assault rife and a 9mm handgun. Before he committed suicide at the crime scene, Purdy had murdered five children and injured twenty-nine in his horrifying few moments of mass murder.

Table 1.15: Patrick Purdy

Perpetrator	A twenty-six-year-old loner with an extensive criminal history. He held a deep resentment against immigrants, particularly Asian-Americans.
Incident date/location	January 17, 1989, at an elementary school in Stockton, California.
Incident category	Politics and hate.
Weapons	An AK-47 assault rifle and a 9mm pistol.
Deaths/Injuries	Five killed, twenty-nine injured.
Motivation	Racial hatred directed against Asian-Americans.
Disposition	Purdy committed suicide at the crime scene.

In that same year, another man in his twenties grimly murdered over a dozen women whom he considered to be "feminists."[17] Marc Lepine, a Canadian, was born with the name Gamil Gharbi—the son of an Algerian father and Canadian mother. When he was eighteen years old, Lepine formally adopted his mother's maiden name. Throughout his young life, Lepine was unable to form a healthy relationship with women. By his mid-twenties, he had come to the conclusion that women were the cause of all his unhappiness and failures—particularly women who were vocal and assured about their roles in society and the workplace (see Table 1.16).

On a snowy afternoon in December 1989, Lepine decided that he would take final, symbolic revenge against all the women in his life who had become the basis of so much rejection, frustration, and disappointment. Carrying a high-powered rifle and several boxes of ammunition, Lepine went to the campus of Ecole Polytechnique de Montreal (a coeducational engineering school) and entered one of the crowded classrooms. Demanding that the students immediately stop their work, Lepine separated the male and female students, ordering the men to leave the classroom. He shouted at the remaining students in French: "You're women, you're going to be engineers. You're all a bunch of feminists. I hate feminists!"[18] With only female students remaining, he opened fire on the terrified and defenseless women at point blank range. Six of the students died immediately at the scene, and several others were seriously injured.

Table 1.16: Marc Lepine

Perpetrator	A twenty-five-year-old Canadian paramilitary enthusiast who harbored a deep hatred of women.
Incident date/location	December 6, 1989, at the Ecole Polytechnique in Montreal, Canada.
Incident category	Politics and hate.
Weapons	A Sturm Ruger semiautomatic hunting rifle, a sheathed buck knife, two boxes of .223-caliber bullets, and several ammunition clips.
Deaths/Injuries	Fourteen killed, thirteen injured.
Motivation	A pathological hatred of those women whom he perceived as feminists.
Disposition	Lepine committed suicide at the crime scene.

Lepine then roamed the halls of the school, randomly targeting other women for death. At the end of his rampage, he had managed to murder fourteen and injure another thirteen individuals. All those killed and nine of the injured were women. Finding no more women to terrorize or murder, Lepine finally ended his siege by putting the rifle to his own head and pulling the trigger.

Arriving at the brutal scene, law enforcement officials discovered a three-page suicide note that Lepine had prepared in advance of his attack on the school. The note railed against women in general, and in particular, women whom he considered to be feminists. The suicide note also made it clear to investigators that Lepine had carefully planned the crime to include his own death after the murder of as many women as possible. A particular line in Lepine's suicide note made his intentions grotesquely apparent: "I have been unhappy for the past seven years. And, I will die on December 6, 1989. Feminists have always ruined my life."[19]

The actions of Marc Lepine that afternoon in Montreal became the worst mass murder in Canadian history.[VI] Like Patrick Purdy, Marc Lepine knew none of his victims; he struck out in hate and revenge against a symbolically targeted group of innocent individuals.

VI. Although this book deals specifically with the American mass murderer, the crimes of Marc Lepine were so egregious that they could not be omitted from this discussion of the mass murderer who strikes out from a pathological sense of hatred. It should be noted that mass murder in Canada is a much rarer event than it is in the United States.

In 1973, an African-American man who was bitter and angry about the pervasive racial discrimination that he found throughout America went to a luxury hotel that primarily catered to Caucasian tourists. While at the hotel that day, he murdered seven guests and employees. The perpetrator knew none of his victims; however, it was clear to investigators that he had obviously targeted only Caucasians, while consciously bypassing minority employees and guests during his murderous rampage. Like Patrick Purdy, his crime was a clear act of mass murder based exclusively on racial hatred.

Internal terrorism based on politics and hate, such as occurred in Oklahoma City in 1995, has now gained a painful and strong foothold in this country. In recent years, mass murder by terrorism has become a serious concern for both law enforcement personnel and workers in certain public service job categories. To compound the possibilities of political violence, right-wing extremist groups have gained popularity with American youth and often incite their members to acts of aggression and murder, including targeting symbolic groups of citizens based on ethnicity, politics, or affiliations. Each of these elements is now apparent in American society; they are contributing to a general increase in societal violence, as well as an increase in attempted mass murders.

Revenge. Revenge represents the most common motivating factor apparent in the crime of the mass murderer. In fact, this category may be misleading simply because revenge is extremely prevalent in the behavior of most mass murderers, both prior to, and during, the commission of their crimes. Certainly, one could argue that the preceding category—politics and hate—can just as accurately be viewed as a form of twisted, and highly symbolic, revenge. However, there are many incidents of mass murder that are clearly rooted in a singular, personal, and deep sense of revenge which is quite specific. In the past decade, the most striking examples of mass murder based on revenge have been carried out by the lethal employee—an individual who works (or has worked) for an organization and then attacks individuals in the workplace in retribution for actions taken by his employer, supervisors, or coworkers. This particular mass murderer (the lethal employee) has become a significant threat to the American business community in the past ten years because of the alarming increase in victims claimed annually. Perpetrators such as Patrick Sherrill (see Table 1.17), who murdered fourteen coworkers and himself in 1986, or Clifton McCree (see Table 1.14) who, a decade later, in 1996, killed five coworkers and himself a year after losing his job, are typical of the lethal employee who resorts to mass murder as an act of revenge.

However, the lethal employee or ex-employee is not alone in his search for revenge and retribution. There are many other forms of revenge that lead to mass murder, and these crimes are committed by a diversity of perpetrators. In 1996, for example, a fourteen-year-old boy brought a rifle to his high school and murdered two students and a teacher against whom he held a deep grudge, in a highly personalized crime of revenge. Three years earlier, Gian Luigi Ferri murdered eight individuals in a high-rise office building in San Francisco when he attacked a law firm against which he held an equally overpowering grudge (see Table 1.11). However, even though Ferri carried in his pocket a list of previously targeted victims, his crime of mass murder devolved into an indiscriminate act of egregious violence. Once at the crime scene, Ferri never struck out against any of those whom he had previously targeted; rather, his actions became a highly symbolic, depersonalized crime of revenge against the law firm itself. Despite the symbolism of his actions, it was obvious that Ferri's brutal act of mass murder had been carefully planned and executed.

Table 1.17: Patrick Sherrill

Perpetrator	A forty-four-year-old, disgruntled post office employee who was an expert with handguns.
Incident date/location	August 20, 1986, at the Edmond Post Office in Edmond, Oklahoma.
Incident category	Revenge by a lethal employee.
Weapons	Two .45-caliber pistols, a .22-caliber handgun, and in excess of 300 rounds of ammunition.
Deaths/Injuries	Fifteen killed, six injured.
Motivation	Revenge against his employer and symbolic annihilation of the organization.
Disposition	Sherrill committed suicide at the crime scene.

Mass murder motivated by revenge can exhibit many different characteristics and may be perpetrated by a wide range of individuals, from the angry adolescent to the frustrated middle-age worker. It could be argued that most acts of mass murder are based, at least in part, on some element of revenge or retribution. For example, the mass murderer who slays his family or loved ones could be striking out in an act of retribution; however, there appear to be different, and perhaps more complex, motivations to be discovered in the murder of loved ones than in the lethal acts of an angered, vengeful employee or the pathological retribution demanded by an adolescent against his peers or teachers. However, it would be reasonable to assume that elements of revenge play a critical role in many, if not most, categories of mass murder.

Sexual Homicide. Sexual homicide refers to murders that exhibit clear evidence that the crime was sexual in nature. Such evidence is typically derived from the crime scene and involves considerations such as the attire (or lack of attire) of the victim, exposure of the body, sexual positioning of the body, evidence of sexual intercourse or substitute sexual activity prior to or after death, sadistic fantasy, or the introduction of foreign objects into the victim's body.[20] Sexual homicide is often associated with serial killing; it is rarely associated with acts of mass murder. In fact, incidents of mass murder that evidence any of the usual characteristics of sexual homicide are extremely unusual. The most notorious sexual mass murderer in recent American history was Richard Speck who, in 1966, sexually attacked and murdered eight women in an evening of chaotic mayhem that has rarely been experienced in this country or elsewhere.

In at least one characteristic a crime of sexual homicide is often similar to an act of mass murder—the need for absolute and pathological control of the victim is typically paramount in the mind of the perpetrator. However, beyond this shared characteristic, the two crimes differ in significant ways. By definition, sexual homicide is a crime based on very obvious sexual motives which are often brutal in nature and may be carried out over an extended period of time with each victim; alternatively, it may involve a number of victims who are attacked in a serial nature over a significant period of time. On the other hand, mass murder is a singular and discreet incident in which a number of individuals are slain in a unique episode; it is rarely a crime that takes place over any protracted period of time. In those unusual incidents in which mass murder is committed with a clear sexual motive, elements of both crimes (sexual serial murder and mass murder) are present, and notably, the victims are slain in a single episode that tends to be unusually protracted to facilitate the sexual activities of the perpetrator. It could be argued that such a crime is, in effect, a form of serial killing that is not characterized by the typical cooling-off period, during which the perpetrator fantasizes about his crime and plans his next attack. However, the overriding consideration is that multiple victims are slain in a single episode—a primary characteristic of the crime of mass murder. Because the sexual mass murderer combines the intense anger and frustration of the mass murderer with the complex and perverse motivations of the sexual sadist, he is an extraordinarily brutal and atrocious individual whose crimes, by definition, must be among the most heinous.

Mass Murder by Execution. Although rare in this country, mass murders can be crimes that are, for all practical purposes, executions. These crimes generally fall into two categories: (1) the premeditated, highly planned, "contract" execution of multiple individuals, and (2) the typically unplanned execution of witnesses usually committed in an effort to avoid apprehension while the perpetrator is in the pursuit of another crime. The latter category is more common than the former, although neither are frequent occurrences within the strict definition of mass murder. The mass execution of witnesses to a crime is an incident that generally comports with a fairly consistent crime event profile in which the perpetrator is young, aggressive, and may be involved with gang activity, drugs or other illicit activities. Although rare in the context of multiple murders, the execution of witnesses to a crime is a significant problem in incidents of single or double homicides perpetrated in the course of a robbery or similar confrontational crime. These crimes of murder (single and double homicides) are particularly rampant in certain segments of the American economy, such as the retail trades.

Sane or Insane. The question of sanity is a legal issue, not a medical one. From a prosaic point of view, it is difficult to understand the sanity in any act of mass murder. However, from a legal perspective, mass murderers are rarely judged to be insane and unaccountable for their actions. It is difficult to assess the percentage of mass murderers who, at the time of their crimes, were suffering from such severely debilitating psychological disorders that they were unable to fully comprehend the heinous nature of their actions. In the final analysis, our system of jurisprudence rarely finds a psychological disorder, regardless of its debilitating nature, as grounds for justifying murder in any form. Understandably, the medical perspective is generally quite different. Behavioral scientists often determine that mass murderers were suffering from severe psychological disorders, such as paranoid schizophrenia, bipolar personality disorder, or antisocial personality disorder, at the time when they committed their crimes. The psychologist or psychiatrist may argue that the perpetrator was unable to control his behavior, or perhaps even unable to understand the ramifications of his actions, because of such a disorder. However, the American legal system takes a much narrower view of culpability, which often concludes that the perpetrator was well aware of his actions and therefore capable of making an alternative choice of behavior at the time when he committed the crime. Clearly, the question of sanity is not one that can be resolved easily or, possibly, to anyone's satisfaction. Where the behaviorist finds clear psychological deficits or a severe disorder, a judge or jury may see an obvious path to legal culpability.

There are a significant number of cases of mass murder that make the dichotomy between a behaviorist's view of culpability and the decisions made by our court system disturbingly apparent. In the end, the question of sanity or insanity is one that may never be satisfactorily resolved by either school of thought.

The Unexplained. Most incidents of mass murder are planned and, with sufficient knowledge of the history of the perpetrator, can be understood as the culmination of a series of experiences and events that motivated the individual to extreme violence. This is not to say that mass murder was ever a logical inevitability of the perpetrator's experiences. Murder is rarely, if ever, logical or inevitable. However, the crime of mass murder is not an isolated and singular act that happens spontaneously. It is usually the result of a long period of frustration, disappointment, hostile fantasy, rejection, isolation, and anger. Triggering events that precede the crime are usually apparent, although they may, in themselves, be illogical or objectively insignificant. The overwhelming number of incidents of mass murder are at least somewhat explainable, given sufficient understanding of the perpetrator, his history, and his life experiences. However, there remain a few incidents of mass murder that seem to defy all efforts at understanding or explanation.

Occasionally, the mass murderer will strike out in what appears to be a completely random act, without obvious motivation or an apparent precipitating event. Even though these crimes are few in number and remain without explanation today, it does not mean that they would be unexplained under different circumstances. It may be the case that we are simply not aware of sufficient background information about the perpetrator to comprehend what (on the surface) appears to be inexplicable. The crime of mass murder is not well understood because it involves highly complex modalities of human behavior, states of mind, and experiences that (together) form a unique mosaic of motivating factors. There is not now, and will likely never be, a reliable formula for understanding mass murder; it is unlikely that we will ever recognize a dependable method of predicting the crime or a completely satisfactory method of profiling the perpetrator before he commits to violence. There are a number of incidents of mass murder that appear to be without explanation. They are clearly deserving of further research, despite the fact that such investigation is often painful and frustrating. It is unreasonable to expect this situation to change in the near future unless we benefit from a sudden, quantum increase in our understanding of human behavior and of why certain individuals resort to lethal violence in any form. Rare as such inexplicable cases are in the history of this crime, it is an especially troubling category because it defies our best efforts to understand the convoluted and extremely covert motivations of the perpetrator. This uncertainty leaves us all with unanswered questions and increased fear.

ABOUT THE CATEGORIES

These seven categories of mass murder are not traditional by the accepted standards of most criminologists; nor are they meant to be so. Mass murder is more than a quantification of victims or categorizations of the typology of the perpetrator. This is a crime that has an obvious intent—an act that demonstrates purpose and motivation that reaches beyond its actualization at the crime scene. For each mass murderer, whether or not he succeeds in killing sufficient numbers of victims to earn that designation in a traditional sense, there is the reality of *why* he was compelled to commit such a crime. Each perpetrator formulated some concept of the crime prior to his actions; each murderer had a motivation and, to a greater or lesser extent, a plan of action in mind. That his ability to understand his own actions and motivations was lacking in some cases (or completely absent in others) does not diminish the importance of understanding why he became a mass murderer.

Most mass murderers formulate their intentions over time and become hopelessly impaled upon their own obsessions; they are often pathological in their desire for revenge. It is in the *way* that they enact their crimes that we are able to first understand the covert and convoluted psychological process that leads to murder. That is the goal of why we strive to understand this crime. It is a journey into the mind of the mass murderer that is best begun with some understanding of the similarities and differences within the various aspects of the crime itself. In that sense, many ways of categorizing the crime of mass murder may be appropriate, so long as the method accurately reflects the crime itself and can be used as a mirror to help us illuminate the dark and foreboding mind of the perpetrator.

NOTES

1. "Sexual Homicide: Decision Process Models," in Kozel Multimedia, Inc., *Mind of a Killer,* CD-ROM (Chatsworth, CA: Cambrix, 1995).

2. James Alan Fox and Jack Levin, *Mass Murder: America's Growing Menace,* (New York: Plenum, 1985) 139.

3. William Hamilton, "Familiar Echoes of Rage," *Philadelphia Inquirer Online* (Internet edition), 12 December 1993, A01.

4. "Sniper Terrorizes Shopping Center," in AP News Wire, *WWW World News Today* (Internet edition), 14 April 1996.

5. Hal Spencer, "Scary Man Charged in Shooting Spree," *Philadelphia Inquirer Online* (Internet edition), 27 March 1993, A05.

6. John Way Jennings, "Judge Allows Unruh 1 Attendant for Walks," *Philadelphia Inquirer Online* (Internet edition), 21 October 1994.

7. William Hamilton, "Familiar Echoes."

8. Fox and Levin, *Mass Murder*, 137.

9. "Firefighter Gunman: He Was a Time Bomb Waiting to Go Off," in Associated Press, *Nando Times* (Internet edition), 25 April 1996.

10. Ibid.

11. Ibid.

12. Stephen Hawkins, "Mississippi Firefighter Kills Wife and Four Colleagues, Police Say," *Philadelphia Inquirer Online* (Internet edition), 25 April 1996.

13. "Firefighter Gunman."

14. Hawkins, "Mississippi Firefighter."

15. James Alan Fox and Jack Levin, *Overkill: Mass Murder and Serial Killing Exposed* (New York: Plenum, 1994), 199.

16. Michael D. Kelleher, *Profiling the Lethal Employee: Case Studies in Workplace Violence* (Westport, CT: Greenwood/Praeger, 1996), 26.

17. Susan Levine and Michael Matza, "Rage at Women Set Off Massacre," *Philadelphia Inquirer Online* (Internet edition), 8 December 1989, A01.

18. Ibid.

19. Fox and Levin, *Overkill*, 203.

20. Robert K. Ressler, Ann W. Burgess, and John E. Douglas, *Sexual Homicide: Patterns and Motives*, (New York: Lexington, 1988), xiii.

CHAPTER 2

Perverted Love

When love begins to sicken and decay . . .

William Shakespeare
Julius Caesar, act 4, scene 2

Mass murder that is committed in the name of love is perhaps the most unsettling of any form of homicide. It is difficult, if not impossible, to understand or accept the motivations for this crime. The perpetrator attacks those whom he claims to love and, regardless of their age or physical condition, murders them in a perverse and wholly egocentric rage that betrays a trust held sacred in our society. Although the victims are usually family members or loved ones, unrelated and unknown individuals can also be targeted by the murderer if they are unfortunate enough to be in harm's way when he strikes. In some incidents of mass murder motivated by perverted love, it is obvious that the perpetrator was incapable of understanding his brutal actions; however, in many incidents, the murderer has carefully planned his crime and is fully aware of his actions and their ramifications.

When the mass murderer attacks family members, he may or may not take his own life while acting out his aggressions. Because of the possibility of the perpetrator's suicide, criminologists have traditionally identified two classifications of family mass murder: (1) a *family murder/suicide,* in which the perpetrator kills family members and then commits suicide, and (2) a *family killing,* in which the perpetrator, after murdering his loved ones, survives his own actions by design. The motivations for murder within these two categorizations may differ significantly, despite the fact that either crime may be carefully planned. A family murder/suicide will involve the concept of suicide-by-proxy, whereas a family killing certainly will not. Although both of these crimes can be considered as acts of perverted love, a significant difference in motivation is usually apparent, since the question of the perpetrator's survival is a central issue.

An especially chilling and brutal example of the crime of perverted love that was categorized as a family killing took place on November 9, 1972, when John List murdered his entire family in their Westfield, New Jersey, home. He killed his mother, wife, and three teenage children by shooting each of them, execution-style, in the back of the head. After murdering his loved ones, List carefully laid out four of the bodies in the front room of the family home, placing each of them on a sleeping bag, with their faces covered and arms folded across their bodies as they might appear in a funeral home before interment. List then fled the crime scene, leaving his car at the local airport parking lot, and became a fugitive for seventeen years before he was apprehended. Throughout those many years, law enforcement authorities were unsure if he had committed suicide, died of natural causes, or gone on the run. Although most officials considered him to be insane because of the horrendous nature of his crime, after List's apprehension, this would prove to be an incorrect assumption.

Table 2.1: John List

Perpetrator	A husband and father of three children who murdered his entire family.
Incident date/location	November 9, 1972, in the family home in Westfield, New Jersey.
Incident category	Perverted love.
Weapons	A handgun.
Deaths/Injuries	Five killed—all family members.
Motivation	Apparently, List wanted to be free of his family in order to begin a new life.
Disposition	After avoiding apprehension for seventeen years, List was identified through tips provided by viewers of a national television program that aired the details of his crime.

List's arrest came in a way that he could not have foreseen seventeen years earlier when he murdered his family. His profile and the details of his crime appeared on the television program, "America's Most Wanted." The national coverage of his crime spawned a number of telephone tips from viewers, many claiming that they knew List's whereabouts. One of these tips lead to Richmond, Virginia, where List had settled down years before and raised another family—one very much like the family that he had slain. When he was apprehended, it became apparent how very carefully List had planned the heinous attack on his family; his preparation had included all the elements necessary for his escape and a fresh start without the burden of his loved ones. In the end, John List proved to be anything but a crazed murderer. He was a criminal who clearly understood the meaning of his actions and had sufficient capacity to coldly plan his crime and evade apprehension for nearly two decades (see Table 2.1).[1]

Like the crimes of John List, the murders committed by William B. Bishop in 1976 seem to indicate a significant degree of planning, including the perpetrator's prearranged escape from law enforcement authorities (see Table 2.2). His crime was also an extraordinarily brutal act of perverted love.

Bishop was a diplomat with a highly promising career who had received several significant postings overseas. He was considered to be an excellent prospect for a high-level position in the U.S. State Department. However, when he decided to lash out against his family, he did so in a way that was not at all in keeping with his public image. Bishop physically beat to death his mother, wife, three children, and the family dog in their Bethesda, Maryland, home. He subsequently loaded their bodies into his station wagon and drove to North Carolina, where he buried his loved ones in a single, shallow grave. Bishop then disappeared without a trace, leaving behind no evidence that hinted at a motivation for his crime. It is possible that Bishop committed suicide or died of natural causes after the murders; no trace of him has ever been found. However, like John List, Bishop may have predetermined all the critical aspects of the murders, including his escape and evasion of law enforcement personnel.

Table 2.2: William Bishop

Perpetrator	A husband and father of three children who was also a promising diplomat.
Incident date/location	In 1976, in the family home in Bethesda, Maryland.
Incident category	Perverted love.
Weapons	Death inflicted through beating.
Deaths/Injuries	Five killed—all family members.
Motivation	Uncertain, but evidence led to the suspicion that this was a planned crime that involved the perpetrator's escape.
Disposition	Bishop has not been located.

Obviously, not all mass murders that arise from an aspect of perverted love are as premeditated and well planned as those of John List or William Bishop. In fact, some of these crimes are committed by perpetrators who were suffering from such severe psychological disorders that they were not fully aware of their actions at the moment they attacked. However, it is yet another myth surrounding mass murder that the individual who kills his loved ones is always crazed and uncontrolled. In many instances, he is cold, calculating, and careful in his actions.

The family murders committed by Norman Yazzie are an example of mass murder that had its roots in many years of anger, frustration, unemployment, financial hardships, and an addiction to alcohol (see Table 2.3). Yazzie was a thirty-three-year-old Native American who lived with his wife and five children on a small Navajo reservation in Arizona. He had been unemployed for years and was severely addicted to alcohol. Yazzie's wife, Cecelia, supported the family as a full-time health clinic worker in a nearby town. On September 2, 1996, Cecelia left her husband and children in their small trailer to visit a sister in New Mexico. While the five children were watching television, Norman Yazzie shot them multiple times and then attempted to set the home on fire using gasoline and matches. Four of Yazzie's children—all girls ranging in age from five to fifteen years—died from their gunshot wounds; his only son, eleven years old, was critically wounded.

The children's grandparents, who lived nearby, saw the smoke coming from the Yazzie trailer and rushed to the scene, where they attempted to subdue Yazzie by tying his hands behind his back. As the elder Yazzies called for law enforcement personnel, their son escaped and fled the area. Federal Bureau of Investigation (FBI) agents and local police soon caught up with Yazzie in a nearby hogan (a traditional Navajo dwelling), and after a brief struggle, took him into custody.[2]

Table 2.3: Norman Yazzie

Perpetrator	A thirty-three-year-old, unemployed Native American who was severely addicted to alcohol.
Incident date/location	September 2, 1996, at the family home on a Navajo reservation in Arizona.
Incident category	Perverted love.
Weapons	Gun and arson.
Deaths/Injuries	Four killed, one critically injured (all children).
Motivation	Depressed, unemployed, angry, and frustrated, Yazzie lashed out against his children.
Disposition	Yazzie was arrested shortly after the crime and taken into custody.

Although the murders committed by Norman Yazzie had the appearance of a spontaneous crime, this was probably not the real situation. Yazzie had been unemployed for years and was heavily dependent upon alcohol; he was deeply frustrated, depressed, and angry with his life situation. Without question, Yazzie's children were constant reminders of his failure to provide financial support for his family; and they also would have been obvious victims of his inability to control his addiction to alcohol. It is likely that Norman Yazzie found himself without options or an opportunity for positive change. He had probably fantasized for quite some time about the death of his family as a resolution to his own inability to meet the challenges of a life that he could no longer control or accept. Without his wife to intervene or provide any reason to withhold his long-standing anger and frustration, and acting (as reported by arresting officers) under the influence of alcohol, Yazzie lashed out against his own children in an act of murder that he had most likely pondered for quite some time prior to September 2, 1996.

Although Norman Yazzie's crimes were extreme and unforgivable, his motives appear relatively clear and straightforward. However, some incidents of perverted love that have been traditionally categorized as family murder/suicides are troubling, not only in their impact but also because of our inability to understand the true motivation of the perpetrator. For example, five days after Christmas, in 1987, seven members of a family living in rural Iowa were shot to death in what appeared to be a family murder/suicide incident (see Table 2.4). The murders were committed two days after Ronald Gene Simmons had been arrested for slaying fourteen of his own family members in Arkansas (see Table 2.5). The news of the Simmons atrocity was still a front-page headline when Robert Dreesman, at the age of forty, murdered his parents, his sister, and her three children with a shotgun. Investigators later determined that Dreesman had shot the entire family in less than thirty seconds as they sat down to eat a family lunch. He then turned the gun on himself and committed suicide.

Table 2.4: Robert Dreesman

Perpetrator	A forty-year-old, unmarried man.
Incident date/location	December 30, 1987, in the family home in Algona, Iowa.
Incident category	Perverted love.
Weapons	A shotgun.
Deaths/Injuries	Six killed—all family members.
Motivation	Uncertain.
Disposition	Dreesman committed suicide at the crime scene.

Robert Dreesman left no indication why he had murdered his loved ones. It was known that Dreesman had suffered from minor psychological problems earlier in his life; however, he had no criminal history or record of hospitalization. After the killings, he was described by a friend in this way: "He was a genius. He was very, very shy. If you wanted to talk to him he'd look down at the ground. He couldn't stand eye contact. He was very introverted."[3]

The Dreesman family had been well established, successful, and prosperous, enabling their son to attend college and later graduate from the Palmer School of Chiropractics. Dreesman was also completing a degree in veterinary medicine at the time of the murders but had not yet decided which profession to pursue. The Dreesman family, including Robert, was considered steady and well-respected in their community, even though Robert was universally perceived as shy and retiring. The only explanation that family friends could provide for Robert's crimes was one of jealousy. A state senator and close friend of the elder Dreesman said of Robert: "He was living with his parents, kind of the center of attention all the time, and then Marilyn [the murdered sister and mother of three children] and the kids came home. Who knows, but that might have pushed Robert over the edge."[4]

Although it is possible that the return of his sister and her children for the Christmas holidays could have provided a triggering event for Dreesman's rage, this is an unlikely fundamental motivation for his brutal actions. Like most mass murderers, Robert Dreesman probably suffered a long period of frustration, disappointment, and anger that drove him to a final, murderous rampage. No doubt he was aware of the crimes of Ronald Gene Simmons, who had been arrested only days before Dreesman killed his family. It is possible that Dreesman was influenced in coming to his final, brutal decision by the actions of Simmons in murdering his entire family. Unfortunately, as in some other incidents of mass murder in which there are no survivors and no evidence of motive, we will probably never come to a final understanding of Robert Dreesman's crime.

Table 2.5: Ronald Gene Simmons

Perpetrator	A forty-seven-year-old man who was retired from the Air Force and obsessed with controlling those around him.
Incident date/location	December 22-28, 1987, in and near Russellville, Arkansas.
Incident category	Perverted love.
Weapons	A .22-caliber handgun, a crowbar, strangulation, and drowning.
Deaths/Injuries	Sixteen killed, four injured—fourteen victims were members of the perpetrator's family.
Motivation	An angered, frustrated, and sexually disturbed individual with a variety of complex motives. An individual who was unable to cope with life outside of the military.
Disposition	After conviction, Simmons died by lethal injection on June 25, 1990.

Those who murder their family members or loved ones succumb to many of the same imperatives for violence as mass murderers who target other, less personalized, victims. The family mass murderer, like the individual who kills in an act of retribution or revenge, has typically been subjected to years of anger and frustration that are profoundly linked with family members or loved ones.

His ability to cope with the stresses and pressures that he is experiencing in the period just prior to the murders has been completely eroded; he is of the opinion that whatever it is that he is now facing is insurmountable. Even though he may be surrounded by family or loved ones, the perpetrator is typically psychologically isolated and unable to rely on a support network to sustain him through difficult life experiences. Perhaps he is unwilling or incapable of asking for assistance from even those who he knows love him and are, in turn, loved by him. He may have reached a point at which he views his own life as without value and, pondering the possibilities of his own death or suicide, is not willing to permit his family to live with his own disgrace or failures. In such a state of mind, the perpetrator may commit suicide-by-proxy, murdering his family or loved ones as an extension of his own carefully considered suicide. In most incidents, a triggering event that pushes the perpetrator to murder will also be apparent within the dynamics of the family at some point before he finally commits to violence.

Murders that arise from a sense of perverted love typically involve complex emotional factors that are difficult for all but the perpetrator to understand. In some cases, the perpetrator lashes out in an act of revenge because he has been spurned or rejected by a loved one. In these crimes, it is possible that individuals unrelated, or even unknown, to the perpetrator may become indirect targets of his resulting act of retribution. More often, however, the murderer will attack only members of his family or other loved ones, typically in their own home, and continue his killing rampage until all present have been slain. In such crimes, when the perpetrator survives his actions, he will sometimes express a motivational theme that is based on sparing his loved ones from some perceived disaster that is imminent in his own life. The crime in which a man who murders his wife and children because of severe financial difficulties, the loss of a job, an illicit love affair that has been uncovered, or impending legal difficulties is not an unusual scenario. The mother who slays her children because she is simply unable to cope with the stress of raising them has also become an unsettling, but recognizable, form of perverted love.

Regardless of the state of mind of the murderer or his alleged motivations for the crime, mass murder perpetrated against family members or loved ones is a particularly difficult crime to comprehend. The perpetrator of this crime strikes out against that most honored component of American society, the family, in a way that is often extremely vicious and unconscionable. Because this perpetrator frequently murders children, some of whom are only in their infancy, there is little room for understanding or forgiveness in the minds of jurors or the public, regardless of the rationale that may seem so obvious to the murderer. It is a tragic irony of this particular type of homicide that the murderer will sometimes excuse his brutal crime as an act of love that has been carried out to protect his victims from something he perceives as worse than death—their continued survival. Without question, to those who have experienced the genuine depth and meaning of love, this is the most extreme perversion imaginable

"I'VE DONE WHAT I WANTED TO DO . . ."

Over the course of three different days, during the Christmas season of 1987, Ronald Gene Simmons became one of the most brutal family mass murderers in the history of American criminology. Simmons's spree of violence and murder included the death of fourteen members of his own family and six others against whom he held a grudge for one reason or another. Only four of his victims survived their attacker; none of the survivors were family members. One of Simmons's victims was only twenty months old; most were shot, strangled, or both—many with extreme brutality. His three days of carnage were not only incredible in their cruelty but disturbingly calculated and scrupulously planned.

Ronald Simmons was considered a bully in high school and was never popular with his classmates. He wanted to dominate every relationship in which he was involved, particularly those that held any emotional meaning for him. Immediately after graduation, Simmons joined the U.S. Navy, where he served for five years with a level of distinction that would not have been anticipated by his high school reputation. The military provided an environment in which Simmons thrived. He received the respect of his peers and subordinates while serving in the navy—something that had always been missing from his young life. His bullying behavior in adolescence was viewed quite differently in the navy, and perhaps for the first time in his life, Simmons felt at home.

After his term of enlistment came to an end, Simmons briefly tried his hand at civilian life but quickly found it difficult and dissatisfying. He was unable to enjoy the structure and control that was the baseline of all his experiences in the military. Worse, he found himself unaccepted among civilians, in contrast to the ready acceptance that he had received in the navy.

Simmons decided to join the U.S. Air Force so that he could seriously pursue a military career and earn the respect that he felt he deeply deserved but had not yet truly attained. He served in the air force for sixteen years, earning five medals for meritorious service as well as the Bronze Star. While in the military, Simmons managed to find a degree of satisfaction with his life. His passion to control and organize was well rewarded and he seemed to be a relatively happy individual. In 1979, having attained the rank of master sergeant, Simmons decided to retire from the service and once again try his luck in civilian life. He now had a burgeoning family and, although unsure about life outside of the structure of the military, Simmons was determined to find a new career and new opportunities.[5] Unfortunately, civilian life once again proved to be unbearable. Simmons discovered that life away from the air force presented no opportunities for him. The comfortable and predictable structure of the service had given way to a life that seemed chaotic, frustrating, and disappointing to a man who thrived on regimen, control, and certainty.

By 1987, eight years after he had left the military, Simmons was a miserable, frustrated, and angry man. He had been married to his wife, Becky, for over twenty years; however, it had been a stormy relationship that grew dissatisfying and tedious over the years, to the point that they had not regularly slept together in the last six years of their marriage. Simmons was now forty-seven years old and had held nothing but a series of low-paying, menial jobs since his retirement from the air force. None of these jobs provided the satisfaction or sense of importance that Simmons had enjoyed (and on which he had come to rely) throughout his military career.

Simmons's sense of frustration and perceived lack of control was most apparent in the way that he ruled over the members of his family. He censored his wife's mail, forbade his children from any activities outside of school, and isolated his family in a mobile home on thirteen acres of forested land located miles from the nearest town in rural Arkansas. In every way, Simmons was the commandant of what he perceived to be a military unit pretending to be a family. Worse that this, Simmons had severe sexual problems that were tearing his family apart.

In 1981, two years after his retirement from the military, the Simmons family was living in New Mexico. While there, Simmons impregnated his seventeen-year-old daughter, Sheila, after a lengthy incestuous relationship. Sheila and her mother eventually reported Simmons's crime to local authorities in an effort to make him stop the relationship. Simmons responded by forcing his family to flee New Mexico for the isolation of Pope County, Arkansas. Although Simmons never made another attack on his daughter, his incest while in New Mexico and the family's subsequent enforced isolation in Arkansas ripped the family permanently apart. Mrs. Simmons refused to sleep with her husband after the incest was disclosed, and Sheila's siblings never forgave their overbearing and cruel father. Mrs. Simmons and the children deeply resented their father for his behavior and for forcing them to move to the isolated, fortress-like home in Arkansas. From 1981 until 1987, the year in which he murdered sixteen people, Simmons became increasingly frustrated and isolated, demanding that his family obey his every wish and have nothing to do with anyone outside their home. Mrs. Simmons and the children were virtual prisoners to a man whom they both loathed and feared.

In 1987, Simmons became obsessed with a pretty, twenty-four-year-old coworker in the nearby town of Russellville, Arkansas, where he had worked at one of his several low-paying jobs. He pursued Kathy Kendrick with the same intensity that he had applied to every facet of his life, bombarding her with letters, gifts, and flowers in a relentless and dominating fashion. However, Kendrick would have nothing to do with the pudgy, balding man, who seemed to her to be incredibly stilted and demanding. Simmons eventually gave up his overt pursuit of Kendrick; however, he never forgot the rejection and he never forgave her.

That same year, Simmons tried to make amends to Sheila, her husband, and the rest of the family for his incestuous behavior and their impossible living conditions by scripting a lengthy statement to read to the family. However, it was a rambling diatribe of excuses and sentiments of love that was more self-serving than sincere. Gathering the family together to read the prepared statement, Simmons hoped that he would finally be able to make amends for his actions and reestablish a more normal family relationship, particularly with his wife. To his amazement, rather than receiving the forgiveness that he sought and expected, Sheila and the others mocked his statement and refused to accept what they perceived to be yet another insincere effort to control his family in any way that he could. Simmons was furious about this rejection, especially when he subsequently learned that his wife of over two decades was planning to leave him. He filed the scripted statement away in his safe deposit box and said nothing more about it to his family. By late 1987, unbearably frustrated and angry with his family, unable to forgive Kathy Kendrick's rejection, worried about his impending separation, and harboring an insatiable desire for vengeance against a number of supervisors with whom he had worked in the nearby town, Simmons made final preparations to deal with all those he had not been able to control to his satisfaction.

December 22, 1987. This was the last day of school for the Simmons children, who were anxiously looking forward to the school break and to the gifts that had been carefully arranged under the family Christmas tree. Their mobile home had been festively decorated for the occasion, and despite their father's unusually quiet mood, Becky Simmons and the children looked forward to visiting with the rest of the family in a few days.

As was his habit, Ronald Simmons helped get the older children ready for school. Barbara, their three-year-old daughter, was still asleep in the bedroom and Becky was cleaning up the kitchen when Simmons walked Loretta (age seventeen), Eddy (age fourteen), Marianne (age eleven), and Rebecca (age eight) down the hill from their home to the rural road where the school bus stopped each morning. Simmons waited with the children for the bus to arrive and watched them board, warning them to come straight home from school as he did each morning. He then walked back to the mobile home.

As Simmons entered the home, he saw that Becky was busy in the kitchen making coffee. He quietly moved behind her and struck her with two vicious blows from a crowbar that he held hidden behind his back. Becky Simmons collapsed silently onto the kitchen floor. Simmons then went to the bedroom, where their three-year-old daughter lay sleeping. He wrapped several feet of fishing line around her neck and strangled her until she stopped struggling. In the adjoining bedroom was his twenty-six-year-old son, Ronald Gene Simmons, Jr., who was also asleep. Simmons crushed his skull with the same crowbar that he had used on his wife. Unsure if his son was dead and knowing that there was no one in or near the home who could hear his activities, Simmons then shot him five times with a .22-caliber revolver. He immediately returned to the kitchen where Becky lay motionless and pumped two shots from the same revolver into her face.

Several months earlier, Simmons had made his children dig a large, rectangular pit near the back of their mobile home. He told the family that he had planned to build an outhouse over the pit. Their own home was frequently without heat, light, or even a running toilet, and on the morning of the murders, none of these facilities were working. However, the pit had another purpose that Becky Simmons and the children could never have imagined. Simmons now dragged the three bodies of his loved ones to the pit and lowered them down; however, he did not immediately cover their bodies. There were to be more victims that day, and Simmons had worked out his entire plan very carefully.

In the afternoon, Simmons waited, as usual, for the school bus to arrive. The children were more excited than they had been when he saw them that morning. School was over for a week and Christmas had nearly arrived. To the children's amazement, Simmons seemed to be in high spirits. He promised each of them an early Christmas present as they walked together up the hill to their home. Their father told the children to wait in the family car and he would bring each of them into the mobile home to receive their special gift.

Working from the youngest to the eldest in turn, Simmons called each child into the mobile home. As he or she entered their home, he handed them a wrapped gift to divert their attention from his cruel plan. He then strangled the younger children from behind with fishing line and, to be sure they were dead, held their heads under water in a tub in the family bathroom. He bludgeoned and shot each of the older children.

Simmons then dragged the bodies of his four children to the pit behind the family home. He carefully placed each of them in the mass grave and doused all the bodies with kerosene to ward off any predators and to conceal the odor of decaying flesh which he knew would soon present a problem. Simmons then filled the pit with dirt, covered it with corrugated tin strips that he had previously collected, and surrounded the grave site with barbed wire. After he had buried the bodies, Simmons went inside to clean up and wait. For the next three days he did not leave the home in which he had murdered his wife and children.

December 26, 1987. The day after Christmas was a traditional day of reunion for the Simmons family. The children, their spouses, and the Simmons's grandchildren would all arrive to spend the day visiting and sharing Christmas gifts. In recent years, ever since Simmons had raped his daughter, it was not the joyous time it had been in earlier years. However, the older Simmons children had always looked forward to visiting with their mother and younger siblings.

Simmons's twenty-three-year-old son, William, was the first to arrive, accompanied by his wife, Renata, and their twenty-month-old son. Simmons waved to the young family as they pulled up in front of the mobile home, motioning them to follow him inside. As the family entered the home, Simmons shot his son and daughter-in-law in the head; each received several mortal wounds and died instantly. He then strangled their young child with a cord until he was limp, finishing the murder by holding the boy's head under water in the bathtub.

Later that day, Simmons's oldest daughter, Sheila, arrived. She was twenty-four years old and accompanied by her thirty-three-year-old husband and their two children, Sylvia (six years old) and Michael (twenty-one months old). Sheila entered the Simmons home first and, seeing the bodies of her relatives in the living room, tried to scream for her husband. Simmons rushed at his daughter and shot her in the head six times, killing her instantly. Sheila's husband, Dennis McNulty, heard the shots and ran toward the front door of the home. As he entered, Simmons grabbed him from behind and the two men struggled for the weapon. Simmons was able to overcome his son-in-law and, holding the barrel of the .22-caliber gun against McNulty's head, pulled the trigger, killing him instantly. Simmons then chased the two terrified and screaming children around the mobile home, quickly catching them and strangling them as he had murdered the other children.

By now, the Simmons home was an unspeakable vision of mayhem and death. Fourteen family members had been brutally murdered, and the home was littered with bodies. Simmons made no further effort to bury his loved ones or clean up the crime scene. Rather, he waited in the home for Monday morning to arrive—the day that would signal the beginning of his third, and last, murderous rampage. On that day, Simmons would take final retribution against all those in Russellville who had ever caused him anger or heartache.

December 28, 1987. On Monday morning, Simmons drove into Russellville soon after he knew most of the local businesses would be open. He had already worked out a detailed plan of revenge and knew where each of his predetermined victims would be located.

Simmons's first stop was the law offices of Peel, Eddy, and Gibbons, where Kathy Kendrick, the object of his earlier obsession, worked as a receptionist. Without speaking, Simmons entered the offices, walked up to Kendrick's desk, pulled out his .22-caliber revolver, and shot her several times; Kendrick died instantly from her wounds. Simmons then drove across the town of 17,000 residents to the Taylor Oil Company. Entering the office where he knew his former boss would be working, Simmons shot thirty-eight-year-old Rusty Taylor twice in the chest; fortunately, Taylor would survive his wounds. While trying to run from the scene of the shooting, Simmons was confronted by another employee, thirty-four-year-old Jim Chaffin, who had heard the shots and came to offer assistance. Simmons raised his gun and shot Chaffin in the head at extremely close range, killing him instantly.

Simmons once again got into his car and drove to the edge of town to a convenience store where he had worked until a few weeks before Christmas. When he arrived, Simmons blocked the entrance to the store so that no customers would interrupt him and went looking for his former boss. By this time, realizing that the Russellville police were probably looking for someone matching his description, Simmons had changed his jacket and hat in an attempt to alter his appearance. His former boss, thirty-eight-year-old David Salyer, immediately recognized Simmons anyway and knew that there would be trouble. The two men struggled and, during the melee, Simmons shot both

Salyer and a cashier who had reported to the convenience store for her first day of work. Both victims survived their wounds.

Simmons's next destination was only one block away—the Woodline Motor Freight Company, where Kathy Kendrick had worked before being hired by the law firm of Peel, Eddy, and Gibbons. One of her coworkers, thirty-five-year-old Joyce Butts, had been very vocal in her criticism of Simmons for harassing Kendrick. She had embarrassed Simmons in front of Kendrick and the other workers at Woodline, and to Simmons that was unforgivable behavior. He entered the Woodline offices and went straight to where Joyce Butts was working. Again without saying a word, he shot her in the head and heart; incredibly, Butts would also survive her wounds.

Ronald Gene Simmons had finally completed his lethal mission. He placed the .22-caliber revolver on a desk near his last victim and softly asked a shocked female employee of Woodline to call the police, saying, "I've done what I wanted to do and now it's all over."[6] Simmons's murder spree in Russellville had lasted forty-five minutes; he had murdered two individuals and wounded four others. Back at the Simmons home lay the bodies of fourteen members of his family.

Simmons went on trial for his crimes but offered only a weak defense; he demanded that his legal counsel call no witnesses on his behalf. The trial lasted less than two days and he was quickly found guilty and sentenced to death. On June 25, 1990, Ronald Gene Simmons died by lethal injection for the murder of sixteen persons.

The crimes of Ronald Gene Simmons are almost unbelievable in their callousness and atrocity. Simmons was a man who was obsessed by the need to control others—particularly his loved ones. He demanded absolute obedience to his every whim; he was pathological about any form of rejection and perpetually frustrated with civilian life. Simmons was also an incestuous father who was unable to control his sexual impulses. He ruled the Simmons family as one would rule a small army of servants, using each of them for menial work or perverted pleasure, while completely isolating them from the outside world. That Simmons was feared and despised by his wife and children, particularly after the incestuous relationship with his daughter was disclosed, was clear and understandable.

Simmons was a man who was unable to deal with the vicissitudes and responsibilities of his own life after he had retired from the military. His inability to attract anything but menial work was a devastating departure from his military status; it was a turn of events that Simmons could not accept. Once in civilian life, Simmons became obsessed with isolating and controlling his family to every extent possible. In the end, he was unable to obtain the forgiveness and acceptance that he desperately needed from his wife and children. They had simply suffered too much, for far too long, at his hands. Unable to control those around him, about to lose his wife of over two decades, rejected by virtually all who knew him, and a failure at every job that he had held, Simmons reached his breaking point of frustration, anger, resentment, and disappointment. However, he was still quite capable of planning, and he carefully worked out all the details necessary to take revenge on those whom he could no longer dominate. Unlike most mass murders, who kill in a single episode, Ronald Gene Simmons callously and coldly murdered his victims in three distinct episodes (including the annihilation of his entire family) before finally succumbing to the thing he dreaded most—control by others.

AN APOLOGY TO KIRK

Kirk Buckner was a fourteen-year-old, ninety-pound teenager who had spent all his young life in rural Missouri. Kirk's favorite hobby was showing his best Holstein calves at the local county fair. He was a quiet, very hard-working boy, who rose by four o'clock each morning to help with the endless chores on his family's struggling farm in the Ozarks. However, for a period of ten days in 1987, many of those who had known Kirk Buckner all his life believed that he had become a brutal mass murderer of his family.

On the morning of September 25, 1987, James Eugene Schnick, Kirk's uncle, placed a desperate telephone call to the Webster County sheriff, saying that he had been seriously hurt and needed immediate medical assistance. When he made the telephone call, Schnick was wounded and lying in his own farmhouse, which was located about five miles from the Buckner farm (which belonged to his brother-in-law, Steven). The paramedics and the local sheriff rushed to the Schnick farm, where they found James Schnick bleeding from gunshot wounds to his leg and stomach. Despite the fact that his wounds did not appear serious, Schnick seemed to be delirious and began speaking in an artificially low voice while swinging his arms and legs wildly. The confused paramedics had to have help restraining him in order to treat his wounds before transporting him to the hospital.

In the hallway of the Schnick home, Kirk Buckner lay in a pool of blood. He had been shot and stabbed through the heart. In his right hand was a .22-caliber pistol. Buckner's body was sprawled across the hallway of the residence, partially blocking the entrance to the Schnicks' bedroom. In the bedroom, lying as if she were still asleep, was Julie Schnick—Kirk's aunt. She had been fatally shot through the head with a single .22-caliber round that had apparently come from the gun found in the dead boy's hand.

James Schnick told the sheriff that earlier Kirk had burst into their farmhouse carrying the .22-caliber revolver and shot his wife, Julie. Schnick said that he then struggled with the young boy for the weapon. During the struggle, Schnick claimed that Kirk had shot him twice—once in the abdomen and once in the leg. Although wounded, Schnick said he was able to grab a knife from the kitchen counter and stab the young assailant in the heart. Schnick could give no reason why Kirk had been both stabbed and shot in the heart, except to say that it was a violent struggle and that he could not recall every detail. Schnick told the sheriff that he should immediately send officers over to Steven Buckner's farm because he was concerned about the welfare of Kirk's family.

When deputies arrived at the Buckner farm, they were appalled at what they discovered. Mrs. Buckner had been shot to death near the family barn; Kirk's three brothers (ages two, six, and eight) had each been shot to death inside the farmhouse and were found still lying in their beds. Like Julie Schnick, the young boys had each apparently been shot while they slept. Several hours later, in a cemetery a few miles from Kirk's home, Steven Buckner's body was found by the deputies. He had also been shot to death. Each of the victims had died from one or more .22-caliber gunshot wounds to the head; several of the victims had been shot multiple times.

Local authorities tried to piece together the events of that morning. Speaking to the press—and using information based primarily on James Schnick's statements on the day that he was shot—authorities stated their belief that Kirk Buckner had murdered his entire family early on the morning of September 25, 1987. After murdering his loved ones, the ninety-pound boy somehow managed to drag the body of his 250-pound father to the family pickup truck and drive it to the cemetery, where it was later found. After disposing of his father's body, Kirk then went to his uncle's farm, where he fatally shot his aunt and then struggled with Schnick before being overcome by the stronger man.

However, there were fatal flaws in the story. For example, no one could provide any motive for Kirk's actions. The young boy seemed to be universally liked and had never demonstrated any violent or hostile behavior. If anything, he was a shy, retiring, hard-working youngster who was known by neighbors, teachers, and classmates to be calm, honest, and reliable. Nothing about his actions made any sense. There were also elements at the Schnick farmhouse crime scene that made no sense to the local sheriff. As the next week passed and more information became available to law enforcement personnel, the sheriff became convinced that James Schnick had been lying about the events of September 25, 1987. An autopsy on Kirk's body confirmed that he had been both shot and stabbed in the heart. The medical examiner determined that either wound would have caused near-instantaneous death. Schnick had been unable to explain how this could have happened. Also inexplicable was the fact that the .22-caliber revolver—the weapon now known to have accounted for all seven deaths, including Kirk's—was found in the boy's right hand, despite the fact that, within a few days of the shootings, the sheriff had learned that Kirk had been left-handed.

Another aspect of the crime that deeply troubled the sheriff was Schnick's behavior when he was first approached by paramedics on the morning of the shootings. Despite the fact that his wounds were superficial, Schnick reacted with what appeared to be a delirious rage. His voice was artificially low and his flailing seemed inappropriate to his condition. In the words of the sheriff: "We thought he overacted his part. He tried too hard."[7] Moreover, there was Schnick's continuing odd behavior over the next few days. Despite his minor wounds, Schnick had argued vehemently with the medical staff when the local hospital tried to release him; he demanded to stay in the hospital for a few extra days, even though he was physically quite capable of returning to his farm. Most troublesome to the sheriff was the location of Steven Buckner's body. He could not fathom how the young, frail Kirk could have moved the imposing weight of his dead father into the family pickup truck and, once at the cemetery, then moved it out again.

The sheriff had far too many doubts about the case to let matters stand as Schnick had described them. He contacted James Schnick and asked him to take a polygraph test on Monday, October 5, 1987. Schnick politely agreed and the time was set. However, when he arrived at the sheriff's office for the polygraph test, Schnick confirmed the sheriff's suspicions by suddenly confessing that *he* had murdered all seven family members and Kirk was not to blame. The sheriff immediately videotaped his confession and, later that same day, had seven charges of capital murder filed against James Eugene Schnick.

On April 11, 1988, Schnick went to trial. He was formally charged in three of the slayings—those most likely, in the opinion of the prosecutor, to produce a quick conviction. It had been decided that, if needed, Schnick could later be charged with the remaining four murders. As the prosecutor expected, the additional charges would not be needed. On April 14, 1988, Schnick was convicted on all three counts of first-degree murder.

At Schnick's trial, the true events of what happened that day were finally made public. Early on the morning of September 25, 1987, he had driven to the Buckner farm and brutally shot and killed each family member. Kirk had apparently been away from the farmhouse when his uncle had arrived, doing his usual morning chores. Returning to the farmhouse sometime later that morning, Kirk found his family dead and immediately went to his uncle's farm for help. By the time Kirk arrived, Schnick had already shot his wife while she slept. Schnick then murdered the young boy and self-inflicted two gunshot wounds in an effort to validate his cover story before calling the sheriff (see Table 2.6).

James Schnick never spoke about why he had murdered seven members of his family. However, there was a great deal of speculation about his motives in and around the small farming community. It was generally known that James Schnick and Steven Buckner had been engaged in a long-standing family feud. What was later learned by law enforcement personnel was that Schnick's wife carried a $50,000 life insurance policy that named her husband as the beneficiary. However, this could not explain why Schnick had murdered the entire Buckner family. It was clear from both his confession and the trial that Schnick had carefully planned his crime and prepared an elaborate cover story to avoid apprehension. However, Schnick never personally disclosed his motivations for the murders. Schnick's prosecutor, himself trying to come to some understanding of the brutal crimes, said of the defendant: "He really didn't explain why it happened. I don't know if we will ever know exactly why it happened."[8]

Table 2.6: James Eugene Schnick

Perpetrator	Uncle of a fourteen-year-old boy, who was originally identified by Schnick as the murderer of seven family members.
Incident date/location	September 25, 1987, at two locations in rural Missouri.
Incident category	Perverted love.
Weapons	A .22-caliber pistol and a knife.
Deaths/Injuries	Seven killed.
Motivation	Perpetrator never disclosed the reasons for the murders.
Disposition	Schnick survived his crimes, later confessed, and was convicted of multiple counts of first degree murder on April 14, 1988.

REJECTION AND REVENGE

Rejection and revenge can be powerful motivating factors that lie behind the most brutal family killings. These two elements are critically linked, and for a few individuals, can provide all that is necessary to set the stage for mass murder. When an act of rejection is insurmountable or it is followed and compounded by fantasies of revenge and retribution, a potentially violent or unbalanced individual may become obsessed with the injustices that he feels were thrust upon him by others. Pathologically pondering these injustices and, in some cases, with the added fuel of an addiction to alcohol, drugs, or both, the compulsion for revenge can become overwhelming and irresistible. Ramon Salcido was just such a family mass murderer. Obsessed with rejection and jealousy, possessed by pathological fantasies of revenge, and a frequent abuser of alcohol and cocaine, Salcido lashed out against his family in a crime of incredible brutality and callousness.

In April 1989, Ramon Salcido received the worst news that he could imagine. He had been involved in a long and bitter child-support case with his ex-wife that had left him intensely angered and frustrated. Salcido had refused to pay child support for his two children, and his ex-wife would not give up the struggle for her rights. By April, Debra Ann Salcido had managed to win a court decree against her ex-husband; it ordered Salcido to pay his ex-wife $511 a month in child support, as well as $6,000 in back payments which he had persistently ignored. When Ramon Salcido learned this news, he was furious. This was, he thought, more than any man could take.

Salcido's relationship with his current wife, twenty-four-year-old Angelia, was also collapsing around him. He was convinced that Angelia was having an affair with one of his coworkers at the winery where Salcido was employed as a forklift operator. His relationship with Angelia had deteriorated to the point that she was planning to leave him. This also made Salcido furious and depressed. In an effort to escape the injustices that he perceived all around him, Ramon Salcido would often turn to nights of heavy drinking and cocaine use, frequently making the rounds of a number of nightclubs until they closed their doors.

On the evening of April 13, 1989, Salcido was once again drinking heavily, using cocaine, and deeply angered about the women in his life. It seemed to him that they *all* had conspired to betray him in one way or another. On that night, he could think of nothing but revenge and feel nothing but anger and hatred.

On Friday morning, April 14, 1989, Salcido drove to the small, northern California town of Glen Ellen, where the winery that employed him was located. He had come to a final decision about the future of all those who had rejected or threatened him in the past—this day was to be his for revenge. Salcido entered the winery, looking for the man who was allegedly having an affair with his wife. As he began searching for his rival, Salcido angrily brandished a gun and threatened all who were nearby. Moving quickly through the winery to locate his target, Salcido shot and killed his boss and seriously wounded the coworker whom he suspected of being Angelia's lover. He then raced from the scene, driving back to his home in nearby Boyes Hot Springs, where he knew his wife would be waiting.

When he arrived home, Salcido angrily confronted Angelia, as he had often done in the past. However, this time there was nothing to stay his violence—he had already committed murder that day. Within moments, his wife lay dead, shot and bludgeoned in a fearsome display of brutality. She was only twenty-four years old on the day she died.

Fleeing the family home, Salcido abducted their three young daughters, aged one, three, and four years. He then drove about a dozen miles to the small town of Cotati, where Angelia's mother lived with her two other daughters. Salcido bludgeoned and shot his mother-in-law, raped and sodomized the two daughters (ages eight and twelve), and then shot and killed the two children.

Salcido's last victims were his own daughters. In an unbelievable act of cruelty, he cut the throats of his three daughters and threw them into an isolated garbage dump by the side of the road. Two of the little girls died immediately. Miraculously, and despite the fact that her neck was slashed from ear to ear, three-year-old Carmina Salcido survived the attack and was discovered by a passerby the day after her father's rampage. She was able to tell authorities of her ordeal and named her father as her attacker and the murderer of her sisters.

Law enforcement officials began a massive manhunt for Ramon Salcido. Knowing that he was a native of Mexico and had family in the small town of Guasave, local police worked closely with Mexican authorities to trace Salcido's movements. On April 19, 1989, Salcido was captured by Mexican law enforcement personnel. When questioned, he immediately confessed to the brutal murders. Salcido told the Mexican authorities that he had murdered his family because he was jealous of his wife and suspected she was having an affair with one of the men he had shot at the winery five days earlier. He went on to explain that he had fled to Mexico to visit with his parents one last time, knowing that he must face his crimes and probable execution back in the United States.

On April 21, 1989, Salcido was formally charged with seven counts of murder and three counts of attempted murder. The prosecutor for the case made it clear that he believed Salcido to be sane and that he would diligently work for the maximum sentence allowed under California law—the death penalty. On May 5, 1989, Salcido pled not guilty to all charges. Many months later, he went to trial and, once in court, was faced with overwhelming evidence of his guilt. On October 30, 1990, Salcido was convicted of six counts of first-degree murder. Just before Christmas of that year, on December 17, 1990, he was sentenced to death for his crimes.

Although sane, Ramon Salcido was a man who appeared to be completely out of control on the day that he murdered his family. Rejected by two women, crazed with jealousy, obsessed with fantasies of revenge, and abusing drugs and alcohol, Salcido struck out with incredible ferocity against the female members of his family and the man whom he thought was involved with his wife. The female victims, including the children, were murdered in a deeply personalized manner by slashing or bludgeoning, as well as shooting. Two of the young girls were raped and sodomized. The extent of this brutality is unusual in the case of mass murder, except in the rare instance of mass sexual homicide. Salcido's murders were acts of inconceivable passion and rage; they were designed to dominate, humiliate, dehumanize, and annihilate his victims. These murders were significantly more heinous and brutal than those usually attributed to the mass murderer—they exhibited many elements that are often linked to sexual homicides. Most incredible were the ages of the victims, with the youngest daughter meeting her death at the age of one.

As is typical of most mass murderers, Ramon Salcido's attacks were planned. He expected to leave no witnesses behind. That his three-year-old daughter was able to survive his brutal onslaught and name him as the murderer was something Salcido could never have foreseen. No doubt, Salcido had long fantasized about revenge against those he so deeply despised. The rejection that he had experienced by his ex-wife and Angelia, the legal difficulties that he brought on himself by failing to support his children, and the rage that he felt at the thought of another man making love to his young wife combined to ignite a cauldron of hostility and anger that must have been simmering for years (see Table 2.7).

The hideous nature of the crimes of Ramon Salcido hinted at a man who must have been insane or severely mentally disabled. In fact, he was neither. He was a man who was angry and resentful beyond comprehension—a man who fueled his obsession for revenge with drugs and alcohol and who had no understanding of the meaning of family or love. In the end, he could only perceive of the death of his loved ones as a resolution to his own, uncontrollable life.

Table 2.7: Ramon Salcido

Perpetrator	A husband and father who went on a rape and murder spree against his own family and coworkers.
Incident date/location	April 14, 1989, at various locations in northern California.
Incident category	Perverted love and revenge.
Weapons	A handgun, knife, blunt instruments, strangulation, and bludgeoning.
Deaths/Injuries	Six killed, four injured, two raped and sodomized. Many of the victims where children.
Motivation	Salcido was addicted to alcohol and drugs, pathologically jealous, and had a history of aggressive and erratic behavior.
Disposition	Convicted of multiple counts of first-degree murder on October 30, 1990. Sentenced to death on December 12, 1990.

"I GOT ANGRY"

Like Ramon Salcido, Julio Gonzalez was a pathologically jealous man who was often aggressive; he was also completely incapable of dealing with rejection. His definition of love was sadistically simple—if he could not have the woman of his choice for himself, on his own terms, than she must die. It did not matter to Gonzalez who would stand in the way of his need to possess Lydia Feliciano—they must also die. For him, it was a matter of pride, control, and absolute domination.

Gonzalez was a Cuban refugee who came to the United States on the Mariel boatlift of 1980. He settled in New York City and eventually developed an intimate relationship with Lydia Feliciano. By 1990, Gonzalez and Feliciano had been together for seven years; however, many of those years had been stormy ones because of his incessant jealousy and overwhelming need to control their relationship. In that same year, Feliciano told Gonzalez that the relationship was over and that he must leave her alone in the future. Gonzalez flatly refused to accept her decision and made repeated attempts to reestablish the relationship. However, Feliciano remained determined to have a life free of his controlling attention.

Lydia Feliciano worked as a coat checker and part-time bartender at the Happy Land social club in the Bronx. The Happy Land was an illegal, but popular, after-hours club that catered primarily to Honduran and Dominican immigrants. Located near the Bronx Zoo in a poor Latino neighborhood, the club was one of over 150 illegal clubs in New York that operated on a shoestring budget and catered to people from a variety of ethnic groups who enjoyed socializing and dancing until the early morning hours. Happy Land charged five dollars for admission and three dollars for the average drink (also illegal), and it would pack as many patrons as possible into its cramped and substandard premises every night.

On the evening and morning of March 25-26, 1990, the Happy Land social club was filled with patrons at the upstairs bar and dance floor. Nearly one hundred customers were at the club, most of whom had been drinking and dancing to Latin music throughout the night. At approximately 3:00 in the morning, Julio Gonzalez went to the club to once again try to convince Feliciano to renew their relationship. The ex-lovers quickly got into a heated argument and Gonzalez was forcefully ejected from the club shortly before 3:30 in the morning.[9] Witnesses to the argument later claimed that they heard Gonzalez say, "I'll be back," and angrily vowing to "shut the place down." [10,11]

Furious and out of control, Gonzalez ran to a nearby, all-night gas station, where he purchased a dollar's worth of gasoline and put it into a plastic container. He ran back to the social club and poured the gasoline around the club's only functional door, igniting it with two matches. As the flames spread quickly around the frame of the door and began to ignite the surrounding wooden structure, Gonzalez stepped away from the scene to watch the results of his handiwork. After he was sure the building would be fully engulfed by fire, Gonzalez went back to his apartment, which was just a few blocks from the club.[12]

The patrons inside the Happy Land social club had virtually no chance of surviving the ensuing fire. The structure was old and substandard, with only a single exit that could be reached via a steep, narrow stairway. (Ironically, Lydia Feliciano was not among the victims who died in the fire that morning. She had left the club shortly after her encounter with Gonzalez and was already at home when the fire began.) At 3:41 in the morning, the first alarm was sounded, and firefighters were quick to arrive on the scene. Unfortunately, because of the unsafe structure and overcrowded conditions, eighty-seven patrons of the Happy Land social club (sixty-one men, twenty-six women) perished that morning; only five customers survived the fire. The majority of those who were killed succumbed to smoke inhalation or trampling, as terrified customers tried to race for the only available exit (see Table 2.8).[13]

Twelve hours after the fire, Julio Gonzalez was arrested at his apartment. During questioning by detectives, Gonzalez gave only this terse explanation for his crime: "I got angry. The devil got into me and I set the place on fire." At the time of his interrogation, detectives noted that Gonzalez "smelled of gasoline, and he admitted setting the fire. His clothes and sneakers were soaked with gas."[14] Gonzalez was immediately arrested and placed in the Brooklyn House of Detention under a suicide watch. The following day, he was preliminarily charged with eighty-seven counts of capital murder and a grand jury began to hear the evidence of the case. The perpetrator was subsequently transferred to the psychiatric ward at Bellevue Hospital for evaluation. On March 30, 1990, Gonzalez was indicted on 176 counts of murder, arson, and other charges.[15]

Table 2.8: Julio Gonzalez

Perpetrator	A thirty-six-year-old, unemployed Cuban refugee.
Incident date/location	March 26, 1990, at the Happy Land social club in New York.
Incident category	Perverted love.
Weapons	Arson.
Deaths/Injuries	Eighty-seven killed, five survived the arson.
Motivation	Gonzalez attempted to take revenge against his girlfriend of seven years by setting fire to the social club at which she worked.
Disposition	Gonzalez was found guilty of eight-seven counts of murder, eighty-seven counts of depraved indifference to human life, and one count each of arson and assault.

In February 1991, the city of New York brought charges against the owner of the building that housed the Happy Land social club, as well as the individual who leased the space and rented it back to the club owners. One month later, on March 25, 1991, a $5 billion lawsuit was filed against the city of New York on behalf of the patrons who had been killed and injured at the club exactly one year earlier.

Julio Gonzalez also went to trial in 1991. Although he had earlier tried to convince authorities that he was insane at the time of the crime, officials had a videotaped confession of his crimes in their possession. On the videotape, which was shown to the jury at his trial, Gonzalez was heard saying to detectives, "I knew that I was going to do damage, but not of that intensity."[16] During court testimony, a psychologist and a psychiatrist testified that Gonzalez was lying when he had earlier told officials that he had heard a voice commanding him to set the fire. Two other psychologists testified that they believed he was suffering from a temporary psychosis when he committed the crime.[17] In the end, the evidence against Gonzalez was overwhelming and the nature of his crime, unforgivable. The jury was convinced that he was sane on the morning of March 26, 1990, and that he had acted out of revenge against Lydia Feliciano. On August 19, 1991, Gonzalez was found guilty of eight-seven counts of murder, eighty-seven counts of depraved indifference to human life, and one count each of arson and assault.

Although the actions of Julio Gonzalez on the morning of March 26, 1990, appear to have been a spontaneous crime of revenge by a scorned lover, this was probably not the case. Gonzalez had been engaged in a stormy relationship for a number of years, and the evidence suggests that he had lost the one element in the relationship that he could not live without—control of Lydia Feliciano. Prior to his crimes, Gonzalez had made repeated attempts to regain control over Feliciano and renew their relationship. Regardless of how he tried to cajole, harass, or intimidate his ex-girlfriend, she would not comply. Obsessed with the need to control a defunct relationship and unwilling to deal with Feliciano's repeated rejections, Gonzalez succumbed to a final triggering event when he was once again rejected by Feliciano at the Happy Land social club. Although it is uncertain whether Gonzalez specifically planned his crime of arson that night, the evidence of his relationship with Feliciano, combined with his inability to deal with her rejection, was certainly at the heart of many fantasies of revenge and retribution that must have plagued Gonzalez for some time before he finally committed to violence. That his feelings for Lydia Feliciano were both perverse and deadly can easily be evidenced by his complete disregard for the nearly one hundred innocent lives that he took at the Happy Land social club.

"I JUST WANT THIS TO BE OVER"

Lawrence John DeLisle's life was never easy; in fact, it was filled with emotional tragedy, even from his early childhood. Born in Lincoln Park, Michigan, the catastrophes that would befall him throughout his life began even before he was born. DeLisle had been named after his uncle, who drowned while swimming in a lake in 1957—years before DeLisle was born. The young DeLisle's father, Richard, had watched his brother drown while making frantic but futile efforts to save his life. Richard DeLisle was never able to overcome the death of his brother and incessantly discussed the tragedy when he was feeling depressed or morose. The death of the elder Richard left Lawrence DeLisle's father an embittered and cold man, who was unable to give his young son the love or attention that he desperately needed. To compound matters, Richard DeLisle's marriage had failed and his business was in financial ruin. Finally, in 1988, at the age of forty-eight, Richard DeLisle could no longer stand the years of guilt, depression, setbacks, and social isolation. In February of that year, Lawrence DeLisle's father committed suicide in the family Ford station wagon, using a .38-caliber pistol.

Lawrence DeLisle, whose mother had left him when he was but a year old, was not living with his father at the time of the suicide; he had been living with his grandparents since his mother abandoned him years earlier. Throughout his childhood, Lawrence's father never played a meaningful role in his son's life—except to leave his son the Ford station wagon in which he had committed suicide. To Lawrence DeLisle, the Ford station wagon represented all the rejection and lack of love that he had experienced throughout his young life. Later, when recalling his father, DeLisle would say: "He was a son-of-a-bitch, an asshole. He blew his fucking brains out and didn't say goodbye."[18] His bitterness toward his father and the memories of the family tragedies were always with Lawrence DeLisle. However, his anger was most obvious when speaking of the hostile relationship between him and his father: "I could never measure up to him. You know what he called me? Pussy. I couldn't hit him back. I wanted to. I should have."[19]

Lawrence DeLisle married and eventually fathered four children—two boys and two girls. However, by 1989, at the age of twenty-eight, DeLisle's life had become as untenable as the life of his father before him. DeLisle's children were young and needed a good deal of attention from their parents: Brian was eight, Melissa was four, Kadie was eighteen months, and Emily less than ten months old. The family's financial situation also needed a good deal of attention. DeLisle owed over $18,000 in credit card debts, thousands in medical bills, and thousands more in loans. His family finances had deteriorated to the point where DeLisle was unable to pay the premiums on his life insurance policy or the rent on the family home. By 1989, DeLisle and his family had been forced to move into his brother's home, where they paid no rent. Working as a service manager for a tire store, DeLisle's salary of $33,000 per year was just not enough to begin to deal with the bills and debts that he had to face, even though he often worked fifty-hour weeks.[20] However, despite these many hardships, Lawrence DeLisle was considered by all who knew him to be a hard-working family man who was devoted to his wife and children. When he was not working, DeLisle took obvious pleasure in spending time with his family and arranging whatever simple outings their meager income would allow.

Table 2.9: Lawrence John DeLisle

Perpetrator	A twenty-eight-year-old, troubled man who murdered his four children.
Incident date/location	August 3, 1989, in Wyandotte, Michigan at the Detroit River.
Incident category	Perverted love.
Weapons	Attempted family murder/suicide by drowning, using the family automobile.
Deaths/Injuries	Four killed (all the DeLisle children), two injured (DeLisle and his wife).
Motivation	DeLisle, faced with a variety of life challenges, wanted to end his life and those of his wife and children.
Disposition	DeLisle and his wife survived the family suicide attempt. DeLisle was convicted of four counts of murder and one count of attempted murder. He was sentenced to life in prison without the possibility of parole.

On August 3, 1989, DeLisle took his wife and children for a late afternoon drive—an activity that had become somewhat of a family tradition and an opportunity for them to spend some time together. On this afternoon, the DeLisles did as they had often done in the past and drove to the drug store for something sweet for the children. When Suzanne DeLisle returned to the car with their four children, each with a treat in hand, Lawrence DeLisle had already made up his mind about his life—and theirs. As DeLisle would later tell law enforcement officials, he thought to himself, "I just want it to be over. There has got to be an afterlife that's better than this hellhole."[21]

After he was sure that his wife had used her seat belt and that the children were safely in their car seats, DeLisle jammed his right foot on the accelerator and aimed the family car straight down the road that led to the shores of the Detroit River. As the automobile picked up speed, DeLisle shouted, "I can't get my foot off; I can't get my foot off!"[22] Traveling at over forty miles per hour, DeLisle's car smashed through a wooden barricade at the end of the road and plunged headlong into the river. The car, with all its occupants trapped inside, flipped over and sunk immediately in thirty feet of water. After a brutal struggle, both DeLisle and his wife were able to free themselves from the sinking car and swim to the surface. However, their children, who were still secured in their car seats, all drowned (see Table 2.9).

Lawrence DeLisle's first reaction when interviewed by law enforcement personnel was to confess to the horrible murder/suicide attempt. Later he retracted his confession and claimed that the incident was an accident. However, witnesses to the event made it clear that DeLisle had deliberately aimed his car toward the river and made no effort to brake the vehicle or turn it from its course. Despite eyewitness accounts, Suzanne DeLisle believed in her husband's innocence—she was, perhaps, the only individual sympathetic to his version of the tragedy that had befallen her children. The jury hearing the case against Lawrence DeLisle was strongly convinced of his guilt and found him responsible for four counts of murder and one count of attempted murder. DeLisle was subsequently sentenced to serve the remainder of his life in prison, without the possibility of parole.

NOTES

1. "Sexual Homicide: Decision Process Models," in Kozel Multimedia, Inc., *Mind of a Killer,* CD-ROM (Chatsworth, CA: Cambrix, 1995).

2. "Navajo Man Shoots His 5 Children—4 Dead," *San Francisco Chronicle,* 3 September 1996, A6.

3. "7 Members of Iowa Family Dead in Murder-Suicide," *Philadelphia Inquirer Online* (Internet edition), 21 December 1987, A01.

4. Tom Seery, "Friends Think Iowa Killing Suspect Was Jealous of Kin," *Philadelphia Inquirer Online* (Internet edition), 1 January 1988, A04.

5. James Alan Fox and Jack Levin, *Overkill: Mass Murder and Serial Killing Exposed* (New York: Plenum, 1994), 145-162.

6. Ibid., 153.

7. Bill Peterson, "Relief Felt as Farm Boy Is Absolved," *Washington Post* (Internet edition), 7 October 1987, 1.

8. J. Michael Kennedy, "Missouri Slayings: Doubts, a Probe, then a Confession," *Los Angeles Times* (Internet edition), 12 October 1987, 1.

9. Larry Celona and Stuart Marques, "Evidence Airtight in N.Y. Arson," *Philadelphia Inquirer Online* (Internet edition), 27 March 1990, 14.

10. Raul Reyes, "Arson Torches N.Y. Club, Kills 87," Philadelphia Inquirer Online (Internet edition), 26 March 1990, 3.

11. Celona and Marques, "Evidence Airtight in N.Y. Arson."

12. Ibid.

13. Reyes, "Arson Torches N.Y. Club, Kills 87."

14. Celona and Marques, "Evidence Airtight in N.Y. Arson."

15. Larry Neumeister, "Club Arson Suspect Indicted," *Philadelphia Inquirer Online* (Internet edition), 31 March 1990, 4.

16. Marlene Aig, "Cuban is Guilty in Fire Killing 87," *Philadelphia Inquirer Online* (Internet edition), 20 August 1991, 12.

17. Ibid.

18. Fox and Levin, *Overkill*, 129.

19. Ibid.

20. Ibid., 130.

21. Ibid., 131.

22. Ibid.

CHAPTER 3

Politics and Hate

The price of hating other human beings is loving oneself less.

Eldridge Cleaver
Soul on Ice

Terrorism and mass murder based on the politics of hate are rampant throughout the world. Americans have traditionally considered this country to be immune from this form of violence; however, in the past few years, this traditional perspective has been shattered by domestic acts of terrorism that were previously considered unthinkable in this country. In particular, several recent incidents of terrorism have shocked Americans into a realization that our shores are no longer protected from many forms of violence. It has become obvious to the public that our most highly treasured landmarks and national events often make prime targets for individuals with an agenda based on the politics of hate.

On February 26, 1993, a bomb weighing over half a ton was detonated in the parking garage beneath the World Trade Center (WTC) in New York City. This enormous explosive device created a five-story crater under the WTC, caused some $500 million dollars in damages, killed six, and injured another 1,042 individuals who were in the building at the time of the explosion. The Federal Bureau of Investigation (FBI) was quickly able to arrest four radical Muslims and charge them with the crime. The speedy apprehension of the terrorists was allegedly due to information provided by an informant, Emad Salem, who had infiltrated the inner circle of the terrorists and participated in the planning of the WTC bombing. Salem was allegedly paid $1 million for his testimony against the radical Muslims—testimony that included tape recorded conversations with the terrorists that left no doubt about their guilt.

In 1994, the four terrorists were brought to trial and found guilty of crimes that resulted in prison terms of 240 years for each perpetrator. A fifth terrorist escaped from the United States immediately after the bombing and fled to Pakistan. In early 1995, he was apprehended and extradited to face the same charges as his coconspirators (see Table 3.1).

Table 3.1: New York World Trade Center Bombing

Perpetrator	Muhammad Amim Salameh, Nidal Ayyad, Mahmud Abouhalima, Ahmed Ajaj, and Ramzi Ahmen Yousef.
Incident date/location	February 26, 1993, at the World Trade Center in New York City.
Incident category	Politics and hate.
Weapons	Explosives.
Deaths/Injuries	Six killed, 1,042 injured.
Motivation	Terrorism by detonation of a 1,200-pound bomb made of high explosives that was hidden in a vehicle in the underground parking area of the building.
Disposition	Salameh, Ayyad, Abouhalima, and Ajaj were convicted on March 4, 1994, and sentenced to 240 years (each) in prison and a $500,000 fine. Yousef fled to Pakistan after the bombing but was subsequently arrested on February 7, 1995, and turned over to the FBI.

POSSIBILITIES AND INTENTIONS

Two incidents took place in July 1996 that may have been prompted by the opening of the centennial Olympic Games, which were held in Atlanta, Georgia, later that month—the crash of TransWorld Airlines (TWA) flight 800 (July 17, 1996) and the bombing that occurred in the Olympic Park public venue at the height of the Olympic Games (July 29, 1996). Although the complete details surrounding these incidents have not yet been made public by the investigating agencies, it is apparent that the Olympic Park bombing was an act of terrorism designed to disrupt one of the most significant events to be held in this country in the past several decades. The tragedy of TWA flight 800 remains an enigma and the topic of persistent national controversy.

If the downing of TWA flight 800 is eventually determined to be the result of a terrorist act, it will be labeled a crime of mass murder unparalleled in U.S. history in terms of the number of lives lost. The Olympic Park bombing only resulted in the deaths of two individuals and would not be traditionally considered a crime of mass murder. However, the failure of the perpetrator of the Olympic Park bombing to achieve his or her formal designation as a mass murderer was only due to a fortunate set of circumstances and poor terrorist tactics. Regardless of the low mortality rate resulting from this crime, the evidence is clear that this was an intended act of mass murder.[VII] Unfortunately, the evidence surrounding the demise of TWA flight 800 is not so clear; the facts of this tragedy remain confusing and, in great measure, sequestered by the government. It appears that the implications of the investigation are not yet known, even to the officials investigating the crash.

On July 17, 1976, TWA flight 800 departed John F. Kennedy International Airport in New York City for Paris. Eleven and a half minutes after takeoff, the airliner suddenly exploded, broke into two major sections, and plummeted into the ocean from an elevation of 13,700 feet. All 230 passengers and crew onboard the airplane were killed.[1] The National Transportation Safety Board (NTSB) and the Federal Bureau of Investigation (FBI) were immediately called to the scene to begin an investigation of what was, at first, considered to be a possible terrorist attack. The crew onboard flight 800 had only engaged in routine conversation with air traffic controllers and gave no indication of any mechanical problems with the aircraft before it suddenly broke in two and disappeared from the radar screens. Data recorders onboard the aircraft gave no indication of the cause of the crash.

The investigation of the crash was made extremely difficult because the wreckage of the airliner was submerged in 120 feet of water and strewn over an area two miles long off the coast of Long Island, New York. More than a month after the crash, only half the wreckage had been recovered and more than twenty of the victims' bodies had not yet been located. However, during that month of investigation, evidence had been accumulated indicating that the airliner may have been brought down by (1) mechanical failure, (2) a bomb planted near one of its massive fuel tanks, or (3) a missile that struck the airliner and detonated in the passenger cabin.

On August 23, 1996, the *New York Times* reported that investigators had determined that there was evidence that an explosive device of some type may have been placed in the cabin of the airliner, possibly between seating rows 17 and 27.[2] The *Times* reported that chemists at the FBI laboratories had discovered traces of pentaerythritol tetranitrate (PETN) on a piece of the wreckage corresponding to the area of the passenger cabin where the breakup of the airliner was known to have occurred. The substance PETN is a component that is common to terrorist bombs and a variety of surface-to-air missiles; it is a key component in the detonator of many explosive devices. One week later, the *New York Times* reported that traces of a second explosive substance had been located by investigators among the wreckage. This second substance was found to be RDX, a major ingredient in Semtex (as is PETN), a

---

VII. If the demise of TWA Flight 800 is determined to be a criminal act, it will become the deadliest crime of mass murder in U.S. history (see "Appendix 4: The Five Most Deadly U.S. Mass Murders").

plastic explosive known to be used by terrorists.[VIII] Semtex is used in a variety of high-powered explosive devices; it can be mixed into a puttylike substance that is easily concealed by molding it into virtually any shape. It is also undetectable by X-ray devices, making it a weapon of choice for those perpetrators who target transportation systems.[3] Both substances were located in the same area of the aircraft that was shown by computer simulation to be the probable point of origin of the explosion that downed TWA flight 800. However, this presumed evidence of an explosive device onboard the airliner was later brought into question when it was discovered that the aircraft had been previously used for a bomb training operation. This training exercise involved the placement of packages containing explosive chemicals that were designed to be detected by bomb-sniffing dogs. Even though these packages were removed from the airliner after the exercise and could not have been the cause of the explosion that was known to have occurred onboard the airliner, it is possible that residue of the explosive chemicals remained behind and was subsequently discovered during the crash investigation activities.[4] This new information caused crash investigators to reverse their earlier position that the crash was probably the result of a terrorist attack and "[lean] toward mechanical failure as the cause" of the tragedy.[5]

Whatever the final determination of the fate of TWA flight 800, it is clear that this catastrophe presented difficulties to investigators and law enforcement officials that were unprecedented in the history of aviation tragedies. The uncertainty of crash investigators, and the shifting positions of government officials involved in the criminal investigation of the downing of TWA flight 800 can only exacerbate the grave concern shared by those who recognize the real possibility for future tragedy inherent in the crime of mass murder for political purposes. Although no official and final determination has yet been released regarding the demise of the airliner, at least some of the evidence points to an act of terrorism. If the downing of TWA flight 800 is eventually determined to be an act of terrorism, one possible theory is that this crime was related to the opening of the centennial Olympic Games, which occurred shortly after the incident (see Table 3.2).

On July 29, 1996, at 1:25 in the morning, a homemade pipe bomb was detonated at Centennial Olympic Park, a free venue of the Olympic Games in Atlanta, Georgia, where attendees at the games gathered nightly to enjoy music and dancing (see Table 3.3). The bomb was spiked with shrapnel of compressed nails and screws in an obvious attempt to kill and injure as many individuals as possible. Just prior to the detonation of the bomb, its existence was discovered by security personnel at the Centennial Olympic Park venue and an effort was made to move individuals away from the area of danger. However, before the area could be completely cleared, the device exploded. One woman was killed

VIII. RDX is also known as cyclonite. It is an explosive substance more powerful than TNT and was used throughout World War II in a variety of munitions.

by shrapnel and a journalist died of a heart attack while covering the incident; over one hundred spectators were injured. Fortunately, only eleven of the injured required hospitalization, and all completely recovered. What could have been an incredible act of mass murder was averted only by luck and circumstances that morning.

Table 3.2: TWA Flight 800

Perpetrator	Unknown. It has not yet been determined whether the airliner succumbed to mechanical failure or it was brought down by an act of terrorism.
Incident date/location	July 17, 1996, while in flight to France.
Incident category	Politics and hate (if the incident proves to be an act of terrorism).
Weapons	Explosives, missile or mechanical failure (not yet determined).
Deaths/Injuries	230 killed, no survivors.
Motivation	Uncertain. One theory is that this was an act of terrorism related to the centennial Olympic Games. The facts of the crash, if known, have not been made public.
Disposition	Not yet determined.

Sometime between 12:58 and 1:08 in the morning, local authorities received a telephone call warning them that the bomb was about to explode. The call had been placed from a public telephone within the Centennial Olympic Park itself—in fact, within sight of where the bomb had been placed, near the music stage. The caller, whose voice was described as belonging to a "white American," said to officials: "There is a bomb in Centennial Park. You have thirty minutes."[6] Unfortunately, due to several delays in relaying this information to field personnel at the bomb site, many individuals were injured in the ensuing explosion.

The Federal Bureau of Investigation (FBI) quickly took charge of the crime scene and declared the explosion an obvious terrorist attack. A security guard fell under immediate suspicion and became the prime target of the ensuing investigation; he had been one of the first on the scene to recognize the pipe bomb and instruct bystanders to leave the area. However, more than three months after the bombing, no suspect had been arrested and the FBI remained silent about the status of its investigation. Despite the silence of authorities, it seems obvious that this was a terrorist attack spawned from the politics of hate and directed at one of the most significant public events ever held in this country. Fortunately, it did not have its intended effect, either in terms of casualties or the disruption of the Olympic Games.

Table 3.3: Olympic Park Bombing

Perpetrator	Unknown.
Incident date/location	July 29, 1996, at Centennial Olympic Park in Atlanta, Georgia.
Incident category	Politics and hate.
Weapons	Explosives (pipe bomb).
Deaths/Injuries	Two killed, 110 injured.
Motivation	Probably an act of terrorism related to the centennial Olympic Games.
Disposition	Perpetrator(s) have not been identified or captured.

RACIAL HATRED

Racially motivated murders have plagued this country since the early days of its formation. Unfortunately, they continue unabated at the end of the twentieth century. On December 11, 1995, an African-American activist murdered seven individuals and then committed suicide, in a crime of mass murder that was apparently motivated by racial hatred (see Table 3.4). The perpetrator, a fifty-one-year-old male, had been upset for some time because a Caucasian-owned, Harlem clothing store was expanding and would soon displace a popular, African-American-owned music store located next door. Prior to the December attack, there had been weeks of demonstrations against the store expansion, many of which echoed a "loot and burn" theme.[7] The perpetrator had been actively involved in these threatening demonstrations.

Table 3.4: Roland Smith

Perpetrator	A fifty-one-year-old African-American who was upset because of the impending closure of a neighborhood music store.
Incident date/location	December 11, 1995, in a retail store in Harlem.
Incident category	Politics and hate.
Weapons	A .38-caliber revolver and arson materials.
Deaths/Injuries	Seven killed, three injured.
Motivation	Perpetrator was actively involved in protesting the closure of a popular retail music store. He had been previously vocal about his dissatisfaction with the closure.
Disposition	Smith committed suicide at the crime scene with his handgun.

On December 11, 1995, the perpetrator entered the clothing store carrying a .38-caliber revolver and a container of paint thinner. He immediately shot four individuals working in the store and then set the premises on fire. After the fire had been ignited, the perpetrator shot himself in the head with his revolver, dying instantly at the scene and making difficult his subsequent identification by law enforcement personnel. Two other individuals in the store at the time of the attack died in the ensuing fire. Witnesses who survived the shooting rampage and fire told law enforcement personnel that the perpetrator warned all African-American customers to leave the store before he began shooting.[8]

OKLAHOMA CITY

On April 19, 1995, at 9:02 in the morning, a truck bomb containing approximately two tons of explosives was detonated in front of the Alfred P. Murrah Federal Building in Oklahoma City, Oklahoma. The blast virtually destroyed the high-rise building, ripping half of it away instantly. The explosion and ensuing collapse of the structure killed 168 individuals and injured over 400 others. Among the fatalities were nineteen children, who were attending a day care center located on a lower floor of the building (see Chapter 1, Table 1.12).

The explosive used in the bombing was comprised of approximately 4,000 pounds of ammonium nitrate (fertilizer), combined with racing fuel and other additives. This material was tightly packed into the rear cargo area of a twenty-foot rental van, which was detonated directly in front of the federal building. The van had allegedly been rented two days earlier by Timothy McVeigh. On the day of the tragedy, McVeigh was arrested for a traffic violation in Perry, Oklahoma; he was later charged with the bombing. McVeigh's alleged coconspirator, Terry Nichols, surrendered himself to authorities in Kansas and was initially held as a material witness. However, Nichols subsequently confessed to authorities about his role in the bombing and implicated McVeigh. A third individual, Michael Fortier, also implicated both Nichols and McVeigh in the bombing with this handwritten statement, which he provided to authorities:

On December 15th and 16th I rode with Tim McVeigh from my home in Kingman, Arizona, to Kansas. There I was to receive weapons that Tim McVeigh told me had been stolen by Terry Nichols and himself. While in Kansas, McVeigh and I loaded about twenty-five weapons into a car that I had rented. On December 17, 1994, I drove the rental car back to Arizona through Oklahoma and Oklahoma City. Later, after returning to Arizona and at the request of Tim McVeigh, I sold some of the weapons and again at the request of Tim McVeigh I gave him some money to give to Terry Nichols.

Prior to April 1995, McVeigh told me about the plans that he and Terry Nichols had to blow up the federal building in Oklahoma City, Oklahoma. I did not as soon as possible make known my knowledge of the McVeigh and Nichols plot to any judge or other persons in civil authority. When FBI agents questioned me later, about two days after the bombing, and during the next three days, I lied about my knowledge and concealed information. For example, I falsely stated that I had no knowledge of plans to bomb the federal building.

I also gave certain items that I had received from McVeigh, including a bag of ammonium nitrate fertilizer, to a neighbor of mine so the items would not be found by law enforcement officers in a search of my residence.[9]

Fortier, like McVeigh and Nichols, is currently incarcerated and will be held until the two primary perpetrators are tried for the bombing. On August 10, 1995, an indictment was filed against McVeigh and Nichols, which among other charges, alleged the following:

> Beginning on or about September 13, 1994, and continuing thereafter until on or about April 19, 1995, at Oklahoma City, Oklahoma, in the Western District of Oklahoma and elsewhere, Timothy James McVeigh and Terry Lynn Nichols, the defendants herein, did knowingly, intentionally, willfully and maliciously conspire, combine and agree together and with others unknown to the Grand Jury to use a weapon of mass destruction, namely an explosive bomb placed in a truck (a "truck bomb"), against persons within the United States and against property that was owned and used by the United States and by a department and agency of the United States, namely, the Alfred P. Murrah Federal Building at 200 N.W. 5th Street, Oklahoma City, Oklahoma, resulting in death, grievous bodily injury and destruction of the building.[10]

The events leading up to the bombing of April 19, 1995, were uncovered by the grand jury in its investigation and indictment; they have been summarized in "Appendix 5: Timeline of the Oklahoma City Bombing." There is strong evidence to support the contention that McVeigh and Nichols began planning their heinous crime prior to September 1994. The two perpetrators carefully used fictitious names and documents, rented various storage units, robbed in order to finance their activities, and purchased 4,000 pounds of ammonium nitrate to construct the massive bomb. Their planning took over six months to complete, and it is still unknown if other perpetrators were involved. However, to date, the only two individuals who have been specifically charged with the bombing are McVeigh and Nichols.

Based on what authorities have learned from McVeigh, Nichols, Fortier, and others, the apparent motivation for the bombing was retribution for the siege upon the Branch Davidian compound in Waco, Texas, by the Federal Bureau of Investigation (FBI) and the Bureau of Alcohol, Tobacco, and Firearms (ATF) exactly two years earlier, on April 19, 1993. In the Waco incident, eighty members of the Branch Davidian religious sect were killed in a rampaging fire that started during a siege by authorities. In a possible ironic confirmation of this motivation, the grand jury learned that McVeigh had obtained a false driver's license under the name of "Robert Kling" in March 1995. On this license, McVeigh had claimed a date of birth of April 19, 1972— the anniversary day of both the Waco incident and his planned bombing of the Oklahoma City federal building. The rental truck that was used to deliver the deadly bomb to Oklahoma City had been delivered to the fictitious Robert Kling two days before the bombing.

The bombing of the federal building in Oklahoma was a clear act of terrorism—mass murder motivated by politics and hate. Although the two key perpetrators, McVeigh and Nichols, have not yet been found guilty of this crime, there is overwhelming evidence of their participation and planning in an act that became the second worse incident of mass murder in U.S. history.

A NAZI CULTIST IN NEW YORK

Frederick Cowan idolized the Nazi party and its leaders; he believed deeply in the racist theories of white supremacy and the inferiority of virtually all minority groups. Cowan lived in an attic room that was adorned with Nazi paraphernalia and filled with Nazi literature. He was also a paramilitary enthusiast, who collected weapons and surplus military mementos, particularly those that were related to the activities in Germany prior to, and during, World War II. So controlling was his obsession that Cowan even adorned his body with tattoos of iron crosses, death head skulls that were symbolic of elements of the Nazi party, and a large swastika. On the walls of his small room were large posters of such notorious Nazis as Adolph Hitler, Heinrich Himmler, and Reinhard Heydrich, the commander of the concentration camps in Germany during the 1930s and 1940s. In one of his many books on fascism, Cowan had inscribed this note: "Nothing is lower than blacks or Jews except the police who protect them."[11]

By the age of thirty-three, Cowan was a 250-pound weight lifter with a lengthy history of aggression and hatred against a plethora of ethnic and religious minority groups. His racism and Nazi cultist activities were known to everyone who came into contact with him, and it was not unusual to hear Cowan express such violent fantasies as his persistent desire to "shoot up a synagogue."[12] That he was a man who believed in settling issues with violence was also made clear by the bumper sticker on his automobile, which read: "I will give up my gun when they pry my cold, dead fingers from around it."[13] These words proved to be prophetic in the life of Frederick Cowan.

Cowan had a history of aggressive behavior that dated back to when he was a teenager. Although he was an excellent student throughout high school, he dropped out of college in his first year, ending his hopes of becoming an engineer. Even by this young age, Cowan was known by his acquaintances as an individual who harbored a deep hatred of virtually all minorities; however, his fury was particularly obsessive and uncontrolled in any matter that dealt with the subjects of African-Americans or Jews. After quitting college, Cowan joined the U.S. Army, where he immediately ran into serious trouble. His aggressive and insubordinate behavior eventually led to two courts-martial and his premature discharge from the military.

Cowan was never able to find work that satisfied him, and he was always quick to blame others (particularly Jews and African-Americans) for his meager financial situation and poor employment outlook. Eventually, he found menial work as a laborer with the Neptune Moving Company—a business that was owned by a Jew, Norman Bing. It did not take long for Cowan's racist, aggressive tendencies to become obvious to his coworkers and his boss. Shortly after joining the company, Cowan refused to move a refrigerator when he was asked to do so as part of his routine job responsibilities; rather, he became aggressive with his coworkers and insubordinate to his supervisor. Unable to convince Cowan to cooperate with his coworkers, Bing suspended him for two weeks without pay.

For the next two weeks, Cowan was enraged and isolated; he fantasized about nothing but revenge against Bing and the other minority employees at Neptune. Surrounded by symbols of hate and words of racism, he carefully planned for his return to the Neptune Moving Company. Cowan reported back to work on February 14, 1977, at the end of his two-week suspension, and entered the business offices before 8:00 in the morning. He was armed with over fifty pounds of various weapons and ammunition. Yelling for all of the Caucasian employees to get out of the way, Cowan went looking for Bing and the other minority employees while firing his weapons indiscriminately. During his fruitless search for Bing, Cowan shot and killed five individuals outright, mortally wounded a sixth (who would die several months later from his injuries), and seriously wounded four others. Five of those killed were minorities (three were African-Americans) and the sixth was a white police officer who had responded to the scene. Norman Bing, the primary target of Cowan's wrath, was able to hide under a desk and eventually flee the premises without injury (see Table 3.5).

Table 3.5: Frederick Cowan

Perpetrator	A thirty-three-year-old Nazi cultist with a history of aggression.
Incident date/location	February 14, 1977, at his place of work in New Rochelle, New York.
Incident category	Politics and hate.
Weapons	Carried over fifty pounds in various weaponry, including guns, to the crime scene.
Deaths/Injuries	Six killed, four injured.
Motivation	Ethnic hatred. Cowan was intent on murdering his Jewish boss and also targeted other minority individuals during his rampage.
Disposition	After a lengthy standoff with police, Cowan committed suicide at the crime scene.

After the shootings, Cowan refused to leave the premises and an all-day siege ensued, with the moving company offices surrounded by law enforcement personnel. Shortly after noon, Cowan called to police negotiators for food and apologized to the mayor of the city for his actions. However, despite several conversations with negotiators, Cowan refused to leave his stronghold and surrender his weapons. Later in the afternoon, at approximately 2:40 in the afternoon, officers heard a single gunshot from inside the building. Special Weapons and Tactics (SWAT) personnel waited for more than two hours (attempting to establish contact with Cowan) before they entered the premises. At about 5:00 that afternoon, officers stormed the building and discovered Cowan's body. He had shot himself through the head while wearing a black beret that was adorned a Nazi-style skull and crossbones.[14]

It is clear that Frederick Cowan was a man who was obsessed with hatred and driven to violence. He was obsessed with ideation of revenge against a variety of ethnic groups and surrounded himself with symbols to maintain and perpetuate this obsession. Isolated, frustrated, angry, and pathological in his need for retribution, Cowan lacked only the triggering event of a suspension from his job to find a reason for mass murder. There is every reason to believe that he was an individual who was seeking a reason to commit mass murder and determined to arrange the circumstances of his life in such a manner as to guarantee the outcome that he sought.

POLITICS AND PREJUDICE

Early in his presidency, Bill Clinton ordered that homosexuals be allowed to serve in the military, without prejudice, provided they did not reveal their sexual orientation to military authorities or recruitment personnel. This came to be known in the media as the "don't ask, don't tell" rule, which was enacted to answer the military establishment's desire to address the controversial issue of gays serving in the armed forces. This was an issue that caused heated debate throughout the nation and, in particular, among the ranks of military personnel, many of whom were strongly opposed to any policy that would openly permit homosexuals to serve in the armed forces. Although it was obvious that gay men and women had long served this country with distinction in the military (while keeping their sexual orientation a carefully guarded secret), a number of officers and enlisted personnel had openly proclaimed their homosexuality in the years preceding Clinton's ruling. These disclosures brought the subject of gays in the military to the forefront of the American media and transformed the issue into one that could no longer be ignored by politicians or the military. Unfortunately, some very dedicated and courageous military personnel lost their careers because of these disclosures and the long-standing opposition to homosexuality that was rampant throughout the various branches of the armed services.

In 1993, an army sergeant who had often and vehemently spoken of his opposition to Clinton's "don't ask, don't tell" policy decided that he would make someone pay for what he perceived to be a ruling that was immoral and completely unacceptable. By that year, Kenneth Junior French was twenty-two years old and had served in the army since June 1989. A native of Florida,

French was a mechanic stationed at Fort Bragg, North Carolina; he had attained the rank of sergeant through hard work and a spotless service record. He had served the military overseas in South Korea and, later, in Fort Jackson, South Carolina. French had no weapons training, no criminal history, and no record of disciplinary action against him. However, he was an angry young man who drank too much and harbored a pathological hatred against homosexuals.

Table 3.6: Kenneth Junior French

Perpetrator	Kenneth Junior French, a twenty-two-year-old army sergeant who had a history of hating homosexuals.
Incident date/location	August 6, 1993, in a family-style Italian restaurant near Fort Bragg, North Carolina.
Incident category	Politics and hate.
Weapons	Two shotguns and a .22-caliber rifle.
Deaths/Injuries	Four killed, seven injured.
Motivation	French was allegedly protesting President Clinton's policy on gays in the military.
Disposition	French was wounded by police personnel at the scene of the crime but survived to stand trial. On April 1, 1994, he was convicted of multiple counts of first-degree murder.

On August 6, 1993, Kenneth French drove to Luigi's Italian Restaurant, located about a mile from Fort Bragg; he had never been to the restaurant before that night. Arriving at about 10 P.M. that Friday evening, he entered the family-style restaurant wearing a hunting vest and carrying two shotguns and a .22-caliber rifle. As French burst into the restaurant, he screamed: "I'll show you, Clinton! You think I'm not going to do this. I'll show you about gays in the military!"[15] The sergeant lowered his .22-caliber rifle and shot the restaurant owner and his wife to death. The elderly couple died in the front booth of their business with their arms wrapped around each other in terror. He then began randomly shooting the patrons at Luigi's as they scrambled for whatever cover they could find. French alternately used the two shotguns and the .22-caliber rifle, pausing to reload the weapons as he continued searching out his victims. A waitress at the restaurant was able to avoid French by hiding under a booth, from where she witnessed the horrifying scene. The employee later told police that she believed French was drunk and that as he was shooting, he continually rambled incoherently about his hatred for gays and the president's policy about homosexuals in the military. During his rampage, French killed four individuals and wounded another seven; only the waitress who had hidden under the booth was left uninjured.

Across the street from Luigi's, an off-duty policeman was working at his part-time job in a grocery store. Christopher Pryer heard the shooting from

Luigi's and, to his horror, noticed several bullets striking the side of the building in which he was working. The officer ran across the street to the restaurant and, seeing a gunman inside who was shooting at the patrons, fired at him through one of the restaurant windows. French was hit in the leg and fell to the floor; however, still in an uncontrollable rage, he immediately got back up and attempted to reload his weapon. By this time, local law enforcement personnel had arrived on the scene; one of the responding officers crawled through the rear door of the restaurant and wounded French a second time. Now shot in the leg and jaw, French was finally subdued and taken into custody.

After French was arrested, he refused to talk to police without legal representation. Two days after the shootings, he was charged with four counts of first-degree murder and six counts of assault with a deadly weapon. French went to trial in early 1994 where, for the first time, he admitted his responsibility for the murders. His attorney offered the defense that French had been in a rage since the age of eight, when his father had raped a female relative and then threatened his son with death should the younger French ever disclose his father's crime. However, the jury was not persuaded by the defense argument. On April 1, 1994, Kenneth French was convicted of four counts of first-degree murder and all counts of attempting to kill eight other individuals.[16] He never disclosed why he randomly attacked the owners and patrons of Luigi's restaurant in 1993, other than to reiterate his lifelong anger at gays, his father, and the policies of President Clinton (see Table 3.6)

NOTES

1. "TWA Probe Turns to Plane's Center, Fire Damage," *Reuters News Service* (Internet edition), 12 August 1996, 1.

2. Don Van Natta, Jr., "Prime Evidence Found That Device Exploded in Cabin of Flight 800," *New York Times* (Internet edition), 23 August 1996, 1.

3. Don Van Natta, Jr., "Crash Investigators Report More Traces of an Explosive," *New York Times* (Internet edition), 31 August 1996, 1.

4. "FBI: TWA Jet Had Been Used for Bomb Tests," *Reuters News Service* (Internet edition), 20 September 1996, 1.

5. "TWA Crash Probers Look to Mechanical Fault," *Reuters News Service* (Internet edition), 19 September 1996, 1.

6. "FBI Releases Chilling Bomb Warning Text," *Reuters News Service* (Internet edition), 30 July 1996, 1.

7. Tom Hays, "Police ID Harlem Man Who Killed 7, Himself," *San Francisco Examiner Online* (Internet edition), 11 December 1995, 1.

8. Ibid.

9. "The Confession of Michael Fortier," KWTV Internet (http://www.kwtv.com), 10 August 1995 (entered as part of Fortier's plea agreement of the same date).

10. "Indictment against McVeigh and Nichols." KWTC Internet (http://www.kwtv.com), 10 August 1995 (United States District Court for the Western District of Oklahoma).

11. James Alan Fox and Jack Levin, *Mass Murder: America's Growing Menace* (New York: Plenum, 1985), 49.

12. Ibid., 50.

13. Ibid., 51.

14. Ibid., 49-51.

15. Martha Waggoner, "Gunman Kills 4 in Restaurant Rampage," *Philadelphia Inquirer Online* (Internet edition), 8 August 1993, A03.

16. "Man Who Opened Fire in Restaurant Guilty of Murder," *Philadelphia Inquirer Online*, News in Brief (Internet edition), 2 April 1994, A10.

CHAPTER 4

Revenge

Revenge is the naked idol of the worship of a semi-barbarous age.

Percy Bysshe Shelley
A Defence of Poetry

Without question, the crime of mass murder is most often an act of ultimate revenge. Assuming that the perpetrator of the crime is capable of understanding his actions, which is true with the vast majority of mass murderers, revenge stands out as a common thread in this category of crime. Ideation centered around revenge and retribution can be pervasive, debilitating, and remorseless. Preoccupation with revenge against those perceived as harmful or dangerous is an acutely dangerous state of mind that can eventually lead to acts of aggression and violence. A state of severe depression, long periods of disappointment and frustration, or intolerable situations of stress can combine with fantasies of revenge to create a potent and unpredictable potential for unbridled violence or self-injury. It is against this background of frustration, anger, depression, stress, and fantasies of retribution that the planning for mass murder may occur. The murderer is caught in an inescapable web of emotions and ideation that coalesces around the individuals, group, or organization that he holds responsible for the hopeless situation he perceives to be his fate. Entrapped in this foray of psychological and emotional imperatives, the mass murderer may find no option but to lash out in a final act of revenge directed against those whom he holds directly responsible for his plight; and, when he does strike out, his victims may be personal, symbolic, or even himself.

"TO THE FAMILIES OF THE VICTIMS"

Gian Luigi Ferri was a fifty-five-year-old real estate investor whose business had fallen on hard times. He was involved in pending litigation in which the opposing side was represented by the prestigious San Francisco law firm of Pettit and Martin. Ferri lived in an apartment complex in Woodland Hills, near Los Angeles. He was the owner of his own business, ADF Mortgage Inc., which had never performed well and was now failing. His neighbors rarely saw Ferri, who was socially isolated and aloof, but they certainly recognized the many eviction notices for nonpayment of rent that had been posted on his apartment door. Ferri also had severe tax problems and was fending off a California Franchise Tax Board lien that had been filed in May 1993; in addition to the lien, his business operations had been suspended because Ferri had failed to file corporate tax returns as far back as 1988.

Neighboring business owners and employees wondered how Ferri could manage to keep his doors open at all. They were openly suspicious of the man himself, and one later commented: "He was strange, very strange. We all used to talk about it. How does this guy stay in business and pay his rent?"[1] By the summer of 1993, Gian Luigi Ferri was an isolated, angry, and near-destitute man who had little left to lose in his life. He also harbored an abiding grudge against dozens of individuals, including all who were bringing suit against him.

On July 1, 1993, Ferri traveled to San Francisco, to the law offices of Pettit and Martin, in search of revenge. In his pocket he carried a typed list of more than forty potential victims against whom he demanded retribution for his financial ruin. On the cover sheet to this list, he had written, "To the families of the victims"; next to some of the names, he had made various angry notations, such as "rapist" and "communist."[2] When Ferri arrived at the skyscraper that housed the law offices of his rival, he immediately took the elevator to the thirty-fourth floor—the headquarters for Pettit and Martin. He was armed with two 9mm semiautomatic pistols, a .45-caliber automatic handgun, and a briefcase full of ammunition.

As soon as the elevator doors opened, Ferri began roaming the adjoining floors of the huge office building, randomly shooting at those who crossed his path. During his rampage, he managed to fire off nearly 100 rounds of ammunition, kill eight individuals, and wound another six. Eventually, finding himself trapped between floors of the high-rise and surrounded by law enforcement personnel, Ferri put one of the handguns to his head and pulled the trigger. Ironically, none of the individuals who were mentioned in Ferri's list of victims had been injured during his rampage. Rather, it was painfully apparent from the crime scene (and later interviews with survivors) that the murderer had selected his victims at random. On that day, Gian Luigi Ferri became the most prolific mass murderer in the history of San Francisco, despite the fact that he never attacked one of the victims whom he had determined to kill long before he began shooting.

The murders perpetrated by Gian Luigi Ferri exhibited not only a high degree of planning, but also a deep and pathological sense of revenge. Ferri had obviously been obsessed with his financial failings and blamed a wide range of individuals for a plethora of unsubstantiated reasons. His obsession with retribution was intensely deep and lethal; however, it was also diffuse and symbolic. In his final moments, Ferri lashed out against anyone who was unfortunate enough to be in his path. So overwhelming was his need for retribution that those victims whom he finally did murder had become symbolic of all whom he so deeply hated and had earlier marked for death. It was a tragic irony of this brutal crime that none of his victims knew Gian Luigi Ferri, and in turn, he had never met any of them (see Chapter 1, Table 1.11).

A SHORT LIFE OF FAILURES

An act of mass murder is frequently the result of many years of frustration and anger that relentlessly erode the ability of the perpetrator to cope with the pressures and stress of daily life. In time, without any release from these frustrations and pressures, the potential murderer may focus his anger and thoughts of revenge on specific individuals whom he holds responsible for his intolerable situation. With sufficient frustration, encountered over a continuing period of time, the individual may eventually react to a final, intolerable incident—a triggering event—with explosive and deadly fury. In part, such long periods of debilitating frustration account for the fact that most mass murderers are well beyond their youth when they commit their crimes. However, there are also exceptions to the general age-range profile of most mass murderers. There are cases in which young men, who were faced with even a short life of insurmountable frustrations and anger, and then experienced a final and irresistible triggering event, acted out their ultimate aggressions against those whom they deemed responsible for their unhappiness. Harry De La Roche, Jr., proved to be such a frustrated and angry young man.

Throughout his young life, Harry Jr. could never be any of the things that his father demanded. As a boy, and later as a young man, Harry was unpopular and unaccepted by his peers, a poor student, and a constant focus of his father's relentless demands to do more and to be better. He was socially isolated and considered to be a failure by his father, despite the obvious fact that Harry worked incessantly to please the elder De La Roche in every way that he could. It seemed that whatever he tried to accomplish only resulted in a disappointment to his father and himself. He was the boy who just could not get it right.

Despite his many failures, Harry did have one remarkable skill—he was an expert marksman. This was something that clearly pleased his father and constituted the boy's single source of praise. However, by the time Harry was a teenager, there was also something burning deep within him that his father had never recognized or given serious consideration: Harry was deeply angry, blatantly unappreciated for who he was, and completely incapable of living the life that his father had incessantly demanded of him.

The thing that Harry De La Roche wanted most in his life was to be proud of his three sons, Harry Jr., Ronald, and Eric. However, of the three, he wanted his firstborn, Harry, to be nothing short of outstanding. To the senior De La Roche, this meant that his eldest son must be successful in every endeavor that he undertook, regardless of the boy's desires or feelings. Whether it be in the area of academics, on the social circuit, or in his knowledge and use of weapons (which were plentiful in the De La Roche household), Harry must always be the best of the best. Unfortunately, Harry never came close to realizing his father's expectations, and the elder De La Roche persistently made his disappointment known to his son and the rest of the family.

Young Harry was not particularly good-looking and had few friends. He was withdrawn in his social encounters and unpopular in high school. In fact, he was so unpopular that one of the few inscriptions in his senior yearbook read: "You're the stupidest kid I met."[3] However, Harry's skill with weapons was remarkable for his age, and to Harry Sr., this was not only a singular source of pride but a clear indication that his son might do well in a military academy rather than a traditional college after he graduated from high school.

Even as he graduated from high school, Harry continued to be a disappointment to his father. Because of his poor eyesight, the young man was unable to gain entrance to West Point or the Air Force Academy, as his father had wished. Rather, he had to settle for the Citadel in South Carolina—a private military school that was known for its tough approach to cadets and its significant tuition. Attendance at the Citadel did not guarantee that Harry would be able to eventually attain a commission in the military, as his father had demanded, but it would help. To his father, admission to the Citadel signified that his son might finally be making some headway in his life. It was a concession that Harry's father could live with; but only if his son proved himself to be the best cadet in his class.

The young De La Roche was unsure about attending the Citadel and worried that he could not make it through the notoriously tough first year, much less eventually graduate. It was an expensive proposition for his parents, and the academy was very far away from his home in Montvale, New Jersey. In fact, there was nothing about the idea that appealed to Harry. However, his father had insisted, and as always, Harry had reluctantly submitted to his father's will.

Once he arrived at the Citadel, Harry knew that his worst fears had been realized. He hated everything about military school. He despised the strict military regimen, the seemingly limitless rules and regulations, and his insensitive and often cruel classmates. Harry was unable to make any friends and remained completely isolated; in fact, he had quickly developed a growing number of classmates who did what they could to add to his daily misery. Shortly after arriving at the Citadel, Harry knew he had reached the end of the line. He could take no more of the academy and its demanding lifestyle. His brief experience at the academy also made him realize that it would be impossible to accept any more of his father's incessant demands. However, Harry was afraid to face his father with the truth about his latest failure. Certainly, he would never be able to confront his father with the genuine depth of his anger and frustration.

Near the end of 1976, Harry quit the Citadel without warning or notice, telling his mother that he could no longer attend because he had been diagnosed with cancer. In fact, he was physically fine; Harry simply could no longer live the life that his father demanded, and he had reached his limit in trying. He asked his mother to say nothing to Harry Sr. about the Citadel, and she respected his wishes. Harry now had to decide what to do—how to approach his father with this latest disappointment.

On November 28, 1976, Harry visited a few acquaintances from his old high school and returned to his parents' home after 3:00 in the morning. Entering the house as quietly as he could, Harry picked up one of the half-dozen pistols that were always loaded and accessible in the De La Roche household. He had decided it was time for revenge—time to be free of the unending demands that he could never meet, and would never be able to meet, as long as his father was alive. Harry's many years of dark fantasies of revenge were about to be realized in a few moments of incredible rage and brutality.

Harry moved silently to his parents' bedroom and held the revolver to his father's head. With its barrel resting lightly against his father's temple, Harry considered what to do. For fifteen minutes he held that position, with his finger poised on the trigger, unsure of his decision. As his father finally stirred gently in sleep, Harry suddenly pulled the trigger, killing his father instantly. The noise of the shot awakened his mother in obvious terror. Harry quickly shoved the pistol in her direction, shooting and killing her where she lay. He then pumped a final shot into his father's body to be absolutely sure that he was dead.

In a quiet panic now, Harry moved swiftly to his brothers' bedroom. Ronald, fifteen years old, had been awakened by the noise from his parents' room but was still lying in his bed when Harry opened fire and killed him. The youngest brother, Eric, who was twelve years old, jumped out of his bed as the gun fired and rushed toward his older brother. Harry wheeled around to confront Eric, pulling the trigger and hitting him twice in the face and once in the chest. Eric immediately fell to the bedroom floor, writhing in pain. Seeing that his brother was still struggling for life, Harry finished his work by bludgeoning the boy to death with the butt of his revolver. He then stuffed his brother's body in a cabinet, in the attic of the family home.[4]

On the day that Harry De La Roche killed his family, he was eighteen years old—one of a small number of mass murderers who commit their crimes while under the age of twenty-five. However, even by that young age, Harry had suffered the frustrations and anger of a lifetime and, like so many of his older counterparts, he finally lashed out with explosive and incredible violence against those whom he held responsible. Sadly, he also attacked and killed those loved ones who had supported and nurtured him throughout his young life (see Table 4.1).

Table 4.1: Harry De La Roche, Jr.

Perpetrator	An eighteen-year-old family murderer who was never able to please his demanding father.
Incident date/location	November 28, 1976, at the family home in Montvale, New Jersey.
Incident category	Revenge.
Weapons	A handgun and bludgeoning.
Deaths/Injuries	Four killed—all were family members.
Motivation	Revenge for a lifetime of submission to his father.
Disposition	Perpetrator survived his crimes to stand trial.

REVENGE BY LETHAL EMPLOYEES IN THE PUBLIC SECTOR

In 1986, a letter carrier by the name of Patrick Sherrill, who worked in Edmond, Oklahoma, killed fourteen of his colleagues and ended his day of mass murder by committing suicide. Sherrill was a socially isolated, depressed, middle-age, white male who had a history of erratic employment, exhibited evidence of poor job performance at the Edmond Post Office, and had an overpowering fetish for weaponry. A day prior to his murderous rampage, Sherrill was counseled by his supervisor about his erratic work performance. Even though postal authorities claimed that they had no intention of firing Sherrill, he could no longer tolerate the years of rejection, isolation, frustration, and anger, which had become the mainstay of his life. When he left the workplace for his home on the evening of November 27, 1986, he could think only of revenge.

By the next morning, Sherrill had finalized his plans. Armed with weapons that he was able to borrow from a nearby national guard armory, Sherrill reported to work early, went looking for his supervisor, and fatally shot him. After murdering the primary target of his revenge with a high-powered handgun, Sherrill began to shoot his coworkers at random, in an apparent symbolic attempt to annihilate the organization against which his years of anger and frustration had finally coalesced. After felling over a dozen colleagues, Sherrill turned one of the three handguns that he was carrying on himself and died just a few feet from his former supervisor and first victim (see Chapter 1, Table 1.17).

Patrick Sherrill's crime in 1986 inaugurated the modern era of the violent workplace and forever changed the traditional American view of a safe work environment. Because of his shocking crime, Sherrill became the instant prototype of the lethal employee—the behavioral standard against which subsequent lethal employees were compared and contrasted. Since that day in August 1986, the lethal employee has become a near-tradition in the American labor force. In the decade since the Edmond Post Office massacre, workplace homicide has become a major category of crime, which has impacted a wide variety of organizations in both the public and private sectors of our economy.

Although most workers who are slain on the job are incidental victims of perpetrators engaged in another crime, such as robbery or extortion, nearly 50 percent of the employees and supervisors who are slain each year were targeted by disgruntled employees or ex-employees. By the mid-1990s, the number of workers murdered on the job each year exceeded 1,000. While the number of workplace victims slain in the course of another crime has indicated a slight decrease in recent years, the number of employees and supervisors slain by coworkers or ex-employees has significantly increased. Even more alarming is the fact that the lethal employee often murders multiple colleagues in an indiscriminate manner, frequently using powerful, paramilitary weapons. The lethal employee has become one of the most significant threats to the workplace ever experienced in this country; moreover, there is every indication that he will become more lethal, and his crimes more frequent, as we approach the new millennium.

The American economy has experienced profound economic and workplace changes in the past decade. This economic upheaval has resulted in unexpected organizational shifting, aggressive profit-seeking and cost-cutting tactics, widespread business failures and reorganizations, pervasive waves of downsizing, and an unprecedented number of layoffs. This national disruption to the work environment has created unexpected and significant stress for vast segments of the American workforce. Frequently, middle-age employees, who may have worked for the same organization for many years (or even decades) or who find themselves with a single skill that is no longer in demand, are most affected by the continuing economic changes of the past decade. These workers view their jobs as crucial to their sense of well being and vital to their economic survival. Deprived of this critical life connection, and with a vision of the future that may be considerably more bleak than they ever expected it could be, some of these individuals may perceive no option but retaliation and revenge.

GOING POSTAL

In recent years, the term *going postal* has become synonymous with mass murder committed by the lethal employee in the public sector of our economy. Like so many of the issues surrounding the crime of mass murder, this characterization embodies both truth and myth. The U.S. Postal Service has received a great deal of notoriety because of the number of employees who have turned against their colleagues in highly publicized incidents of violence and death. In part, this is due to the crimes of Patrick Sherrill, who shocked the nation with his siege on the Edmond Post Office; however, this belief is also due to the persistence of workplace multiple homicides that have plagued the postal service over the past decade in a variety of other locations.

There is little question that the working environment at postal stations across America has been less than ideal for some time. The organization is steeped in bureaucracy and known for a workforce that suffers from low morale and an arcane management style. The U.S. Postal Service has recognized these basic managerial shortcomings and continues to make efforts to improve both working conditions and management techniques. Like many other organizations, the postal service has suffered from the strain of massive reorganization in recent years.

In 1970, the Postal Reorganization Act was passed by Congress; by 1982, the U.S. Postal Service was operating without any government financial assistance. This legislation mandated increased independence for the postal service and forced the organization to work toward financial autonomy, thereby eliminating its historical reliance on taxpayer subsidy. The traditional environment of the postal service was forever changed by this legislation. The result was massive reorganization, downsizing, and the introduction of wholly unfamiliar constraints of free-market competition. Inevitably, such pervasive change affected many long-term post office employees in ways that were both unexpected and unwelcome. Many employees lost their jobs, while those fortunate enough to keep their employment found themselves in a rapidly changing and unstable work environment. In many ways, and for all these reasons, the postal service has come to exemplify the type of working environment that can quickly become a breeding ground for discontent and violence.

However, it must also be recognized that mass murder committed by the lethal employee is not unique to the postal service. This crime victimizes workers in both the public and private sectors and in organizations both large and small. Mass murder is not indigenous to any single agency or work environment. In recent years, the U.S. Postal Service has become the focus of much workplace violence that is extreme because of the media attention it has received; however, the postal service is not unique in the weaknesses that have contributed to its victimization.

Three years after Patrick Sherrill inaugurated the modern era of the violent workplace, John Taylor, another postal service employee, murdered three individuals, and wounded another five, in an incident that remains an enigma in the history of mass murder (see Table 4.2). Taylor worked for the postal service nearly all his adult life. He was considered to be an exemplary employee by all who knew him, especially his coworkers and supervisors. Taylor had often received commendations from his supervisors, and throughout the twenty-seven years that he worked for the post office, he was never the subject of a disciplinary action. To all who knew him, John Taylor was considered a model employee.

Taylor was also a devoted husband who spoke lovingly of his wife to friends and coworkers. His neighbors held Taylor in high regard and often commented about the ideal relationship that he appeared to share with his wife. He was a man who never complained about his problems; he was reliable to a fault and always quick to help others. If there was anything bothering Taylor at all, it was that he was disappointed about the deteriorating morale that he (and others) had experienced at the Orange Glen Post Office, where he worked as a letter carrier.

Because Taylor had spent so much of his life at the post office, he had developed a close personal relationship with many coworkers, and two in particular. For years he would report early to work so that he could spend a few moments chatting with these two colleagues before they started their daily rounds of work. It was a workplace tradition that the three men seemed to enjoy very much.

On August 10, 1989, Taylor arrived early, as usual, to meet his two friends. However, on this day he carried with him a loaded, .22-caliber semiautomatic pistol and a box of 100 rounds of ammunition. Taylor approached the table where he customarily met with his two colleagues and immediately shot them to death, without speaking a word. He then entered the post office through a side door that was reserved for employees and began shooting randomly at coworkers. Throughout his rampage, Taylor did not target a specific individual (as is usual with workplace mass murderers) but fired indiscriminately, for approximately twenty minutes, without ever speaking a word. After wounding an additional five coworkers, John Taylor put the gun to his own head and committed suicide. When police investigated the incident later that morning, they discovered that, before leaving for work, Taylor had also murdered his wife as she slept.

Table 4.2: John Taylor

Perpetrator	A fifty-one-year-old postal employee with an excellent work record and an apparently stable, loving domestic life.
Incident date/location	August 10, 1989, at two locations (home and work) in and around the Orange Glen post office in California.
Incident category	Revenge by a lethal employee (presumed).
Weapons	A .22-caliber semiautomatic pistol and a box of 100 rounds of ammunition.
Deaths/Injuries	Three killed, five injured. One of those killed was Taylor's wife.
Motivation	Uncertain. There appears to be no certain motive for the murder of his wife or his subsequent rampage at the Orange Glen post office, although he had been concerned about workplace morale and working conditions.
Disposition	Taylor committed suicide at the crime scene.

Unlike Patrick Sherrill, who had exhibited several warning signs of potential violence such as depression, social isolation, a weapons fetish, and pathological blaming of others, John Taylor demonstrated no indication that he was a potential murderer. He was a respected employee with a stable and full home life. If there was anything troubling Taylor at all, it seemed to have been his disappointment about working conditions and morale at the Orange Glen post office. All who knew Taylor and were later interviewed after his murderous rampage were unanimous in their opinion that he was the most unlikely of murderers and that his actions that day were wholly inconsistent with the man that many had known for decades.

In stark contrast to John Taylor was another postal employee, Thomas McIlvane, who exhibited persistent and obvious indications that he was a man who was driven to violence throughout his adult life. On November 14, 1991, McIlvane smuggled a sawed-off, .22-caliber semiautomatic rifle, hidden under his coat, into the Royal Oak, Michigan, post office. Once inside, McIlvane sought out his former supervisor and killed him instantly. He then began to fire indiscriminately at coworkers as they scurried for any cover they could find. During his rampage, McIlvane managed to murder an additional three employees and wound four others, none of whom he had targeted before the start of his onslaught. Like John Taylor, Thomas McIlvane also committed suicide at the scene of his crime, dying a few feet from his first victim and original target (see Table 4.3).

Unlike Taylor, McIlvane was a man who enthroned violence and was obsessed with dominating every relationship into which he ventured. While serving in the military, McIlvane had been demoted several times because of his aggressive and violent behavior. He was finally discharged without honors because his behavior had become uncontrollable. After he left the military, McIlvane joined the postal service and continued his violent ways. He received numerous warnings for unauthorized leave from his job, fighting with supervisors, and arguing with customers. In fact, he had a five-year history of disciplinary problems, most of which involved some form of violence, before he was eventually fired from his job at the Royal Oak station. During the course of McIlvane's employment, and even after he was fired, he continued to make threats against his supervisor and various coworkers. McIlvane made it clear he would seek revenge; he frequently and openly stated that he would murder those against whom he held a grudge.

As is often the case with mass murderers who make good on their threats, Thomas McIlvane planned his crime carefully and made sure that he dealt first with his former supervisor and the primary target of his revenge. After killing his supervisor, McIlvane murdered and injured his colleagues indiscriminately, in a symbolic effort to annihilate the organization against which he harbored so much hatred and anger.

Patrick Sherrill, John Taylor, and Thomas McIlvane shared several characteristics that have come to be associated with the American mass murder; however, each was also exceptional in his own way. Each was a white, working-class male aged between thirty-one (Thomas McIlvane) and fifty-one (John Taylor)—the age grouping most common to the mass murderer. Each was familiar with weapons and skilled in their use, electing to use a gun to commit their crimes—the weapon of choice for the mass murderer. In fact, Sherrill and McIlvane were both highly trained in the use of handguns. Sherrill had been a handgun instructor and member of a National Guard marksmanship team. On the other hand, John Taylor exhibited no unusual interest in weapons, even though he was obviously familiar with handguns.

Table 4.3: Thomas McIlvane

Perpetrator	A thirty-one-year-old postal worker with a history of violent behavior.
Incident date/location	November 14, 1991, at the Royal Oak, Michigan, post office.
Incident category	Revenge by a lethal employee.
Weapons	A sawed-off, .22-caliber semiautomatic rifle.
Deaths/Injuries	Five killed, four injured.
Motivation	An enraged employee who had been terminated for misconduct.
Disposition	McIlvane committed suicide at the crime scene.

All three of these men murdered (or attempted to murder) their coworkers indiscriminately. While Sherrill and McIlvane specifically identified individuals against whom they held a known grudge, it is uncertain why Taylor attacked his close friends and coworkers. No satisfactory explanation has ever been offered as to why Taylor murdered his wife. He was not socially isolated and appeared to have a strong support network of family and friends, unlike McIlvane and Sherrill, who were both socially isolated and had no support network available to them. However, despite their differences, all three men made the decision to strike out against their coworkers in an indiscriminate manner; in other words, all three desired the symbolic destruction of their employers, in some manner.

None of these three perpetrators was known to suffer from any significant psychological disorder for which they were receiving treatment at the time they committed murder. If all of these perpetrators had survived their crimes, it is likely that they would all have been found legally sane and able to stand trial for their actions. This awareness of their actions, as evidenced by the planning and execution of their crimes, is a common characteristic of the contemporary American mass murderer and, in particular, the lethal employee.

Patrick Sherrill and Thomas McIlvane exhibited several behavioral warning signs that are frequently associated with potentially violent behavior. McIlvane's behavior gave clear evidence that he was a man of violence whose behavior was often out of control. On the other hand, John Taylor's motives remain unclear; he showed no significant behavioral warning signs that would lead anyone who knew him to suspect the violence he wrought on others.

It is unknown what may have triggered John Taylor's violent outburst. His actions and motivations remain a mystery. However, for Sherrill and McIlvane, the triggering events that led to murder were more clear. Sherrill had been counseled by his supervisor the day before he returned to murder his coworkers. His job performance had been questionable for some time and he knew that he was in trouble with his employer. Thomas McIlvane was the prototypical problem employee. He perennially encountered difficulties at work, and his unacceptable performance and uncontrollable behavior led directly to his termination. After McIlvane learned he had lost an appeal for reinstatement to his job (the final triggering event), he wholly committed himself to lethal revenge.

REVENGE BY LETHAL EMPLOYEES IN PRIVATE INDUSTRY

Private industry is also significantly impacted by the crimes of the lethal employee, who at times will resort to mass murder in an effort to achieve the retribution that he demands. As with the homicides that have plagued the U.S. Postal Service, most of the mass murders committed by employees of private industry are acts of revenge against supervisors, coworkers, or the organization itself. Feelings of abandonment, frustration, and hopelessness often follow in the wake of strategic corporate decisions that leave workers unemployed, socially adrift, financially devastated, and uncertain about their futures. Mismanagement and strategic errors in judgment occur in private industry with at least as much frequency as they do in the public sector. Employees in both sectors of our economy are subject to innumerable stressors, which may be related to their work environment or brought into the workplace from home. It would be a mistake to believe that only the public sector is impacted by workplace violence, homicide, or mass murder. Each year, a growing number of American organizations in the private sector are held hostage by the employee or ex-employee who is hell-bent on revenge. Sometimes this revenge takes the form of mass murder.

Lethal employees such as Willie Woods (see Chapter 1, Table 1.9), Joseph Wesbecker (see Chapter 1, Table 1.10), or Clifton McCree (see Chapter 1, Table 1.14), represent the most common and prolific perpetrators of mass murder in America in the past several years. These are murderers who plan their acts of revenge with care; they are often incredibly bold and wholly committed to extreme violence when they enact their crimes.

One of the most horrendous incidents of revenge exacted by a lethal employee occurred in 1987, in California. David Burke worked for Pacific Southwest Airlines (PSA) as a ticket agent in Los Angeles. Prior to his California assignment, Burke had worked for USAir, the parent company of PSA, for thirteen years in New York. His reputation on the job was one of a mild, easygoing individual who had a good performance record; however, not everyone who knew Burke on a more personal basis agreed with that assessment. Away from the job, he had the reputation of a man with a hair-trigger temper who would sometimes skirt the law if the opportunity presented itself. He was known as someone who could move easily from relationship to relationship, having fathered several children in four different relationships, and would sometimes exhibit an aggressive side of his nature to those closest to him. However, despite this somewhat dark side to his personality, those who were close to Burke considered him to be a good father who was unquestionably devoted to his children—all seven of them.

Burke was born in Britain, to Jamaican parents, and emigrated to the United States as a young man. Even though he was eventually investigated for a variety of questionable activities while he lived and worked in New York, Burke had no criminal record and no documented history of violence. While working for USAir and PSA, Burke apparently experienced no difficulties with his supervisors and was not subject to any questionable performance issues until 1987. In November of that year, he was accused of stealing $69 from in-flight cocktail receipts after security personnel made a routine review of videotaped employee activities. It was obvious from the videotape that Burke had stolen the cash—an offense that could result in his termination. When he was confronted with the videotaped evidence, Burke did not deny the charges; instead, he pleaded for leniency for his children in an effort to keep his job. Despite his pleas, Burke was terminated by Raymond Thompson, the USAir customer service manager, in Los Angeles on November 19, 1987. Upon learning that he was to be fired, Burke became angry and violent, threatening Thompson and others with death for their actions.

A few days after he lost his job, Burke held his female companion and her six-year-old daughter hostage, at gunpoint, for over six hours. He forced the terrified woman to drive him aimlessly around the Los Angeles basin while he incessantly raged about his termination and vocalized fantasies of revenge against his former employer and, in particular, Raymond Thompson. Over the next few weeks, both at home and to his acquaintances, Burke incessantly complained about the injustice that had been done to him; he obsessively vowed to get even with Thompson and PSA. It was clear to all who knew him that Burke's behavior was wheeling out of control and that he was pathologically obsessed with thoughts of retribution for the loss of the job that he had held for thirteen years.

On December 8, 1987, David Burke boarded PSA flight 1771, which was on a routine run from San Diego to San Francisco with a stopover in Los Angeles. This was a regularly scheduled flight, which Raymond Thompson always took, and Burke knew that Thompson would be onboard that day. Using his PSA identification badge, which (incredibly) had not been confiscated when Burke was fired, he was able to bypass normal airport security and board flight 1771 with a .44-magnum handgun that he had borrowed from a former coworker a few weeks earlier.

After the flight left Los Angeles and attained cruising altitude, Burke removed an air sickness bag from the pocket of the seat in front of him and wrote a final message to Raymond Thompson, who was seated ahead of him near the front of the airplane. The message read: "Hi Ray. I think it's sort of ironical that we end up like this. I asked for some leniency for my family, remember. Well I got none and you'll get none."[5] After writing this ominous message, Burke moved forward to where Thompson was seated, withdrew his handgun in front of terrified passengers, and shot Thompson twice, probably killing him instantly. Burke then forced his way onto the flight deck of the airliner and shot the entire flight crew, emptying his handgun in the process. Flight 1771, which was at an altitude of four miles when Burke attacked the crew, immediately went out of control and plummeted in a near-vertical trajectory into a muddy pasture near the town of San Luis Obispo. All forty-three passengers and crew perished in the crash (see Table 4.4).

Table 4.4: David Burke

Perpetrator	A thirty-five-year-old airline worker with a stable employment history but who was also known to have a quick temper outside of the workplace.
Incident date/location	December 9, 1987, onboard an airliner in flight over San Luis Obispo, California.
Incident category	Revenge by a lethal employee.
Weapons	A .44-magnum handgun.
Deaths/Injuries	Forty-three killed, no survivors.
Motivation	Burke was angered and seeking revenge for having been was terminated from a job that he had held for thirteen years.
Disposition	Burke was killed with his victims in the crash of an airliner after he shot his former supervisor and the entire flight crew.

With his incredible crime of revenge, David Burke became the most lethal employee in American history at that time. Today, his crime still ranks as one of the worst mass murders in U.S. history (see "Appendix 4: The Five Most Deadly U.S. Mass Murders") and one that remains incomprehensible in the murderer's callous disregard for innocent lives.

Burke experienced a triggering event of such personal impact (the loss of his job) that he was driven to an extreme act of retribution. Clearly, however, there was much more to his motivations than the termination from a job that he had held for over a decade. Burke's reaction to this final triggering event was unbelievably extreme and must have embodied a lifetime of anger, frustration, and disappointment that proved overwhelming. However, in a certain way, his reaction to the loss of his job was consistent with the behavior that he had exhibited for many years—it was just more extreme. He was known to be a man with a violent temper who exhibited mildly antisocial behavior whenever it met his needs or desires. However, in the final analysis, no one could have foreseen the vehemence of his reaction or the depth of his need for retribution when he found himself without employment. Burke's callous disregard for the lives of so many innocent individuals, with each victim brought to such a horrible end for the sake of revenge, stands apart from even the usual horror wrought by lethal employees who ultimately resort to mass murder.

Most lethal employees do not react with the extreme and unpredictable violence of a man like David Burke. In fact, the majority of lethal employees telegraph their intentions to exact revenge well before they act out violently. In some instances, such as the case of Valery Fabrikant (see Table 4.5), the individual will give many warning signs over a long period of time that cumulatively indicate him to be angry and intent upon revenge. At times, these clues will be subtle and easily disregarded by coworkers; at others, they will be overt and obvious. Some employees, like Paul Calden (see Table 4.6), provide warning signs that are unmistakable in their meaning and obviously frightening to coworkers. Whether the signals given by the potentially lethal employee are obvious or not, they are almost always present in some form, usually well before the individual strikes out against the workplace or its occupants.

Table 4.5: Valery Fabrikant

Perpetrator	A fifty-three-year-old university professor who was socially isolated, culturally displaced, and had a lengthy history of aggressive behavior.
Incident date/location	August 24, 1992, on the campus of Concordia University in Quebec, Montreal, Canada.
Incident category	Revenge by a lethal employee.
Weapons	Three handguns and a briefcase filled with ammunition.
Deaths/Injuries	Four killed, one injured.
Motivation	Fabrikant was angered about a variety of ethical and scientific issues and was seeking revenge against several coworkers.
Disposition	Fabrikant survived his crime and went to trial. He was found guilty of four counts of murder and sentenced to life imprisonment in 1993.

Valery Fabrikant's crime of mass murder was preceded by years of behavioral warning signs that gave every indication of a man who was driven to aggression and unwilling (or unable) to control his hostility against others. Fabrikant was a Russian émigré who possessed a U.S. green card (giving him status as a permanent resident alien) and was traveling on Italian papers when he arrived at Concordia University in Quebec in December 1979, in search of a research or teaching position with the school of mechanical engineering. Although he was unknown to university officials and was unable to provide routine background confirmation from his homeland, Fabrikant was able to secure a job as a research assistant at the university, on December 20, 1979.[IX]

Over the next thirteen years, Fabrikant proved to be a worthy researcher and a competent instructor who received regular promotions and salary increases. Unfortunately, he also proved to be a man who was aggressive, argumentative, prone to violence, and unable to control his behavior. By 1982, Fabrikant had alienated a host of coworkers at the university because of his foul temper, aggressive tactics, and threatening behavior. In that year, a female student complained to university officials that she had been raped by Fabrikant. The woman had suffered a dislocated shoulder and subsequently filed a police report about the attack, but she was terrified to pursue the matter further because of Fabrikant's unpredictable behavior.

This incident apparently only served to bolster Fabrikant's propensity to intimidate those around him to an even greater degree. Within the next few years, Fabrikant was banned from certain university classes because of his erratic, aggressive behavior and his intimidating tactics with other instructors; the university purchasing services department refused to do business with him because of his unreasonable and aggressive behavior; and many of his colleagues had extra dead bolts installed on their office doors or panic buttons installed on their desks because of his continuing threats. By the late 1980s, Fabrikant's behavior was legendary on campus; by 1989, his tenth year on the job, he began to vocalize clear and obvious threats of massive, indiscriminate violence, such as: "I know how people get what they want, they shoot a lot of people."[6]

By 1992, Fabrikant had made a formal request to university administrators to be allowed to possess and transport a handgun on campus. His request was forcefully turned aside in a written reply by university officials; however, no other action was taken to protect the university, its students, or his colleagues. Fabrikant still had full access to the campus, all of its offices, and all of its facilities; in fact, it is likely that he was already carrying a handgun on campus by the time he was denied permission to do so by the university administrators.

Ironically, throughout the many years of harassment, hostility, and aggression, Fabrikant continued to earn academic recognition and regular salary increases, even while university administrators frequently met in closed session about how to deal with his uncontrollable behavior. These administrators were eventually compelled to consult an outside psychiatrist about how to deal with Fabrikant; unbelievably, they were never able to come to a consensus about how to put a stop to his threatening and disruptive behavior.

On August 24, 1992, Fabrikant came to the Hall Building on the university campus. This building housed his own office as well as those of

---

IX. Although the crimes of Valery Fabrikant took place in Canada, they are used in the book as an example of the long-term nature of behavioral warning signs that can sometimes indicate the potential for violence.

several other researchers and instructors. When he arrived on campus, Fabrikant was armed with three handguns and a briefcase filled with ammunition. During a ninety-minute siege of the Hall Building, Fabrikant shot five of his coworkers and took a student hostage. Four of his victims died from their wounds and the fifth survived; the student who was taken hostage was released unharmed. At the end of his siege, Fabrikant was taken into custody and subsequently charged with four counts of murder (see Table 4.5).

Prior to his trial, Fabrikant was examined by two court-appointed psychiatrists and found to be sane. He went on trial in 1993 and, during the course of the proceedings, received six contempt-of-court citations for his persistently uncontrollable behavior. Before the trial ended, he had hired and then fired ten lawyers; in the end, Fabrikant had won the right to represent himself in court. At the conclusion of the trial, he was found guilty of four counts of murder and sentenced to life imprisonment—the maximum penalty under Canadian law. Until the end of his trial, Fabrikant continued to exhibit the same hostile and aggressive behavior that had become his trademark at Concordia University. For well over a decade, he was a man who had made it clear, to all who knew him, that he had few limits on his behavior and an intense obsession for revenge.

Table 4.6: Paul Calden

Perpetrator	A thirty-three-year-old claims adjuster who had a history of aggressive behavior in the workplace and who was severely socially isolated.
Incident date/location	January 27, 1993, in a cafeteria located on the premises of his former employer in Tampa, Florida.
Incident category	Revenge by a lethal employee.
Weapons	A .9mm semiautomatic handgun and a .357-magnum revolver.
Deaths/Injuries	Three killed, two injured.
Motivation	Angered because he had been terminated from his job, Calden vowed to return and take revenge against those whom he blamed for his termination.
Disposition	Calden committed suicide on a nearby golf course after the shooting rampage.

Like Valery Fabrikant, Paul Calden also telegraphed his intentions to be violent. However, Calden's threats were even more overt than Fabrikant's and occurred much earlier in his working career. After Calden graduated from college, he held a number of short-term jobs before he eventually went to work for the Allstate Insurance Company as a claims manager. While he worked at Allstate, Calden quickly developed a reputation as an unpredictable, aggressive, and often hostile employee. He was argumentative with coworkers and would frequently resort to threats of physical violence when things did not go his way.

His behavior became completely unacceptable to management when he got into the habit of bringing a handgun to work and displaying it to supervisors and coworkers in obvious attempts to intimidate them. The management at Allstate was very concerned about Calden's erratic behavior, and they were apparently afraid to take any overt disciplinary action against him. In an effort to rid themselves of a troublesome and dangerous employee, the company's management offered Calden a generous severance package and a positive written recommendation, provided he agreed to voluntarily resign from the organization.

Calden accepted Allstate's offer and pocketed his generous severance pay. The written recommendation that he now carried with him provided Calden with the opportunity to work at one of Allstate's competitors. Calden approached Fireman's Fund for a job and, based largely on the Allstate recommendation, he was hired as a claims manager. From 1990 until 1992, when he was fired from his job at Fireman's Fund, Calden continued his aggressive and intimidating tactics with coworkers. He also continued to bring a handgun to work and threaten others by displaying it in the workplace. In 1992, the management of Fireman's Fund was forced to take action to protect the work environment and terminated Calden from his job. At the time he was fired, Calden made it clear that he would return to take revenge on those who had participated in his termination.

Ten months after he was fired, on January 27, 1993, Paul Calden returned to his former employer's offices. Partially disguised, Calden waited for his predetermined victims in the ground-floor cafeteria of the building that housed Fireman's Fund offices. He knew that the members of management who had been involved in his termination would soon arrive to eat their lunch together, as they often did. For over an hour Calden waited, sipping on a soft drink and pacing from the cafeteria to an adjoining patio. Eventually, his intended victims arrived and Calden was able to put his well-considered plan into action.

As the managers sat together at a table, Calden approached and pulled a .9mm semiautomatic handgun from underneath his jacket. Yelling, "This is what you all get for firing me!" Calden raised his gun to the heads of the stunned employees sitting at the table and, in rapid succession, pumped bullets into each.[7] Within thirty seconds, he had fired off ten rounds, killing three of his former colleagues outright and seriously wounding another two. During the rampage, he passed over one woman who was sitting at the same table as the other victims—she had had nothing to do with Calden's termination nearly a year earlier. He had carefully considered who should die that day, and he kept unerringly to his plan.

Calden unhurriedly left the cafeteria, depositing his weapon next to a cash register near the exit. He then left the crime scene in an automobile that he had rented especially for that day. However, it was never Calden's intention to escape from authorities. Rather, he drove to a nearby golf course, left his vehicle in the parking lot, and walked to the thirteenth hole. There, he sat underneath a large tree and produced another weapon from inside his jacket—a

.357-magnum revolver. Paul Calden put the barrel of the gun to his head and pulled the trigger, dying instantly.

In many ways, Paul Calden was a prototypical lethal employee who turned to mass murder in seeking revenge. According to his neighbors, Calden was severely socially isolated and was never seen in the company of another person. His only social network was in the workplace—an environment in which he had no friends because he thrived on threats, aggression, and intimidation. He was also a man who gave clear and obvious warning signs that he intended to do violence. His was a life of frustration, anger, and loneliness that became so intolerable that he ceased to give it any value. So obvious were the warning signs exhibited by Calden that one of his employers took whatever course they could devise to be rid of him. Unfortunately, his next employer was not able or willing to take that same course and, after firing Calden, suffered the loss of three senior employees and serious injury to two others as a consequence.

Most lethal employees who resort to mass murder commit their crimes in the workplace. Occasionally, however, the perpetrator will kill elsewhere; on rare occasions, the perpetrator will seek out his victims in multiple locations and engage in a murder spree against those whom he has targeted for revenge. Even though such a murder spree is quite rare, its impact can be devastating because of the intensity of the obsession for revenge that is typically demonstrated by the murderer. Jerry Hessler is an example of a lethal employee who went on a murder spree to attack former coworkers in their own homes—an extremely unusual and deeply disturbing form of murder for revenge (see Table 4.7).

Table 4.7: Jerry Hessler

Perpetrator	A thirty-eight-year-old bank employee who had been terminated from his job for harassing coworkers.
Incident date/location	November 19-20, 1995, in four different locations in and around Columbus, Ohio.
Incident category	Revenge by a lethal employee (outside of the work environment).
Weapons	A handgun and a bulletproof vest.
Deaths/Injuries	Four killed, two injured.
Motivation	Hessler attacked those he believed responsible for the loss of his job.
Disposition	Perpetrator survived his crimes and was arrested.

Hessler worked in the credit card operations department of a large bank. By all accounts, he was a rather nondescript employee who rarely socialized with coworkers. In October 1994, after only eighteen months of service, he was fired from his job for harassing other employees. Several of Hessler's colleagues had brought his unwelcome activities to the attention of the bank management, and Hessler quickly came to the conclusion that these coworkers were directly responsible for the loss of his job.

For the year following his termination, Hessler was unemployed and completely socially isolated. He had lost his girlfriend (also a former coworker) and occupied his time at home by making anonymous, threatening telephone calls to one of the women who had been instrumental in his termination. On the evening of November 19, 1995, Hessler decided that he would exact revenge against all those whom he perceived as responsible for his plight. Arming himself with a handgun and donning a bulletproof vest, Hessler had already planned out a driving route that would take him to the residences of his predetermined targets. It was a Sunday night, and Hessler was sure that each victim would be at home. He had planned his attack very carefully.

Hessler first drove to the residence of the woman he had been threatening with telephone calls for a year. Both Tracy Stevens and her husband, Brian, had been coworkers of Hessler, and both had been involved in the events that led to his termination. When he arrived at the Stevenses' home, Hessler broke in without warning and confronted the family with his handgun. Visiting with the Stevens family that night was another bank employee and former coworker, Ruth Canter. Hessler immediately shot and killed Tracy Stevens, Brian Stevens, and their four-month-old daughter; he also shot and wounded Canter before racing from the Stevenses' home to his next planned location. Driving north for less than a mile, Hessler arrived at the home of Mark Campolito, another bank employee and former coworker. Hessler broke through the front door of Campolito's home and immediately shot him. Although wounded, Campolito survived the attack. After shooting Campolito, Hessler fled to the suburb of Worthington, outside of Columbus, and broke into the home of P. Thane Griffin, a local charity executive. For reasons that were not clear to authorities (and never explained by the perpetrator himself), Hessler shot and killed the sixty-four-year-old man in his home.

Hessler's final target was his former girlfriend (now married), Judy Stanton. He drove about seventy miles to reach Stanton's home and banged loudly at the door, demanding to confront the terrified woman. When the Stantons refused to let him in, Hessler fired three shots at the front door and knocked it off its hinges. Stepping into the Stanton home with his gun poised to fire, Hessler was shocked to find himself confronted by Mr. Stanton, who was armed with two handguns of his own. Stanton immediately opened fire at Hessler and hit him in the chest; however, because he was still wearing the bulletproof vest, Hessler was able to escape without injury. Stunned by his encounter with Stanton, Hessler quickly fled the scene in his car. However, by this time authorities were in pursuit of him, and he was arrested before he could leave town. Hessler was subsequently charged with multiple counts of murder and felonious assault.

Jerry Hessler's crimes were unusual in at least two key aspects. As a lethal employee, he attacked former colleagues whom he considered to be responsible for the loss of his job—a common scenario for this type of crime. However, he attacked these individuals in their own homes in a well-planned, carefully executed manner. In effect, these attacks were crimes involving home invasion by a lethal employee seeking revenge—an extremely rare occurrence. Also unusual, was the fact that Hessler's actions on the night of November 19, 1995, constituted a murder spree because they took place at several different locations and were connected by motive (and linked by the relationship of his victims to each other and himself). These elements of Hessler's crime differentiate it from the usual activities of the lethal employee who is seeking revenge against supervisors or coworkers.

Hessler's murder of Griffin remains unexplained and is an enigmatic element in this crime. Griffin had no apparent connection with Hessler's other victims, his former employer, or the loss of his job. Why Hessler should have targeted Griffin that night remains a troubling question. In other aspects of the crime, Jerry Hessler fit the profile of a lethal employee who resorts to murder. He was a socially isolated, angry, and frustrated man who had suffered two major triggering events—the end of an important personal relationship and the loss of his job. Hessler obsessively pondered his options for a year before acting upon his compulsion for retribution. During that time, he was able to carefully plan his crime and dwell incessantly upon the only thing that mattered to him—revenge.

NOTES

1. Adrian Croft, "California Gunman Sought Revenge, Officials Say," *San Francisco Examiner Online* (Internet edition), 3 July 1993, A03.

2. Ibid.

3. James Alan Fox and Jack Levin, *Overkill: Mass Murder and Serial Killing Exposed* (New York: Plenum, 1994), 55.

4. Ibid., 58.

5. "Mass Murder in the Clouds," *U.S. News and World Report*, 21 December 1987, 14.

6. John S. Cowan, "Lessons from the Fabrikant File: A Report to the Board of Governors of Concordia University," (Concordia University, Montreal, Canada. 1 May 1994), 27.

7. Fox and Levin, *Overkill*, 167.

CHAPTER 5

Sexual Homicide

Sexual homicide, a crime of increasing concern in our society, is the killing of a person in the context of power, sexuality, and brutality.

Ressler, Burgess & Douglas
Sexual Homicide: Patterns and Motives

Sexual homicide may involve a single victim in a single incident or multiple victims slain in a number of incidents, each separated by a cooling off period. In the latter case, the perpetrator is generally described as a *serial killer*. Crimes of sexual homicide have increased as a percentage of all homicides in the past few decades and now constitute a significant challenge to law enforcement personnel. In their book, *Sexual Homicide: Patterns and Motives*, authors Ressler, Burgess, and Douglas present an exhaustive study of the crime of sexual homicide, its perpetrator, and the complex life experiences and motivations that are critical to the eventual enactment of this crime. In particular, this book delves into the crimes of the serial killer—a sexual predator of brutal proportions and a perpetrator who has become increasingly common throughout America in the past few decades. It is the serial killer who is most often associated with the crime of sexual homicide in the press and in the minds of most Americans.

Examples of some of the most notorious serial killers in America include an individual known only as "The Green River Killer," who assaulted and murdered at least forty-eight women between 1982 and 1984 in the Seattle-Tacoma area of Washington, dumping many of their bodies in or near the Green River, outside of Seattle; he has never been apprehended (or even identified), and authorities are uncertain why his murders spontaneously came to an end.

John Wayne Gacy was a sexual predator who victimized boys and young men; he tortured, raped, and finally murdered thirty-three victims, most of whose bodies he buried in the basement of his own home. Gacy carefully selected his victims and lured them to his residence with offers of money, a job, or sex. Once in his home, Gacy had complete control over his victims and would have his way with them without fear of interruption. He was executed by lethal injection in 1994.

Theodore Bundy sexually assaulted and murdered at least twenty-two women, who were generally selected based on their similar physical appearance. Bundy planned his crimes with extraordinary care and perfected his ability to interact with his intended victims in a way that gained their trust. Once the victim was in his control (usually inside his vehicle), Bundy became a vicious sexual predator who bit, raped, and brutally murdered her. He was executed in a Florida gas chamber in 1989, leaving law enforcement personnel uncertain how many women he had actually attacked and murdered over his many years of criminal behavior.

There are a great many other examples of serial killers who have been active throughout America in the past few decades. They are the most representative perpetrators of the crime of sexual homicide, whose actions clearly demonstrate the driving compulsion for sexual control and domination that is so characteristic of this offense. The vast majority of serial killers share the unmistakable characteristics of a sexual predator who is relentlessly driven to murder until he is captured or otherwise forced to end his activities because of illness, incarceration for other crimes, or death.

The crime of sexual homicide arises from a mosaic of disturbing experiences that begin in childhood and involve a lethal combination of aggressive and sexual fantasies, which are typically lifelong and pervasive in nature. Activities and experiences such as uncontrollably aggressive behavior, perverse sexual experiences, pathological fantasies, social isolation, acts of animal brutality, and a variety of childhood traumas, combine to build a complex psychological view of others that leads, in a few individuals, to a predatory and brutal association of sex and violence. For these individuals, the only missing element is a triggering event that impels them to the actualization of long-established, pathological fantasies in which sex, violence, and homicide are interwoven into a tangled and uncontrollable obsession. Given the right triggering event, the perpetrator of sexual homicide begins the process of selecting a victim, acting out the crime, and experiencing a cooling off period of fantasy, growing frustration, and renewed planning until he is compelled to repeat the process again with a new victim. This is the classic pattern of the sexual serial killer with which Americans have become all too familiar and against whom law enforcement personnel often face their most strenuous challenges.

The sexual predator who murders in a repetitive pattern typically plans his crimes quite carefully and is obsessed with the fantasy process that this planning implies. He strongly desires to survive his crimes and experience them again and again. He may even engage in a complex, covert interaction with law enforcement personnel as part of his fantasy-driven criminal strategy to prove his ability to control and dominate the situation that he has created. This perpetrator is compelled to exercise pathological control over his victims, often prolonging their suffering as an integral part of the perverse pleasure that he experiences in actuating his fantasies. His crimes demand the maximum degree of victim domination that he can possibly muster; his activities typically exhibit sophisticated planning that allows the murderer to have his way with his prey for the time that is required to fulfill the fantasies that have driven him to murder in the first place. Sexual homicide is often a secret, time-consuming crime that demonstrates an obvious and dominating orientation as a primary motivating element.

On the other hand, the typical mass murderer is not driven by the need for sexual gratification as a primary motivating element; however, he will often be motivated by the same compulsion to control, dominate, or overpower his victims. The mass murderer is typically motivated by the obsession to annihilate his victims, even if they are so depersonalized as to be wholly symbolic in his mind. However, the sexual serial killer is often very specific in selecting his victims, even if he depersonalizes them within the context of his actions. His victims must often meet certain preordained criteria that have arisen from the darkness of his pathological fantasies over a long period of time.

It is extremely rare to encounter a case of mass sexual homicide in which a number of victims are murdered in a single incident and in which the element of sexuality was the primary motivating factor. However, there are a few such cases, and they are extremely disturbing. The case of Richard Speck is notorious as the most heinous example of a sexual mass murderer in American history. His crimes were clearly motivated by a sexual obsession that was perverse and overwhelming. He was also a career criminal, who was addicted to alcohol and illicit drugs and who demonstrated many of the behavioral characteristics of an individual suffering from a severe psychological disorder. Richard Speck was both a sexual predator of the most incredible brutality and a mass murderer by virtue of the number of victims that he murdered in a single episode (see Table 5.1). Fortunately, crimes of this magnitude and complexity are rare in America.

BORN TO RAISE HELL

Richard Speck's left forearm sported a tattoo that not only led to his capture for the mass murder of eight women in Chicago in 1966 but was a near-perfect affirmation of his life of mayhem and murder. The jagged, irregularly lettered tattoo read, "Born to raise hell."

Speck was born in Kirkwood, Illinois, on December 6, 1941. By the age of twenty, he had been arrested over three dozen times for a variety of offenses, including public intoxication, fighting, disorderly conduct, assault, and burglary. By the time he was twenty-five, Speck had been married to a fifteen-year-old girl, fathered a child, held innumerable low-paying jobs, escalated his lifelong record of deviant behavior, and finally been separated from his wife and family after innumerable bitter arguments. By this time, he had also been charged with at least one felony crime in which he assaulted a woman in Dallas by holding a knife to her throat and demanding that she submit to him sexually. At the time of his felony arrest, Speck was severely addicted to drugs and alcohol; when he was not in jail for one of his many offenses, he spent most of his free time frequenting bars, where he would meet a variety of women who offered sex for little or no money. By his mid-twenties, Speck was pathologically obsessed with sex, deeply angry and frustrated about the failure of his marriage, and unable to control either his behavior or his addictions.

Table 5.1: Richard Speck

Perpetrator	A twenty-five-year-old, separated male with a long criminal history, chronic addiction to drugs and alcohol, and indications of a severe psychological disorder.
Incident date/location	July 13, 1966, in Chicago, Illinois. Possibly other (earlier) dates in separate incidents of murder fitting the same profile.
Incident category	Sexual homicide.
Weapons	Knife, strangulation, and a variety of other methods.
Deaths/Injuries	Eight killed during the July 13, 1966, rampage. Possibly four others killed previously. All of the victims were female; some were sexually assaulted.
Motivation	A sexual sadist with a long criminal history and severe chemical and alcohol addictions.
Disposition	Apprehended and sentenced to death in 1967, Speck avoided execution when the Supreme Court later overturned the death penalty. He died while in custody in 1991.

In 1966, Speck was living alone in Chicago and laboring to fuel his persistent addictions to alcohol, drugs, and sex; he was also obsessed by a pernicious and uncontrollable hatred of women that he later attributed to the failed relationship with his wife. Speck earned barely enough money to sustain himself by working sporadically on ore barges that were harbored on the Great Lakes. At this point in his life, he was a man who recognized no bounds on his behavior or sexual impulses; he was willing to submit to even the most outrageous fantasies that were persistently dredged up from his troubled mind.

During a three-month period in 1966, Speck murdered twelve women in a series of particularly sadistic murder sprees. Eight of his victims were slain in a single incident on July 13, 1966—a crime that became the most notorious incident of mass sexual homicide in American history.

Throughout the summer of 1966, Speck spent a good deal of time at the Chicago National Maritime Union hall in order to find the intermittent work that he needed to survive. Less than one block from the union hall was a two-story building known as Jeffrey Manor. It was home to a dozen student nurses who were attached to the South Chicago Community Hospital, located in the same neighborhood. On July 13, 1966, Speck had been drinking heavily and was high on drugs when he banged on the door of Jeffrey Manor, demanding to be let in.

"I'm not going to hurt you," Speck said to Corazon Amurao, a twenty-three-year old student nurse and resident of the building. "I'm only going to tie you up. I need your money to go to New Orleans."[1] Speck held a gun in one hand and a knife in the other as he forced his way inside Jeffrey Manor with Amurao as his first hostage.

Once inside the residence, Speck went from room to room, looking for any other occupants. He forced five other student nurses (in addition to Amurao) into a single room on the second floor, where he bound each and ordered them to lay quietly, side-by-side, on the floor. Over the next hour, three other nurses arrived at the residence; each was taken hostage, bound, and made to lie on the floor with the other terrified women. Speck now held nine nurses captive at Jeffrey Manor.

One after the other, Speck untied each of his victims and led them to other rooms on the second floor of the residence. He murdered his first victim, a twenty-year-old, by stabbing her in the chest and strangling her with a strip of bed sheet. Speck then returned to the room where the frightened nurses lay motionless and weeping. He selected two more victims and led each to separate rooms on the upper floor. His second victim, another twenty-year-old, was stabbed fatally in the heart, neck, and eye. Speck then stabbed his third victim, a twenty-one-year-old, eighteen times before he strangled her. Unlike his first two victims, Speck did not rape his latest victim, but instead, ripped away her undergarments and shredded them with his knife.

Speck's fourth victim was twenty-four-year-old Nina Schmale. He ordered her to lie across a bed in a nearby room, where he raped her and then slashed and strangled her to death. Speck then returned to the room where the remaining nurses were held captive and noticed that they were wriggling around on the floor, crying hysterically, and desperately trying to find anyplace they could to hide. He ordered them to be quiet; however, he did not bother to account for each hostage. One of them, Corazon Amurao, had managed to slither under a nearby bed, where she pressed her body hard against the wall of the room in an effort to keep out of sight. Unconcerned, and unaware of the missing hostage, Speck took his next two victims into a separate room. There he murdered his fifth victim by slashing her throat and the sixth by stabbing her four times. These two women were murdered together, in the same room and on the same bed.

The seventh victim was still bound as Speck forced her into a nearby bathroom. He threw her to the floor and kicked her repeatedly in the torso before strangling her to death. Returning to the room where the nurses had been held, Speck now realized he had lost count of the number of captives he had originally held. As he would later testify, he was never absolutely sure of the number of hostages he had originally taken and finally decided that each victim had been accounted for.

Speck forced his eighth victim to submit to rape, at one point pausing to plead with her, "Would you mind putting your legs around my back?"[2] His chilling request was overheard by Speck's original hostage, Corazon Amurao, who remained silent and motionless, hidden under the bed upon which Speck's last victim lay. After brutally raping his final victim, Speck forced her into a room on the first floor of the residence and again sexually assaulted her, after which he mutilated and strangled her to death. Speck then left Jeffrey Manor believing he had murdered all his original hostages; but he was wrong.

Corazon Amurao waited for some time to be sure that the intruder had left before she struggled out from under the bed that had been her salvation. She was eventually able to make her way to the balcony of the room and scream for help to passersby on the street below. When police arrived on the grizzly scene of the mass murder, Amurao, despite her incredible ordeal, was able to give an accurate description of the suspect. Her description included the infamous tattoo on Speck's forearm. Law enforcement officials were also able to gather a significant amount of forensic evidence at the scene of the crime, and an immediate and intensive manhunt for the mass murderer was put into effect.

On July 17, 1966, four days after the murders, Speck attempted suicide but bungled his effort and found himself in the emergency room of a local hospital. His tattoo, a description of which had been widely disseminated in the press and on television throughout the Chicago area, was immediately recognized by emergency room personnel. The Chicago police responded to the hospital and arrested Speck for the murders of eight women.

In 1967, Speck was convicted of multiple counts of murder and sentenced to death; however, his death sentence was subsequently overturned when the U.S. Supreme Court ruled that capital punishment was unconstitutional. Speck's sentence was eventually amended to multiple life terms without the possibility of parole. In December 1991, Speck died while in custody.

Law enforcement officials spared no effort to investigate the crimes of Richard Speck, including a review of other, unsolved homicides in the Chicago area that had been committed during the time he lived there. It was later determined that Speck was probably the murderer of four other women, each of whom had been brutally raped and slain in the same manner as the victims at Jeffrey Manor.

The horrific crimes of Richard Speck captured front-page headlines throughout the nation. He became (and remains) one of the most notorious, brutal, and sadistic mass murderers in the history of American criminology. A man who was a true sociopath and sexual sadist, there remains a disturbing and loathsome truth to the words tattooed on his arm—"Born to raise hell." Unlike the sexual sadist serial killer, who carefully selects his victims and plans his brutal crimes in detail, Speck capped off his life of deviance by indiscriminately attacking a group of women in their own residence, in a manner that was unspeakably horrific and apparently unplanned. He was a criminal who truly knew no bounds on his behavior, who was pathologically obsessed with anger and hatred toward women, and who was a sexual deviant of unparalleled magnitude.

MASS SEXUAL HOMICIDE IN CANADA

Although this book is concerned with the crimes of the American mass murderer, there is an example of mass sexual homicide that took place in Canada only a few years after the horrible crimes of Richard Speck that must be included here. This incident helps to shed more light on the true horror of this form of mass murder. Even though the crime of mass sexual homicide is rare, this second incident, involving Dale Merle Nelson, demonstrates the similarities of the course of the crime and helps to elucidate many of the characteristics that are common to the profile of the perpetrator of mass sexual homicide (see Table 5.2).

Dale Merle Nelson was a Canadian lumberjack who lived in West Creston, British Columbia. Although generally considered to be a friendly, outgoing individual, Nelson was known to suffer from periods of deep depression and was a frequent abuser of alcohol and illicit drugs, especially LSD. He was also known to suffer from sexual impotence and would often drink to excess in a vain effort to overcome his feelings about this disability.

On September 5, 1970, Nelson had been drinking heavily and was in a morose state of mind. Late that night, he entered the home of a neighbor, Mrs. Shirley Wasyk, who lived alone with her three daughters: Tracey, seven years old; Sharlene, eight years old; and Debbie, twelve years old. As Nelson would later testify, he was also under the influence of LSD and carrying a loaded rifle when he forced his way into the Wasyk home.

After entering the home, Nelson immediately battered Shirley Wasyk to death. During the lengthy beating, Debbie was able to escape from the home to summon help; however, the other two daughters were not so fortunate. Nelson choked Tracey into unconsciousness and then mutilated her across the abdomen with a large knife. He then attacked and sodomized Sharlene.

Nelson left the Wasyk home and traveled a short distance to the residence of another neighbor, the Phipps family. After forcing his way into the Phippses' home, he shot and killed Ray Phipps and his common-law wife, Isabelle St. Amand. Nelson then turned his attention to their four children and shot each of them. As he left, Nelson took the body of eight-year-old Cathy St. Amand with him.

Table 5.2: Dale Merle Nelson

Perpetrator	A twenty-eight-year-old Canadian lumberjack who was socially isolated and severely addicted to alcohol and LSD.
Incident date/location	September 5, 1970, in the homes of two neighbors near West Creston, British Columbia.
Incident category	Sexual homicide.
Weapons	Bludgeoning, beating, shooting, slashing, sodomy, strangulation, and mutilation.
Deaths/Injuries	Eight killed and two injured in two different locations on the same night.
Motivation	A sexually impotent male with severe addictions.
Disposition	Nelson turned himself into authorities and was convicted of murder. He was sentenced to the maximum penalty under Canadian law—life imprisonment without the possibility of parole.

Nelson somehow managed to avoid the police, who had been immediately summoned to both homes. However, a short while later his car was located in the deep woods near the town of West Creston. Close to the car, police found the remains of Tracey Wasyk scattered around the area. Many of the child's organs were missing and were never located. Approximately thirty-six hours after the murders, still armed with the rifle that he had used to shoot several of his victims, Nelson surrendered to authorities.

Dale Merle Nelson went to trial in March 1971 for the murders of Tracey Wasyk and Cathy St. Amand, claiming that he was insane at the time of the crimes due to his addiction to alcohol and LSD. However, the jury rejected this line of defense and found him guilty. Nelson was given the maximum sentence under Canadian law—life imprisonment without the possibility of parole.[3]

NOTES

1. "Hunting Humans: Richard Speck," in Kozel Multimedia, Inc., *Mind of a Killer* CD-ROM (Chatsworth, CA: Cambrix, 1995).

2. Ibid.

3. J. H. H. H. Gaute, *Murderers Who's Who*, (New York: Methuen, 1979), 173.

CHAPTER 6

Mass Executions

Every murder turns on a bright hot light, and a lot of people have to walk out of the shadows.

Mark Hellinger
The Naked City

Mass murder by execution is a rare crime in this country. However, when it occurs, it is sometimes committed by perpetrators for very specific reasons, such as to eliminate witnesses to a crime or as a "contracted" act of murder that targets several specific individuals in a single incident. Occasionally, but with increasing frequency in recent years, gang-style killings devolve into crimes of mass murder by execution because several victims are slain in a single incident. Within this category of crime, the most common type of incident involves the killing of witnesses to a felony action that has gone wrong and in which the perpetrators fear that they will be identified by their victims. Such mass executions may involve multiple perpetrators, who will often be young, aggressive males who are unsure of their actions and unable to control the situation that they have created. Gang activities and drug or alcohol abuse may also play a prominent role in the commission of such a crime.

Although contracted mass executions are typically well planned and obvious, they are rare in this country. This form of murder is most often committed against one or two individuals, and not against larger groups of victims; it is generally accomplished in a manner that does not draw notice to the perpetrators and minimizes potential crime scene evidence. However, there are exceptions to the quiet, secretive "contract hit."

The most notorious crime of contracted mass execution in the history of American criminology is the infamous St. Valentine's Day Massacre, which occurred in 1929 (see Table 6.1). On February 13, 1929, George "Bugs" Moran, the head of a powerful Chicago gang, and rival to the notorious Al Capone, received an anonymous telephone call offering to hijack a truckload of Capone's whiskey for his gang operations. The offer included the delivery of the whiskey to Moran's warehouse the next day—St. Valentine's Day. The following day, Moran ordered seven of his gang members to help unload the whiskey at his warehouse. However, when Moran and the gang approached the meeting place, Moran saw a police vehicle and what he believed to be uniformed and plainclothes law enforcement officers gathering near the warehouse entrance. Thinking that it was a police raid, Moran drove quickly away; however, the other members of the gang did not leave the scene.

Four of the would-be police officers herded the seven members of Moran's gang into the warehouse and ordered them stand against a wall. The officers then shot the gang members repeatedly with machine guns, leaving no survivors. An investigation later disclosed that the men who were masquerading as police officers were, in fact, members of Al Capone's gang—Moran's rival in Chicago for the lucrative bootlegging business. A $100,000 reward was posted for the arrest and conviction of the murderers. Only a single arrest was made—a gangster by the name of "Machine Gun" Jack McGurn. However, the evidence against McGurn was insufficient to result in any formal charges or a trial. In an ironic twist to this early incident of mass murder, McGurn was killed in a shoot-out exactly seven years later—on St. Valentine's Day.

Table 6.1: St. Valentine's Day Massacre

Perpetrator	Uncertain but believed to be members of Al Capone's Chicago gang.
Incident date/location	February 14, 1929, in a warehouse in Chicago, Illinois.
Incident category	Mass execution.
Weapons	Machine guns.
Deaths/Injuries	Seven killed.
Motivation	Gang warfare.
Disposition	Perpetrators were never positively identified or charged.

Gang-style mass executions are now on the rise in America, and when they occur, these crimes are both extraordinarily blatant and brutal. For example, on November 6, 1995, two gunman seeking revenge against their rivals entered a Charleston, Massachusetts, restaurant; they were armed with semiautomatic weapons. Within a few seconds, the perpetrators had fired eight to ten rounds, killing four patrons and critically wounding a fifth (see Table

6.2). The two gunmen were immediately taken into custody and appeared to have specifically targeted their victims, with gang revenge as a motivation.

Table 6.2: Charleston Restaurant and Pub Murders

Perpetrator	Two males who were undisguised and armed.
Incident date/location	November 6, 1995, at a restaurant in Charleston, Massachusetts.
Incident category	Mass execution (probably gang-related).
Weapons	Semiautomatic weapons.
Deaths/Injuries	Four killed, one injured.
Motivation	Probably a gang-related shooting.
Disposition	The two unidentified perpetrators were arrested at the crime scene.

Murders such as these are most often associated with gang warfare, drug activity, and intense turf rivalries among groups of young males. They are premeditated crimes designed to eliminate rivals and establish the perpetrators as revered members of a group. A more familiar form of this activity (and one that is not typically an act of mass murder) is the drive-by shooting of rival gang members—a crime that has become almost legendary in impoverished, urban neighborhoods across America. However, it rare that this form of violence escalates into an organized act of mass murder.

Mass executions that occur during the course of a crime usually indicate that the crime itself was poorly planned or badly botched. These crimes are often linked to young perpetrators—typically under twenty-five years of age—and are frequently gang related or involve drug use. It is not unusual for this category of mass murder to involve two or more perpetrators who may be operating on a crime spree or an impulse. Robbery is the most frequently demonstrated motive in such crimes. These murders are usually incidental to the intent of the original crime and occur because the perpetrators were surprised by witnesses or had not anticipated that potential witnesses would present a problem. Once involved in the crime and subsequently confronted by potential witnesses, the perpetrators, typically in a panic, will lash out to eliminate all who can identify them. When there are two or more perpetrators involved in the crime, there may come a point when one of the perpetrators decides it is vital to eliminate all witnesses. For all the perpetrators, such a decision may then become a mandate in order to maintain group loyalty and cohesiveness. This situation typically occurs in confrontational crimes, such as a robbery that has been unexpectedly interrupted by witnesses.

On December 19, 1995, Michael Vernon, a twenty-two-year-old with a history of aggression and mental instability, entered a Bronx shoe store (as he had done on several preceding Tuesdays), apparently shopping for a pair of shoes of a unique size. Each time he visited the store, he would inquire about the shoes and be told by store personnel that they were not available in his size.

However, on this particular Tuesday, when Vernon was told that the shoes were still not available, he announced that he had come to rob the store. Without explanation, Vernon immediately began randomly firing a shotgun at the individuals inside. Law enforcement personnel later speculated that Vernon's prior visits to the shoe store were nothing more than a diversionary tactic that he used while planning the robbery; they also concluded that once he had initiated the robbery attempt, Vernon lost control of the situation (and himself) and that his instinctive reaction was to indiscriminately shoot at anyone within sight.

In an apparent panic, Vernon fatally shot four customers and the store owner's wife, and seriously wounded another three shoppers. Three of those who were killed at the scene belonged to a single family—a mother and her two sons—who had been Christmas shopping at the store. Vernon immediately fled from the store without any money but with a female hostage. He was confronted on the street outside the shoe store by a passing highway patrol officer, and a gunfight ensued in which Vernon was shot but not seriously injured (see Table 6.3). He was subsequently taken into custody, after again trying to flee the scene, when he collapsed from his wounds.

It was later discovered that Michael Vernon had a history of both violence and psychological problems. He was raised in a drug- and weapon-infested housing project known as Edenwald Houses, where he lived with his mother. Vernon's father had died when he was young and his brother died in 1993, from complications of AIDS caused by intravenous drug use. Vernon himself had been briefly hospitalized for a psychological disorder just a few months before his murderous rampage at the Bronx shoe store.

Table 6.3: Michael Vernon

Perpetrator	A twenty-two-year-old male with a history of violent behavior and possible mental instability.
Incident date/location	December 19, 1995, in a retail store in the Bronx, New York.
Incident category	Mass execution.
Weapons	A shotgun.
Deaths/Injuries	Five killed, three injured.
Motivation	Murders committed in the course of a botched robbery attempt.
Disposition	Vernon was wounded by responding police personnel and taken into custody.

A few months earlier, across the country on the West Coast, another witness-elimination crime took place in the small farming community of Tulare, California. Located in the San Joaquin Valley, the town of Tulare had not experienced a mass murder in its history until July 19, 1995. On that evening, three males, wearing masks to hide their identities, entered a neighborhood bar to rob it and, presumably, any patrons unlucky enough to be inside at the time. The bar was a quiet place that catered to a number of regular customers who gathered to socialize and play pool. The robbers had obviously planned their crime to some extent but had not anticipated the number of patrons who would still be in the bar when they arrived. In the course of the robbery, the perpetrators shot all six of the individuals in the bar. Five died at the scene and the sixth was critically wounded (see Table 6.4). The robbers, who were never identified or apprehended, escaped with money they had taken from the proprietor and several customers.

Table 6.4: Tulare, California, Mass Murder

Perpetrator	Three unidentified perpetrators were involved in the rampage.
Incident date/location	July 19, 1995, in a neighborhood bar in the town of Tulare, California.
Incident category	Mass execution.
Weapons	Multiple handguns from more than a single shooter.
Deaths/Injuries	Five killed, one injured.
Motivation	Murders committed in the course of a robbery.
Disposition	The perpetrators have never been identified or apprehended.

DEATH IN A TEMPLE

In 1991, an exceptionally vicious crime of mass murder by execution took place near the small town of Goodyear, Arizona, approximately twenty miles west of Phoenix. Located on the outskirts of town was a Buddhist temple known as Wat Promkunaram. This religious center housed six practicing monks, one monk in training, and an elderly nun who lived in the temple with her teenage grandson. The monks lived frugally, surviving on small donations from their religious community and food delivered to the temple each day by local residents. The monks were primarily from Thailand and practiced a form of Buddhism known as Theravada—a philosophy that emphasized a lack of worldly attachments, a life of monastic discipline, and the daily practice of prayer and meditation. Their religious beliefs strongly prohibited any form of aggressive behavior or harm to others. The temple and its monks were an important religious and cultural center to the approximately 3,000 member Thai community in and around the Phoenix area.

Early Saturday morning, August 10, 1991, a member of the temple congregation arrived to deliver food for the monks' first meal of the day. Entering the temple (which was always unlocked), the congregation member was horrified to discover that the inhabitants had been murdered, execution-style, with their bodies laid face-down in their living quarters. The entire entourage of the temple, nine in all, had been slain in a similar manner with a small caliber weapon. Several of the rooms in the temple had been ransacked, and the jewelry usually worn by the monks had been removed from their bodies. However, ornate and valuable statues and artifacts that were on display in the main room of the temple had been left undisturbed. At first, law enforcement personnel arriving at the scene were uncertain of the motive for the crime, although they were convinced that there had been two perpetrators present who had each used a different weapon.

The discovery of the nine bodies signaled the beginning of a manhunt by Arizona law enforcement personnel that was, from the start, very poorly handled. Months after the murders, Arizona officials had arrested and imprisoned four suspects; however, because of a combination of inadequate investigative methods and the questionable interrogation of suspects, it was later proved that none of the individuals was relevant to the case. Another suspect, who was mentally disturbed, had been held in custody for fourteen months on charges of murder; however, he was also eventually cleared when Alessandro Garcia, age seventeen, confessed that he and another teenager, Johnathan Doody, eighteen years old, had murdered the Buddhists during a botched robbery attempt. Both of the teenage murderers, who were friends and high school classmates in Avondale, Arizona, had a history of illegal and violent activity in the area. Apparently in a panic, they had murdered the Buddhists after only planning to rob the temple. Neither perpetrator provided a compelling reason for the killings, which were apparently committed on an impulse during the robbery.

Table 6.5: Alessandro Garcia and Johnathan Doody

Perpetrator	Garcia (age seventeen) and Doody (age eighteen) were high school friends who shared a history of aggressive and violent behavior.
Incident date/location	August 10, 1991, in a Buddhist temple in Goodyear, Arizona.
Incident category	Mass execution.
Weapons	Two, small-caliber handguns.
Deaths/Injuries	Nine killed—all members of the Buddhist temple.
Motivation	Mass murder in the course of a robbery.
Disposition	Both perpetrators were arrested after a lengthy, inadequate investigation by law enforcement personnel. Garcia later testified against Doody. In 1993, both were convicted of multiple counts of first degree murder.

On July 12, 1993, Johnathan Doody was convicted of nine counts of murder, nine counts of armed robbery, one count of burglary, and one count of conspiracy.[1] Alessandro Garcia pled guilty to first-degree murder charges and was able to avoid the death penalty by testifying against Doody (see Table 6.5).

The crimes of Garcia and Doody were particularly horrifying because of the nature of their victims. The Buddhists at temple Wat Promkunaram lived a simple, nonviolent life. They had few possessions and were committed to following a strict path of good works and caring for others. The monks were highly regarded by the surrounding community for their willingness to help others who were in need, whether or not they were members of the Buddhist congregation. One of the members of the congregation said of the monks: "People would come at ten o'clock at night to talk about their problems, and the monks would let them in. They trusted people."[2] Law enforcement personnel found no evidence that any of the Buddhists put up a struggle against their attackers. In fact, to do so would not have been consistent with their religious beliefs. Garcia and Doody took an extreme and unforgivable step in executing these people who had committed their lives to all the values that proved meaningless to their killers.

NOTES

1. "Nation in Brief," Associated Press, *Philadelphia Inquirer Online* (Internet edition), 13 July 1993, A04.

2. John Woestendiek, "Tranquil Lives Shattered by Gunfire," *Philadelphia Inquirer Online* (Internet edition), 12 August 1991, A01.

CHAPTER 7

Sane or Insane

Sanity is a madness put to good uses; waking life is a dream controlled.

George Santayana
Interpretations of Poetry and Religion

Although the majority of mass murderers are sane in a legal sense, the literature of this crime is peppered with incidents that clearly indicate that the perpetrator was probably deranged at the time he committed his crimes, at least from the layperson's perspective. From a prosaic and practical point of view, it seems absurd to bother with terms such as *sanity* or *insanity* when discussing the crimes of any mass murderer. Regardless of his state of mind, disability, or disposition, the actions of a mass murderer are always, in a very real sense, insane. From a certain viewpoint, the issue of sanity is irrelevant, when one considers the nature of the crime itself. Mass murder is a horrible offense that claims the innocent and leaves precious little room for understanding or forgiveness under any circumstances.

Despite the heinous nature of the crime, we must come to some understanding of the mass murderer if we are ever to come to grips with the impact of this crime and begin to deal with the motivations and imperatives that allow it to be repeated over and over again throughout America. We must strive for a complete understanding of the mass murderer and his actions, whether or not he is legally sane. The question of sanity is therefore crucial to an understanding of the motivations of the murderer.

The term *insanity* does not derive solely from the behavioral sciences; rather, it is an important legal categorization that is used to define culpability.

In its many variations, the use of insanity as a defense is as ancient as jurisprudence itself; and it has been redefined often over many centuries. The use and success of the insanity defense also varies widely with cultural influences, even among legal systems that share a common basis in theory and practice. For example, the American system of jurisprudence is derived from English law and shares many tenets with it, one of which is the use of the insanity defense. Despite the derivation of our legal system from that practiced in the United Kingdom, American juries are extremely reluctant to recognize insanity as a viable defense, validating its use with a not-guilty verdict in only about 2 percent of all cases in which sanity is raised as an issue. However, in England, juries validate this defense as much as 25 percent of the time it is used as a defense strategy.[1] Despite this disparity, the English and American legal definitions of insanity are based on the same tenet of law—the McNaughton test.

The McNaughton test is the most commonly applied standard for the applicability of a defense based on insanity. It reads, in part:

To establish a defense on the ground of insanity, it must be clearly proved that, at the time of the committing of the act, the party was laboring under such a defect of reason, from disease of the mind, as to not know the nature and quality of the act he was doing, or, if he did know it, that he did not know he was doing what was wrong.[2]

The test has led to the common public practice of determining if the individual in question knew right from wrong as a fundamental determination of sanity in our legal system.

This point of law first arose in the trial of Daniel McNaughton in the 1840s, in England. McNaughton shot and killed the private secretary to the prime minister of England on January 20, 1843. He was subsequently tried for the crime and found to be insane and (therefore) not guilty. Contemporary behavioral scientists who have carefully reviewed the circumstances surrounding McNaughton's life and crime believe that he was a paranoid schizophrenic who suffered from severe delusions and was therefore clinically incapable of understanding the nature of his actions. Because of his obvious dementia, McNaughton's English jury found him *legally* unable to determine right from wrong in shooting the prime minister's private secretary. The McNaughton test, which emanated from his trial and became a formalized point of law, has been the subject of periodic debate ever since it was first established more than a century ago. In the majority of American courts to this day, the McNaughton test stands as a crucial element of jurisprudence by which juries and the court are able to determine legal sanity in a way that is independent of the opinion of behaviorists or medical professionals.

For those mass murderers who survive their crimes, the insanity defense is not an uncommon trial strategy; however, it is rarely successful. American courts, juries, and the public are extremely reluctant to accept an insanity defense when confronted with crimes as heinous as those that are typical of the contemporary mass murderer. This reluctance is understandable and well-grounded in the American court system by the verdicts of many juries over many decades. Nonetheless, from a clinical perspective, there may be a number of mass murderers who suffer from disorders that the layperson would define as insanity.

The question of legal sanity is a point of continuous and pervasive debate between behavioral scientists and experts in the law. Where a psychiatrist or psychologist will immediately recognize elements that constitute the common definition of insanity, when applying the standards of the McNaughton test, legal experts and the courts will typically find the perpetrator to be sane. The case of John Frazier stands as a classic example of an individual who to behaviorists was quite incapable of processing reality in a normal fashion yet in a legal sense was sane enough to stand trial for five counts of murder and be sentenced to life imprisonment. The fact that all who knew Frazier were convinced that he was demented did not persuade a jury to consider his disorder as a practical defense. Ironically, he suffered from the same disability as Daniel McNaughton—the man who lent his name to the test of sanity that was used at Frazier's trial.[X]

JOHN FRAZIER'S MISSION

On the evening of October 19, 1970, firemen responded to the home of Dr. Victor M. Ohta after receiving a report that the residence of the highly respected eye surgeon was burning. What they found at the Ohta residence was not only a number of small fires that had been deliberately set throughout the home, but a scene of incredible mayhem and horror. Victor Ohta, his wife, his secretary, and their two sons had each been tied, blindfolded, shot, and thrown into the family swimming pool. The impressive Ohta estate had become the scene of one of the most brutal cases of mass murder in the history of the small town of Santa Cruz, California.

Parked in the driveway leading to the Ohta home was the doctor's red Rolls-Royce. Pinned under the windshield wiper blade was this incoherent, typewritten note, which proved to be the most critical piece of evidence found at the crime scene:[XI]

halloween . . . 1970
today world war 3 will begin as brought to you by the people of the free universe.
From this day forward any one and ?/or company of persons who missuses the natural environment or destroys same will suffer the penalty of death by the people of the free universe.

X. Both suffered from paranoid schizophrenia accompanied by severe delusions.
XI. The idiosyncratic spelling of certain words is from the original document.

I and my comrads from this day forth will fight until death or freedom, against anything or anyone who dose not support natural life on this planet, materalisum must die or man-kind will.
KNIGHT OF WANDS
KNIGHT OF CUPS
KNIGHT OF PENTICLES
KNIGHT OF SWORDS[3]

In addition to this piece of evidence, law enforcement officials received a number of tips about the Ohta murders; all of them pointed to a man named John Linley Frazier as the individual who had typewritten the message that was found on Ohta's automobile. The informants who spoke to police were all acquaintances of Frazier and had long been concerned about his bizarre behavior and rambling, incoherent speech. For years he had constantly preached about materialism, pollution, the end of the world, and an army of unnamed "people of the free universe."

Frazier lived in a cow shed on property located down the hill from the Ohta home. The Ohta residence had been erected above him, at the summit of a rise that took advantage of a sweeping view of the canyon, the nearby town of Santa Cruz, and the Pacific Ocean. From his isolated hovel, Frazier could easily see the impressive estate of the Ohta family, which was perched far above him. At the age of twenty-four, Frazier was separated from his wife, essentially destitute, and (by the accounts of those who knew him) quite mad. He was also obsessed with the grandeur of the Ohta residence and curious about those who lived there in such apparent opulence.

Frazier had a very troubled childhood. His parents had separated when he was two years old, and at the age of five, he was placed in a foster home because his mother was unable to earn enough money to care for him. After Frazier was separated from his mother, he was in and out of trouble for the rest of his childhood. He frequently ran away from his foster home, was arrested for theft, and was eventually placed in a series of California youth facilities. He had a long history of bed-wetting, horrendous nightmares, and sleepwalking—all of which continued until the time of his arrest for the Ohta family murders.[4]

At the age of twenty-one, Frazier found work as an automobile mechanic and married a local woman. However, marriage did not change his course or ameliorate his growing psychological problems. Frazier's behavior continued to deteriorate, and after a minor automobile accident in 1970, he told his wife he had received a message from God informing him that if he were ever to drive an automobile again, he would be killed. According to Donald T. Lunde, an eminent criminal psychiatrist who became familiar with Frazier's case, this incident was the triggering event for Frazier's psychosis.[5]

After the message from God, Frazier's behavior became even more bizarre. He came to the conclusion that it was his mission to save the earth from materialism and pollution—elements that he found to be pervasive and out of control wherever he turned. Frazier began to have spiritual visions and believed that the Book of Revelations in the Bible had been written specifically for him; he became convinced that it was his personal obligation to interpret this arcane text for the benefit of the rest of humanity. His delusions also involved convoluted aspects of astrology and the tarot; and they were replete with an overriding obsession that the end of the world was imminent.

Frazier tried to recruit disciples for his cause and spoke incessantly about his mission to all he encountered. He frequently wrote of his delusional beliefs in a diary, summing them up in a phrase that read, "The present condition of this world is so that man cannot sustain life as intended by God so I, John Frazier, believe He will intervein (sic) according to the last book or chapter."[6] Clearly, Frazier was ready for the end of the world as portrayed in the Book of Revelations and believed himself to be a critical interpreter and agent of Armageddon.

By October 1970, Frazier was completely isolated and living in the cow shed on his mother's property. In the months preceding the murders, both Frazier's mother and his wife made repeated attempts to persuade him to seek psychiatric help. He persistently refused all offers of assistance and came to believe that the only two people in the world who had showed any interest in his welfare, his wife and his mother, were now aligned against him. In the weeks before his crime, several of Frazier's neighbors witnessed him sitting on top of a water tower near his home with a gun in his hand. He had become completely delusional and unwilling to communicate with anyone unless he was discussing his mission and the end of the world. He had also become obsessed with the Ohta estate, which was visible high on the hill above where he lived in squalor. To his crazed way of thinking, the Ohta home came to represent the ultimate in materialism and pollution.

Frazier came to the conclusion that the occupants of the large home on the hill must die in order for him to complete the mission that had been given to him by God. It did not matter that he had never met the Ohta family and knew nothing of their humanity. He had decided that whoever lived in that home must be slain, and the residence itself must be destroyed in order to return the hillside upon which it was built to a more natural state. This was his mission and his obsession.

On October 19, 1970, Frazier climbed the hill to the Ohta home and brutally murdered all its occupants. He then set a number of fires throughout the residence and, leaving the scene of the murders, carefully placed his typewritten note under the windshield wiper of Dr. Ohta's car. Lost in his delusions and fantasies, Frazier then went back to the cow shed that was his home and waited. Four days after his victims were discovered, Frazier was found, sleeping in the cow shed, by law enforcement personnel.

The question of John Frazier's sanity proved to be a complex one. From a psychiatric point of view, he was clearly psychotic and had been diagnosed as a paranoid schizophrenic who suffered from persistent, debilitating delusions. However, in a legal sense he was found to be sane and able to stand trial for his crimes. Frazier was eventually convicted of five counts of first-degree homicide and sentenced to life imprisonment at San Quentin, in Marin County, California (see Table 7.1).

Table 7.1: John Frazier

Perpetrator	A twenty-four-year-old man who suffered from significant psychological problems.
Incident date/location	October 19, 1970, in a private residence near the town of Santa Cruz, California.
Incident category	Sane/insane.
Weapons	A handgun, drowning, and arson.
Deaths/Injuries	Five killed.
Motivation	Frazier believed that the members of the Ohta family must die in order to fulfill a mission from God involving the end of the world and widespread ecological damage.
Disposition	Frazier was sentenced to life imprisonment.

PARANOID SCHIZOPHRENIA

Schizophrenia is a severely debilitating mental illness that is complex, often misunderstood or misdiagnosed, and difficult or impossible to treat effectively. In some forms it is accompanied by bizarre delusions or hallucinations and characterized by equally unusual, disorganized behavior and speech. There are a range of subtypes of schizophrenia, among which is the paranoid type. Individuals suffering from this form of schizophrenia can sometimes become lethally violent and, by the standards of the layperson, would often be described as deranged.

Individuals suffering from schizophrenia may exhibit very disorganized behavior that is extreme and eccentric; or alternatively, they may react with extraordinary complacency to even the most obvious stimulation. They may also react with a wide range of behavior that varies unpredictably between these extremes. This is a mental disorder that typically attacks the individual after adolescence and most often before the age of forty. In males, the disease is typically first exhibited in the mid-twenties and is usually slow to develop, progressing over time and manifesting itself in an increasing inability of the individual to function effectively in society. The disorder generally effects both sexes equally, although perhaps slightly favoring males.

Schizophrenia tends to be chronic and may run in family groups. First-degree biological relatives of individuals suffering from schizophrenia indicate a likelihood of succumbing to the disorder that is ten times greater than that of the general population. It is also a disorder that affects many Americans annually and, because of its long-term, insidious nature, it can destroy their lives permanently. Several studies of the disease indicate that schizophrenia will be diagnosed for the first time in about 1 in 10,000 individuals each year, and that somewhere between 1 and 2 percent of the population is currently suffering from some type of the disorder.[7]

Schizophrenics are often socially dysfunctional and subject to unpredictable and extreme changes in mood and behavior. The paranoid schizophrenic is subject to overwhelming delusions or hallucinations that are marked by persistent themes of persecution and accompanied by anxiety, anger, and (sometimes) violent behavior. The individual will frequently believe he is the victim of a wide range of conspiracies and plots that are perpetrated by both individuals known to him and complete strangers. In his or her distorted thinking process, the individual will perceive threats everywhere with everyone he encounters, and is therefore compelled to react in ways that are defensive and fearful. A unique aspect of the paranoid type of schizophrenic is that he or she will sometimes experience persistent auditory hallucinations that command him to seek revenge or retribution against those plotting against him. Often, these delusions or hallucinations will have a religious tone or theme that tell the victim he has been specially chosen to undergo and overcome the very persecution that he is experiencing. Ironically, to the casual observer, the paranoid schizophrenic may not appear to be as ill as is truly the case. These individuals may not always exhibit some of the more obvious symptoms of other subtypes of schizophrenia, such as grossly disorganized behavior or speech.

The individual suffering from paranoid schizophrenia can sometimes be violent or lethal with little or no warning. Unable to process reality in an appropriate way (psychotic), and believing that those around him are engaged in a conspiracy to deprive him of his freedom or his life, the individual suffering from this disorder can erupt with a sudden ferocity that may be brutal and overwhelming. He may also become entangled in a long-term web of delusions and hallucinations that lead, slowly but inevitably, to violence against himself or others. Given that these delusions and hallucinations may be persistent, powerful, and bizarre, the paranoid schizophrenic can sometimes perceive life-threatening situations incessantly, and he may eventually succumb to the compelling demand to protect himself or his interests with violent behavior. Because of this disorder, the paranoid schizophrenic may view himself in the role of a savior, redeemer, or instrument of justice, who is compelled by his "voices" to exact retribution against those who threaten him, society, or even the world itself.

Schizophrenia is a disorder that can sometimes be controlled through a strict regimen of medication and psychiatric care. Often, however, the affected individuals are unable to access the health care that they require or they are simply not diagnosed and treated appropriately. Even when they have been provided with medical care and treatment, achieving ongoing supervision and drug maintenance is often difficult and unsuccessful. Many individuals simply stop taking the medication that they so desperately need in order to maintain minimal stability. Worse than even this common situation, recent legislation in many states (such as California) has had the effect of abandoning individuals who are suffering from schizophrenia by closing the facilities designed to provide long-term treatment. Left on their own, individuals suffering from this disorder must try to fend for themselves in a world that is perceived as threatening and overwhelming. The victims of paranoid schizophrenia can sometimes represent an ongoing and significant threat to themselves and others due to a lack of access to the treatment that could otherwise allow them to at least function appropriately in society. The life and crimes of John Frazier are a sad testimony to the insidious effect of this disorder and the inability of our society to provide the kind of support that is necessary to avoid the violence and mayhem that Frazier deemed to be inevitable.

HATE OR INSANITY?

The motivations underlying mass murder are sometimes complex and chaotic, thereby making a reliable understanding of any particular incident difficult or impossible. The crimes of Colin Ferguson provide an example of the uncertainty that is common in categorizing and comprehending some incidents of mass murder. Ferguson, an African-American, shot twenty-five people on a crowded commuter train; not one of his victims was known to him. All his victims were Caucasians or Asian-Americans, despite a significant number of African-American commuters onboard the same train in the immediate proximity of the shooter. Six of Ferguson's victims died of their wounds and another nineteen were injured—several quite seriously. During the trial, it became clear to some observers that Colin Ferguson was suffering from significant psychological problems and may have even been incapable of truly understanding the impact of his actions at the time of the murders. However, the jury did not agree with these observations and found him guilty of most of the charges brought against him. Today, the question remains unanswered as to whether Ferguson's murderous rampage was motivated by racial hatred, a debilitating psychological disorder, or other factors that were more complex and covert. Thus, the Ferguson case raises stark and difficult questions of motivation that sometimes accompany the actions of a mass murder.

On December 7, 1993, Colin Ferguson, age thirty-five, boarded a Long Island Rail Road commuter train that was packed with passengers returning from work. Shortly after 6 P.M., the train was arriving at the Merillon Avenue Station in Garden City, New York, when the conductor passed by Ferguson's seat to check his ticket. The conductor asked Ferguson for additional money because the ticket that he held was only valid for off-peak travel times. Ferguson handed over the additional fare without argument and started to rise from his seat, apparently in anticipation of the Merillon Avenue stop just ahead. As he turned to rise from his seat, Ferguson quickly swiveled around to face the two riders in an adjoining pair of seats and suddenly brandished a weapon that he had previously concealed in a bag on his lap. Ferguson immediately shot both passengers with a Ruger P89, 9mm handgun that he had purchased in California in May of the same year. It was a powerful gun that offered a fifteen-round magazine and could cause massive wounds. He had purchased the gun legally and apparently had a habit of carrying the weapon concealed in a small bag that was often in his possession.[8]

Ferguson then moved rapidly toward the front of the railroad car, looking from left to right and shooting anyone in his path who was either Caucasian or Asian in appearance. In less than ten seconds, Ferguson had managed to empty the fifteen-round clip into as many passengers. As the terrified commuters scrambled for whatever safety they could find, Ferguson paused to reload the Ruger with a second clip and began firing again. Dozens of frightened commuters tried to jam through the front door of the railroad car in an effort to move forward to the next car for safety. Ferguson followed with determination, firing as he went.

Realizing that his second ammunition clip was expended, Ferguson began to retreat, walking backwards through the third car, where he had originally been seated. As he backed through the length of the car, there were bodies of his victims strewn across seats and blocking the narrow walkway. He had fired off thirty rounds and hit twenty-five commuters. Some of the victims, realizing that they had no means of escape, begged Ferguson for their lives before he shot them.

As Ferguson continued to walk backward down the length of the railroad car, three male passengers who had managed to avoid injury by scrambling behind their seats simultaneously jumped on him and wrestled the empty gun from his hand. An off-duty railroad detective, who had been waiting on the station platform for his wife to arrive on the train, noticed the commotion of fleeing commuters and entered the car where Ferguson had been subdued. The officer immediately handcuffed Ferguson and placed him in custody. As he was being handcuffed, Ferguson looked up at the off-duty officer and said: "Oh, God, what did I do? What did I do? I deserve whatever I get." Ferguson had slain six passengers and wounded another nineteen, none of whom were known to him.

While investigating the background of Colin Ferguson, law enforcement officials discovered a significant body of evidence to indicate that the murders were racially motivated. A search of Ferguson's pockets disclosed notes in his handwriting indicating his intention to commit mass murder and outlining his twisted reasoning. In part, these notes stated: "Nassau County is the venue. NYC [New York City] was spared because of my respect for Mayor David Dinkins [an African-American]."[9] Many comments in Ferguson's notes referred to "racists."

Ferguson's apartment contained writings in his own hand that complained about government and institutional racism—an evil that, to the murderer, seemed to be pervasive in American society. Among the writings that were attributed to Ferguson was a compendium of four rambling pages in which he stated the depth of his hatred for Caucasians, Asian-Americans, and what he termed "Uncle Tom Negroes."[10] On the basis of the material found in Ferguson's apartment, law enforcement officials concluded that his brutal rampage had been motivated by a deep hatred for Caucasians, Asian-Americans, and middle-class, conservative African-Americans. Their findings (and opinions) were released to the press, which made much of the racial characteristics of the crime well before Ferguson's trial was even scheduled.

Colin Ferguson was a Jamaican immigrant and the son of a prominent businessman. He came to the United States in 1982, at the age of twenty-four, to pursue an advanced education that he could not obtain in his homeland. Ferguson was raised in a prosperous, well-established, respected family environment, and prior to his shooting rampage, had no criminal record or documented history of mental problems. However, he did have a history of violent behavior. In 1991, Ferguson was twice suspended from Adelphi University in New York for threatening students and faculty members. At the time of the murders, Ferguson was unemployed and had been compulsively harassing the Worker's Compensation Board for additional compensation for a 1989, work-related injury. His record of interactions with the board indicated that he was frequently angry, hostile, and belligerent. On the day he committed mass murder, Ferguson had received a final statement from the Worker's Compensation Board stating that his claim would not be reopened. This rejection of his claim may have constituted the final, intolerable triggering event for Ferguson's murderous actions later that day.

Ferguson may also have been angered by the experience of his immigration to the United States, where, to his astonishment and dismay, he encountered significant and persistent racial discrimination. He was known to be socially isolated, living alone, and with no close friends. Compounding his isolation was the fact that he was unable to rely on any close emotional support from his family in Jamaica. Ferguson eventually came to the conclusion that he had become the target of widespread racial discrimination ever since his arrival in the United States. In addition, many aspects of his personality indicated that Ferguson was suffering from severe paranoia—an assessment that would later be confirmed by several court-appointed psychiatrists who testified at his preliminary hearing.

In January 1994, Ferguson was indicted on twelve counts of second-degree murder and an additional eighty-one other felony counts. The charges ranged from murder to civil rights violations, alleging that Ferguson had shot his victims "because of their race, color, religion or national origin."[11] A year later, in January 1995, Ferguson's trial began in Nassau County, New York.

Even before the first jurors were seated, Ferguson challenged the county's jury system, claiming that it discriminated against African-Americans. He demanded that the presiding judge subpoena the president of the United States and the governor of the state of New York as witnesses to attest to the prejudice and discrimination that was rampant in New York and throughout America. By the first day of his trial, Ferguson had accepted, then fired, and accepted again several volunteer lawyers, among whose ranks was the famous civil liberties attorney William Kunstler. In the end, rejecting his lawyer's suggestions for a defense line of insanity based on the behavioral theory of "black rage,"

Ferguson demanded that he be allowed to defend himself. His favored (but incredible) defense argument was that he had not shot anyone a year earlier; instead, the murders had been committed by an unidentified Caucasian male who had mysteriously left the scene of the crime, unnoticed by any of the witnesses. According to this bizarre theory, the unidentified shooter had removed Ferguson's handgun from the bag underneath his seat while Ferguson was dozing; he then shot twenty-five commuters and escaped the crime scene after returning the gun to Ferguson's bag, without ever waking the defendant. According to Ferguson's theory, all this had occurred without anyone on the commuter train noticing the perpetrator. However, before the trial ended, Ferguson had again shifted his line of defense unpredictably and erratically, finally realizing that his theory of an unnamed, unnoticed Caucasian shooter was preposterous and would never be taken seriously by the jurors.

The trial of Colin Ferguson was bizarre and unsettling from beginning to end. While incarcerated and awaiting trial, the defendant had to be isolated from the general prison population because of the heated public response to what most perceived to be a racially motivated murder rampage. When Ferguson was brought to the courthouse each day, he was protected by seventeen armed court officers and made to wear a bulletproof vest because there was such heightened concern for possible acts of revenge against him.[12] Court-appointed attorneys pleaded with Ferguson and the judge to allow their defendant to enter an insanity plea. Ferguson consistently refused this advice and subsequently fired his lawyers, eventually winning the right to defend himself. The prosecution was able to call forty-three witnesses, many of whom were victims of the shooting. Every witness was able to convincingly testify to the fact that Ferguson was the only shooter on the commuter train that afternoon. Acting as his own attorney, the defendant offered several extraordinary defense strategies, including a repeated attempt to use the scenario in which he was asleep on the train when an unidentified Caucasian male stole the Ruger from his bag and began shooting passengers. The defendant also claimed that he was the target of a complex government conspiracy that led to the massacre. Lecturing the jury on his conspiracy theory and noting that he had been charged with ninety-three felony counts, Ferguson argued: "There were ninety-three counts to that indictment, ninety-three counts only because it matches the year 1993. If it had been 1925, it would have been a twenty-five-count indictment."[13] Finally, he resorted to a defense strategy that claimed that the real shooter was another African-American male who had the exact same name as his own but whom law enforcement officials had elected to ignore in an effort to frame him for the murders.

Throughout the trial, Colin Ferguson seemed to fluctuate in his ability to focus on what was happening around him. At times, he presented the impression of an articulate man who had more than a passing knowledge of the law. On some days his behavior was redundant, incoherent, and confused. However, the judge allowed Ferguson to defend himself, and the defendant, despite his erratic behavior and shifting defense strategy, demanded that he was not only sane, but that he was, himself, a victim of others. At one point during the trial, Ferguson stated to the jury (speaking of himself in the third person): "Mr. Ferguson did not fire a gun. He simply is the victim of a shooting on a train, like any other victim."[14] During the trial, one of Ferguson's court-appointed attorneys, who had been dismissed earlier by Ferguson when he suggested a more plausible defense, characterized the defendant's actions in court as "an exercise in madness."[15] Many others who witnessed the trial also felt that the defendant was clearly suffering from severe psychological problems, or was simply insane. On the other hand, the legal case against Ferguson was overwhelming.

In February 1995, after ten hours of deliberation, the jury found Colin Ferguson guilty on most of the felony counts with which he had been charged. When the verdict was read in court, Ferguson stood mute, staring without emotion at the jurors. He was convicted of twenty-two counts of attempted murder, weapons possession, second-degree murder, and the reckless endangerment of others. However, he was acquitted of twenty-five counts of civil rights violations that alleged he had singled out his victims on the basis of their race.[16] The jury could not conclude that his crimes were racially motivated, despite the ethnic makeup of the victims and court testimony indicating that he deeply hated a range of ethnic groups. In March 1995, Ferguson was sentenced to six consecutive life terms in prison. At the time of sentencing, the judge noted that he would have sentenced Ferguson to the death penalty if that had been an option at the time of his trial. The judge also noted in the record that Ferguson demonstrated "a total lack of remorse" for his crimes.[17]

The case of Colin Ferguson is an enigma, and will likely remain so forever. There is little question that the perpetrator harbored a deep hatred for Caucasians, Asian-Americans, and other groups that he felt were deserving of his wrath. It is also possible that Ferguson was not a psychologically stable individual. All the pretrial information generated from the investigation of his crimes pointed to a racial motivation for the murder rampage. His own writing clearly proclaimed his deep hatred of specific ethnic groups. Law enforcement officials went to extraordinary lengths to protect the defendant against retribution because they were so concerned about the racial overtones of his crime. The press offered a variety of investigative pieces that emphasized the racial aspects of his life and crime. However, Ferguson's jury could not find him guilty of violating the civil rights of those who he injured and killed.

Ferguson was allowed to dismiss capable lawyers who had offered a plausible defense in favor of defending himself. At times, Ferguson presented himself as intelligent and articulate; at other times, however, he was obviously confused, argumentative, and irrational. He was unable to present even a reasonable defense case, calling only a single witness whose testimony hurt his cause far more than it helped. In the end, many of those who witnessed Ferguson's behavior throughout his incarceration and trial agreed that this was a man who was mentally ill. However, in a legal sense, Ferguson was found to be sane and therefore culpable for his crimes.

It will likely never be known to a certainty whether Colin Ferguson was a deranged madman who murdered at random, a mass murderer who was motivated by a deep and abiding racial hatred for others, a charlatan who attempted to convince a judge and jury that he was truly insane, or all these things. It became a tragic irony of this case that the trial of Colin Ferguson did more to obliterate any possible understanding of the murderer's motives than even his own cryptic writing and statements (see Table 7.2).

Table 7.2: Colin Ferguson

Perpetrator	A thirty-five-year-old immigrant from Jamaica who had a history of racial prejudice and aggressive behavior. It is uncertain (but considered likely by many) if Ferguson was suffering from a psychological disorder that may have contributed to his actions.
Incident date/location	December 7, 1993, aboard a commuter train in Garden City, New York.
Incident category	Sane/insane.
Weapons	A Ruger P89, 9mm handgun with multiple clips of ammunition.
Deaths/Injuries	Six killed, nineteen injured.
Motivation	Uncertain. It was believed that Ferguson targeted only racial groups against whom he held a grudge. At his trial, the jury did not support this theory.
Disposition	Found guilty and sentenced to multiple life terms in March, 1995.

THE FEMALE RAMBO

At the age of fifteen, Sylvia Seegrist suddenly developed symptoms of severe mental illness. Almost overnight she had been transformed from a relatively happy child into an adolescent who harbored a deep hatred of all those around her and exhibited a pervasive taste for threatening and violent behavior. Even at that young age, Seegrist was told by a psychiatrist that she had only two options to effectively deal with her illness: a lifetime of debilitating medication or long-term hospitalization. For the next ten years, she struggled with these options but was never able to come to grips with either. With each year that passed, her symptoms became worse, her disorientation more severe, and her fantasies more violent. During that decade, Seegrist was hospitalized twelve times for mental illness; each time, she was subsequently released with a prescription in her hand and little or no follow-up care. She visited several psychiatrists and received any number of medications, which she often failed to use consistently or appropriately. Invariably, Seegrist only grew worse in her behavior and outlook. By the age of twenty-five, she was pathologically angry, fearful, incapable of functioning effectively in society, and completely unable to cope with her feelings. She had long been diagnosed as a paranoid schizophrenic.

Between the ages of fifteen and twenty-five, Sylvia Seegrist developed into a perpetually hostile young woman who hated her parents, other adults, and, particularly, children. She had once tried to strangle her mother, and she had a long history of threatening behavior and unpredictably violent outbursts. Seegrist had a passion for paramilitary themes, which ranged from how she dressed to her political beliefs and incoherent pronouncements to all who would listen. By 1985, she also owned a semiautomatic rifle, which she had purchased in order to complete her self-defined image as a "Female Rambo." Living alone and severely socially isolated, Seegrist was a woman who others avoided at all costs. By the common understanding of the term, she was quite crazy.

Seegrist was well known to many of the store managers at the Springfield Mall, which, along with the public library, was one of her favorite haunts. For the five years prior to her 1985 shooting rampage, Seegrist often visited a variety of stores in the mall to pass away the time or taunt other shoppers with her angry and bizarre outbursts. She had gained a notorious reputation as a disturbed and often frightening visitor. One employee recalled Seegrist's visits to the shopping center as very intimidating, saying, "We've had mall security officers take her out [of the mall] and Springfield police take her out [of the mall]."[18] The summer before her rampage, Seegrist had entered a restaurant in the mall, shouting, "I'm going to shoot the mother-fucking bastard."[19] She appeared to be shouting at no one in particular and, according to witnesses, was completely irrational. She would often complain that clothing in various store windows was too bright in color or looked like outdated merchandise. A week before she visited the mall for the last time, while wearing her customary camouflage clothing, Seegrist got into a heated argument with a pharmacist when she tried to fill a prescription for a tranquilizer without her welfare card.

On October 30, 1985, Seegrist was once again at the Springfield Mall, in the pharmacy, to pick up yet another prescription order for tranquilizers. She was dressed in her usual paramilitary fashion. Shortly after 1 P.M., she left the mall and went to a nearby fitness center, where she had been a member for about a year. Once there, she worked with weights, as she usually did, while still fully dressed in her combat fatigues. The fitness center employees also knew Seegrist as an unpredictable and persistently angry patron. She would sometimes pretend to stalk enemies inside the center or become argumentative and belligerent with other clients. On several occasions, she would go into the sauna room while fully dressed in combat fatigues and sit vacantly, mumbling incoherently to herself. However, on this day, she quietly lifted weights for about thirty minutes and spoke to no none.

After leaving the fitness center, Seegrist went to the Swarthmore Public Library, where she was as infamous as she was at the mall and the fitness center. Seegrist would visit the library several times a week, sometimes being loud and argumentative with patrons and employees; on other occasions, she would hold long, rambling conversations with herself. She was always seen visiting the library alone and always dressed in green combat fatigues. Contrary to her usual behavior, Seegrist was quiet on this day and spent her time leafing through the card catalogues with a blank, aimless expression.

Shortly after 2 P.M., Seegrist left the library and stopped briefly at her apartment. She then drove to a party favor store, where she made a small purchase of napkins and a hand towel. It was the day before Halloween, and the napkins that she purchased were a traditional black and orange motif designed especially for the holiday. She then set out for the mall once again, but this time with murder on her mind.

Seegrist arrived at the Springfield Mall at 3:30 that afternoon. She was still wearing the olive green military fatigues, military-style boots, and a black, knit beret. On this second trip to the mall, she was carrying a loaded, .22-caliber semiautomatic rifle in the trunk of her car. Seegrist parked her car in the mall parking lot and quickly made her way toward the main entrance with the rifle in hand. Along the way, she saw a telephone installer who was just leaving the shopping center to get some tools from his truck. She lowered the rifle to her hip and quickly fired two shots in his direction. Miraculously, both rounds missed their target as the frightened worker scurried for cover. Seegrist then noticed a woman standing near an automated teller machine that was close to the mall entrance. She again lowered her weapon and this time sprayed a half-dozen bullets in the woman's direction. Even though several rounds hit the area surrounding the bank client, including all around the periphery of the automated teller machine, the terrified woman escaped without injury.

Seegrist's next targets were not so fortunate. A group of young children was standing in front of a popular restaurant, near the automated teller machine, when Seegrist opened fire on them. The children and their mothers had been on a shopping trip to buy new clothes when they were attacked. Two of the children were seriously wounded. The third, a two-year-old boy, was killed.

Now running for the mall entrance, Seegrist burst inside and leveled her rifle once again, looking for more targets. For the next four minutes, she fired randomly at shoppers and store employees who were milling about in the central area of the mall. She fired indiscriminately into a number of the mall's businesses, including a furniture store, a shoe store, and the pharmacy. Many of the customers in the mall were slow to react to the shots that they heard ringing from Seegrist's rifle. It was the day before Halloween, and most shoppers thought it was either a prank or some event that the mall was sponsoring. In the past, the mall had frequently hired an entertainer who dressed up like a cowboy; he would walk among the rows of stores, firing a cap gun and twirling a lariat, to entertain the shoppers and their children.[20] Few of the mall patrons could believe what was really happening as Seegrist attacked the shopping center.

Rampaging through the mall, Seegrist noticed a woman standing near an ice cream stand. She fired two shots at the woman, hitting her both times in the stomach. The shooter then ran the length of the lower level of the shopping center, waving her rifle angrily, and randomly firing more rounds. At the far end of the mall, Seegrist shot and wounded two other women before she saw an older man standing in front of a cutlery store. She carefully took aim at the sixty-seven-year-old man and fired three shots. One of the shots struck him in the face and another hit him in the stomach. Her victim was a well-known Springfield gynecologist who would later die from his massive wounds.[21]

By now, seeing the chaos that had erupted in the center of the mall, shoppers and store employees were running everywhere to avoid the shooter and find some cover. Many of the shoppers fled for the safety of the nearest store they could find in fruitless efforts to avoid the shooting. However, the indiscriminate firing continued into several of the storefronts that now harbored terrified shoppers. A retired city employee who was unlucky enough to be at the Springfield Mall that day was too slow to find cover. Standing outside of a shoe store where he had just made a purchase, with his wife nearby and looking on, he was hit by a bullet in the back of the head and fell dead to the mall floor.

Still selecting her targets at random, Seegrist now headed back toward the mall entrance. A twenty-four-year-old college student who was shopping with a friend saw Seegrist heading his way with the rifle in her hand. For whatever reason, John W. Laufer III did not fully comprehend what he had witnessed. Nonetheless, he was determined to put a stop to the chaos all around him, and he headed in Seegrist's direction. As he approached her, Seegrist lowered her rifle again and began to fire at him, with the weapon resting on her hip and pointed squarely in his direction. He could hear the snap of the rounds as they were fired at him. Laufer hurried in her direction while Seegrist continued to shoot; miraculously, none of the rounds hit him. When he finally reached the shooter, Laufer angrily yanked the rifle from her hands, saying: "You picked the wrong person to fool with. I'm going to turn you in now."[22] Seegrist, stunned at his bold action, and clearly unaware of the impact of her own, whimpered, "I'm a woman and I have family problems and I have seizures."[23] Laufer could not believe what he had just heard and witnessed.

John Laufer walked the shooter to a nearby shoe store, put her in a chair, and demanded that she not move from that spot. Now quiet and obviously afraid, Seegrist complied without question. Almost immediately, a mall security guard arrived and took Seegrist into custody, calling for assistance on his radio. When the security guard asked Seegrist why she had randomly shot customers in the mall, she could only reply: "My family makes me nervous. I didn't mean to do it. I didn't mean to do it."[24] Laufer had already left the shoe store to assist the wounded in the mall.

When Laufer was later asked about his incredible act of bravery in putting a stop to Seegrist's rampage, he minimized his heroism with uncommon humility. He told reporters: "I didn't believe at the time she was firing real bullets. She was facing me about ten yards away. She had the rifle on her hip, and she was firing at me. I just took the gun away from her."[25] All who had witnessed the shooting rampage agreed that Laufer's quick action spared many lives that day. A year later, in October 1986 (and perhaps because of his encounter with Sylvia Seegrist), John Laufer graduated from the State Police Academy and became a state trooper. Sadly, and despite his bravery on October 30, 1995, Seegrist had managed to murder three and seriously wound another seven individuals. In under five minutes, she had become one of the most notorious female mass murderers in American history.

Seegrist spent the next year awaiting her trial. Because of her medical background, she was the subject of frequent and extensive psychological evaluations. In late 1985, despite her obvious mental illness, Seegrist was found to be competent to stand trial for her crimes. Her trial began in June 1986 and revealed many incidents in Seegrist's history that indicated the true depth and severity of her long-standing psychological problems. In addition to attacking her mother (who was acting as her primary caretaker at the time), Seegrist had stabbed a guidance counselor, thrown a lighted cigarette into the face of a psychiatrist who was counseling her, set fire to stuffed animals, and painted the walls of her apartment with such phrases as, "Kill them all" and "I hate you."[26]

At the time of her trial, Seegrist was far too ill to provide a coherent explanation for her rampage. However, years later (in 1991), her condition had improved considerably and she was able to discuss her crime more openly. Speaking to a reporter for the *Philadelphia Inquirer*, she said: "My crime came about because I dreaded the medication so much. It [her shooting rampage] was somewhat premeditated, but that [the medications] was the extra push over the edge."[27] Prior to her crime, Seegrist had suffered for nearly a decade from the effects of a wide range of medications, many of which caused her to lose control of her muscles, made her gain and lose weight unpredictably, and blurred her eyesight. Seegrist had also suffered from years of hallucinations that she described as "the most ickiest, ugliest thoughts" imaginable.[28]

On October 31, 1986, Sylvia Seegrist was sentenced to three consecutive life terms and a minimum of ten years each for the seven counts of attempted murder for which she had been found guilty. Delaware County Judge Robert F. Kelly, in passing the sentence, said: "It is my feeling that the defendant should spend the rest of her life incarcerated. I have imposed these sentences consecutively because it is my opinion that to do anything less would have diminished the seriousness of the offense and diminished the value of each separate life that was taken."[29] After the sentence was passed, Seegrist turned to one of her defense attorneys, Ruth R. Shafer, and asked, "You mean I could die in jail?"[30] Her attorney could only bow her head and tell her "yes." Before imposing his sentence, the judge once again committed Seegrist to the Norristown State Hospital for ninety days—the maximum period allowed by law for an evaluation period. Each ninety days, Seegrist would be evaluated in order to determine her psychological condition. When she was determined to be sufficiently recovered, she would be transferred to prison to serve her consecutive life terms. Seegrist had been in Norristown for almost a year on the day that she appeared before Judge Kelly to learn of her fate.

Prior to sentencing, Seegrist's attorney had argued passionately for a concurrent, rather than a consecutive, sentence in order to allow her client a "glimmer of hope" for the future. Attorney Shafer pointed out that Seegrist had been diagnosed as severely mentally disabled for many years and was therefore unable to understand the meaning of her actions. "She stands before you as a little child. Chronologically she is twenty-six; emotionally, she doesn't understand the enormity of her act," the attorney pleaded.[31] Shafer went on to point out that her client had been cooperative and nonviolent since she had first been transferred to the Norristown State Hospital the previous year. Seegrist's attorney summed up her argument by saying: "I ask you to leave her a glimmer of hope and sentence her concurrently. No one is saying release her—her act was the act of a mentally ill person. From the bottom of my heart I ask you to show compassion for Sylvia."[32]

The opposing counsel, Assistant District Attorney William H. Ryan, Jr., argued that even though Seegrist was obviously mentally ill, she had been blatantly aware of her actions on October 30, 1985. He pointed out to the judge: "She willfully took the lives of three beautiful people she never knew, and tried to kill seven others. She is a person society cannot trust to be in society ever again."[33] The prosecutor passionately argued that Seegrist was still dangerous and would likely remain so in the future. Once again, he pointed out her recurring pattern of hospitalization, remission, and deterioration that inevitably led to the murders a year earlier. Finally, an emotional appeal was made to the judge by the survivors and relatives of those who had been murdered by Seegrist. One of these appeals came from the mother of the two-year-old boy who had been slain in the rampage. The arguments against leniency were overwhelming (and apparently compelling) for Judge Kelly and many of the witnesses and observers in court that day.

There is little question that Sylvia Seegrist was suffering from severe psychological problems on the day when she went on her shooting rampage. She was a woman who had been seriously ill for at least a decade before 1985. Seegrist had a history of bizarre behavior and violent outbursts that were almost legendary to those who came into contact with her. She was known to many of the Springfield Mall employees and feared by them; she had often been physically removed from the shopping center because of her threatening behavior. Incredibly, for over a decade she was unable to make the system work for her. Despite many attempts to ameliorate her obvious and debilitating illness, despite the dozen hospitalizations for her psychological problems, and despite the many health care professionals who were involved with her in one way or another, Seegrist was still able to attack and murder individuals unknown to her in a four-minute rampage of incredible brutality and senselessness. It is unconscionable that in a society that offers the depth and range of services and assistance found in America, a woman as ill and patently dangerous as Sylvia Seegrist could have been ignored until she became lethal (see Chapter 1, Table 1.6).

NOTES

1. Donald T. Lunde, *Murder and Madness* (San Francisco: San Francisco Book Company, 1976), 114.

2. Ibid.

3. Ibid., 49.

4. Ibid., 50.

5. Ibid., 50.

6. Ibid., 51.

7. American Psychiatric Association (APA), *Diagnostic and Statistical Manual of Mental Disorders*, 4th ed. (Washington, DC: APA, 1994).

8. Terence Samuel, "NY Gunman Got Pistol Legally," *Philadelphia Inquirer Online* (Internet edition), 9 December 1993, A01.

9. Pat Milton, "Suspect in Attack on NY Train Lacks Remorse." *Philadelphia Inquirer Online* (Internet edition), 10 December 1993, A16.

10. Pat Milton, "Suspect in Attack on NY Train Lacks Remorse."

11. "Man Accused in Train Shooting in NY is Indicted on 93 Counts," *Reuters News Service* (Internet edition), 19 January 1994, B08.

12. Susan Forrest and Eric Nagourney, "Insanity Defense Is Possibility," *Philadelphia Inquirer Online* (Internet edition), 11 December 1993, A04.

13. David Van Biema, "A Fool for a Client." *Time Domestic* (Internet edition), 145. No. 6 (6 February 1995).

14. "Massacre Trial a Surreal Show," *Reuters News Service* (Internet edition), 30 January 1995, B2.

15. Ibid.

16. Terence Samuel, "Jury Deliberates 10 Hours, Finds Ferguson Guilty in Train Killings," *Philadelphia Inquirer Online* (Internet edition), 18 February 1995, A01.

17. Bill Kurtis, "Long Island Railroad Massacre," in Bill Kurtis *American Justice* series (Arts and Entertainment Network), aired 25 April 1996.

18. Russell E. Eshleman, Jr. and Steve Stecklow, "Step by Step: The Shootings at Springfield Mall," *Philadelphia Inquirer Online* (Internet edition), 25 April 1985, A01.

19. Ibid.

20. Ibid.

21. Ibid.

22. Ibid.

23. Ibid.

24. Ibid.

25. Ibid.

26. Reid Kanaley, "Her Demons Stilled, Seegrist Hopes for Freedom," *Philadelphia Inquirer Online* (Internet edition), 18 March 1991, B01.

27. Ibid.

28. Ibid.

29. Phyllis Holtzman, "Seegrist Gets 3 Life Terms in Mall Spree," *Philadelphia Inquirer Online* (Internet edition), 1 November 1986, A01.

30. Ibid.

31. Ibid.

32. Ibid.

33. Ibid.

CHAPTER 8

The Unexplained

Mystery: something that is not fully understood or that baffles or eludes the understanding; an enigma.

Webster's New Universal Dictionary

Few rational individuals would argue with the statement that mass murder is inherently an insane act, even when it is committed by an obviously sane individual. It is among the most heinous of crimes, often victimizing completely innocent and defenseless individuals who were wholly unprepared for the assault that took their lives. However, the great majority of mass murderers are sane, at least in a legal sense, and plan their crimes, sometimes to a remarkable extent. Certainly, there are incidents of mass murder that clearly indicate that the perpetrator was deranged and unable to fathom the meaning of his actions. There are also gradations of awareness and derangement inherent among the many perpetrators of mass murder. The crimes of someone who seemed clearly deranged although not legally insane (as in the case of John Frazier), or an individual whose sanity remains in question (as in the case of Colin Ferguson) are stunning examples of the notoriously thin line that distinguishes a layperson's definition of sanity or insanity from that used in a court of law. The crimes of Sylvia Seegrist, who was found to be legally culpable after randomly executing three individuals in a shopping center, were clearly the actions of a deranged and uncontrolled person. One of the earliest and most notorious mass murderers in modern criminology, Howard Unruh, who was hospitalized for the random killing of thirteen individuals in Camden, New Jersey, in 1949 (see Chapter 1, Table 1.3), left little doubt that the question of sanity plays a significant role in this crime.

When applied to a crime of the magnitude of mass murder, the issue of sanity, in both the legal and colloquial senses, will likely never be settled to anyone's satisfaction. It will always remain a topic of debate and controversy. Between the obvious and calculated actions of the rational mass murderer, who carefully targets his victims and plans his crime, and the bizarre behavior of the murderer who is clearly insane and unable to comprehend the impact of his actions, lies the unexplained. These are the crimes for which no one can find a reasonable explanation—crimes for which there is no apparent motive and certainly no sense whatsoever. They are not great in number; however, they are acutely painful in the questions that they leave unanswered.

The need to understand the nature of mass murder demands an understanding of the motivations of the perpetrator. Without knowing the reasons why an individual is driven to mass murder, we are left with only the chaos and pain inherent in the scene of this most vicious crime. Knowledge of the crime scene and its details, although crucial, is ultimately inadequate. We must come to an understanding of motive if we are to comprehend the meaning of mass murder. In the vast majority of these crimes, the motivation of the perpetrator is known, if for no other reason than because he *wants* us to know and understand his reasoning. It is usually not sufficient that he simply kill those whom he has targeted as deserving of death; rather, it is often crucial to the perpetrator that the rest of us know *why* he did so. Most of these crimes have a clear purpose to the perpetrator, even though to the rest of us, it is a twisted, pathological, and hateful reasoning that lies behind the crime. However, in a few incidents we remain unable to discover the motivation, despite our best efforts to do so. The dark and complex forces that compel an individual to mass murder remain covert, bizarre or incomprehensible, perhaps even to the murderer himself.

The forces that motivate a mass murderer are never simple; however, they are often accessible if we can understand the history and life experiences of the murderer. Despite this general understanding, from time to time, an individual will murder others and leave nothing by which we can comprehend his motives. Perhaps this is simply because we lack sufficient information about the murderer, or perhaps it is something more complex. Behaviorists have suggested a variety of explanations for these rare cases of sudden and inordinate violence. Reasons range from inexplicable psychological fugue states, in which the murderer simply "goes crazy," to more fundamental explanations that relate to drugs or the effects of certain chemicals that enter the body unexpectedly. In the final analysis, a few cases of mass murder cannot be explained regardless of how hard we try to search for motivation or understanding. In such cases, our comprehension of human behavior falls short or our knowledge of the murderer and his history is incomplete; in a few instances, we may know virtually nothing about the perpetrator. In the latter cases, we are left with little more than speculation and a hope that we can eventually come to a better understanding of the dark nature that we each carry deep within ourselves.

These few, enigmatic mass murders are not only inexplicable by a study of the objective actions of the perpetrator, they also appear to happen without any motivation or warning. Although these crimes are rare, when they do occur they are often particularly disturbing in their explosive nature and brutal execution. The perpetrator acts out in a way that may seem inconsistent with his background or history—in a way that provides no warning or reason.

An example of such an enigmatic case took place in July 1995, in a Washington suburb, when a twenty-year-old house painter and laborer, Bruman Alvarez, brutally murdered his boss and the members of a family whose house he was helping to paint (see Table 8.1). No valuables were taken from the home and no sexual assault had been committed against any of the victims. If there was a dispute between the murderer and any of his victims, it never came to light. After his murderous rampage, the laborer calmly telephoned police emergency services to report the killings, and in that call, he identified himself as the perpetrator. When police arrived at the home where Alvarez was working, they found his boss and another worker dead on the first floor of the residence. Upstairs, they discovered the bodies of the homeowner's three daughters, ranging in age from fourteen to twenty-two years. Each of the victims had been brutally beaten and stabbed to death. Alvarez was never able to provide law enforcement personnel with a coherent motive for his horrendous actions.

Table 8.1: Bruman Alvarez

Perpetrator	A twenty-year old house painter who did not have a history of violence or aggression.
Incident date/location	July 21, 1995, in a residence that he was helping to paint, in a suburb of Washington.
Incident category	Unexplained.
Weapons	Knife and bludgeoning. Victims were beaten and stabbed to death.
Deaths/Injuries	Five killed. Two were coworkers and three were members of the family who employed his services.
Motivation	Uncertain. Alvarez never provided a coherent explanation for his actions.
Disposition	Alvarez survived his crime to stand trial.

Another enigmatic mass murder was committed by Christopher Green on March 21, 1995, in Montclair, New Jersey. Green had been a resident of Montclair all his life. The son of a well-respected, deeply religious family, Green graduated from high school and went to work for a local electrical contractor, where he quickly gained a reputation as a reliable, hard-working individual. In July 1992, Green went to work for the Montclair post office as a janitor. He had also successfully passed the test for the Montclair police department and was waiting for his name to come to the top of the list for an appointment.

Green worked at the post office until April 1993, when he left for a better paying job with the Montclair Department of Public Works (DPW) as a laborer. At both the post office and the Montclair DPW, Green's reputation as a cooperative, reliable employee remained unshaken. Green lived in a fashionable, high-rise apartment building with a woman he loved. To those closest to him, Green seemed to have his life well in order and had distinct plans for his future. He had no criminal record, no history of violence and had never been involved with drugs or any other illegal activity.

On March 21, 1995, Green left his DPW job at the usual time, but he did not return to his apartment. Rather, armed with a 9mm handgun, he went to the Montclair post office. Arriving at the post office around 4:00 in the afternoon, Green entered through the front door and confronted two employees and three customers who were inside the station. The two postal employees were shocked to see Green threatening them with a gun. Green had worked with these two career employees for a year, and both of them knew him as an easygoing, likable young man. Green demanded $5,000 in cash from the post office employees. However, after taking the money, he did not leave the premises. Rather, Green ordered the five individuals into a back room of the postal station and demanded that they lie face-down on the floor. At least one of the employees begged Green not to harm anyone, but it was to no avail. Green placed his handgun to the back of the head of each individual and shot each, in turn, execution-style. Four of the victims died immediately; remarkably, however, one of the customers survived his wounds (see Table 8.2).

The next day, homicide detectives arrested Green at his apartment. When asked what he had done with the money, Green replied that he had paid three months' back rent and had hidden the remainder of the money underneath his refrigerator. He was cooperative with authorities and immediately admitted to all the details of the crime. However, he could give no reasonable explanation for his actions.

On June 8, 1995, Christopher Green pled guilty to the murders and made a short statement to the court, emphasizing his remorse. When asked by the presiding judge why he had so brutally executed four innocent individuals, Green could only reply: "I felt I was over the line, just at the point of no return. I was scared and I was confused."[1]

Theories about why Christopher Green had executed four individuals (two with whom he had shared at least some personal relationship) were abundant in the press. Many believed that Green had panicked during the robbery attempt and reacted by trying to eliminate all the witnesses to his crime; others dismissed this theory on the basis that the robbery itself had been so poorly planned and executed that the very premise of the murders did not make sense. In addition, Green had no history of criminal activity and a very weak motive (unpaid rent) to even consider a crime of robbery. Some theorized that Green's murders were an act of revenge or retribution against former postal coworkers or the post office itself. This theory made even less sense than that of a robbery gone bad. Green's reputation at the post office was excellent, and his relationships with the employees, including those he murdered, was good.

In the final analysis, it is impossible to know why Christopher Green resorted to mass murder. Whether this was a robbery gone bad, or a crime of retribution, or whether there was some other, covert motive will probably never be known. Because Green pled guilty to all charges, and was unable to provide a reasonable explanation for his motives, it is unlikely that we will ever come to an understanding of his actions on March 21, 1995.

Table 8.2: Christopher Green

Perpetrator	A twenty-nine-year-old city worker with no criminal record or history of violence.
Incident date/location	March 21, 1995, at the post office in Montclair, New Jersey.
Incident category	Unexplained.
Weapons	A 9mm handgun.
Deaths/Injuries	Four killed, one injured.
Motivation	Uncertain. Possibly an act of revenge by a lethal employee or an act of mass murder during the commission of a crime (robbery).
Disposition	Green pled guilty to four counts of murder on June 8, 1995. He was sentenced to multiple life terms in prison without parole on September 22, 1995.

In some incidents of mass murder, there are tantalizing leads that suggest a possible motive for the crime; however, in the final analysis, they are washed away in contradictions and uncertainty. The crime is committed, the victims are counted and laid to rest, and the families are consoled; however, the fundamental and overriding aspect of the crime that could lead to some closure and resolution remains uncertain—*why* did this happen? The most notorious case of this kind occurred near San Diego, in 1984, in which twenty-one individuals—mostly children—were murdered in an incomprehensible act of brutality that remains unparalleled in American history.

THE CRIMES OF JAMES OLIVER HUBERTY

James Oliver Huberty was born in Canton, Ohio, in 1943. He was a troubled youngster who was raised by strict Christian parents. From his earliest years, Huberty was both antisocial and socially isolated. The young Huberty was often involved in disputes with his family and neighbors and, early on in his childhood, he developed an obsessive belief that the world was coming to an end very soon. Even as a youngster, James prepared himself for his role when the day of Armageddon would arrive. As he matured, Huberty developed into an obsessive survivalist who collected a number of weapons and hoarded food in anticipation of a final, worldwide conflict that he always thought was imminent. He was known to espouse violence in his conversations with others, although he had only a single, minor offense in his background—a 1980 citation for disorderly conduct that was issued when he became involved in a dispute at a local gas station with the proprietor and another customer.

By other accounts, Huberty was a stable, family-oriented individual who loved his children and worked hard to provide them with the necessities of life. In 1971, he lived with his wife and two daughters in a middle-class section of Massillon, Ohio. While there, he continued to collect weapons and pursue his survivalist ideas, sometimes getting involved in minor confrontations with neighbors and occasionally displaying his weapons on the block where he lived. A few of his neighbors considered Huberty strange; however, none considered him especially bizarre or violent. He was never involved in any criminal activities or acts of violence that brought him to the attention of local law enforcement personnel. During these years, Huberty was completing an internship at a local funeral home, where he was training to get a state license as an embalmer and funeral director.[2] To all external appearance, his home life seemed unremarkable.

In the late 1970s, Huberty gave up on the funeral home business and became a welder in Canton, Ohio. His job as a welder provided significantly more income for his family, and they were able to afford a few luxuries that had been missed in the early years of their marriage. In 1976, Huberty graduated from a Christian liberal arts college that he had been attending since 1961.

In 1982, the facility for which Huberty worked unexpectedly closed its doors, leaving him without income, frustrated, and angry. A former coworker of Huberty's recalled his reaction when he lost his job: "He said that if this was the end of his making a living for his family, he was going to take everyone with him. He was always talking about shooting somebody."[3] However, Huberty never acted out any of his violent fantasies.

Throughout 1983, Huberty was unemployed and continually growing more angry and resentful about his deteriorating financial situation. He was unable to find an acceptable job to support his family. In the fall of that year, he told neighbors that he was going to move his family to Tijuana in search of a better life. In January 1984, Huberty moved his family to San Ysidro, in San Diego County, California, just north of the border with Mexico. Eventually he was able to find a job as a security guard at a condominium complex in the nearby town of Chula Vista. It was a job that paid poorly and left him unable to support his family in a meaningful way; however, it provided more income than he had realized in over a year. A week before James Oliver Huberty became one of the worst mass murderers in modern American history, he was fired from that job.

On July 18, 1984, Huberty went to a McDonald's restaurant in San Ysidro, wearing camouflage trousers and a black T-shirt. He was armed with a

12mm pump-action shotgun, a 9mm Uzi semiautomatic rifle, a 9mm Browning semiautomatic pistol, several hundred rounds of ammunition, and an AM-FM radio concealed in a paper bag. At the time when he entered the restaurant, it was crowded with dozens of young children, who frequented the place each day for an afternoon meal and some fun with their friends. It was 4 P.M. when the gunman entered the restaurant.

Huberty first shot out a large mirror behind the restaurant counter, shouting, "Freeze!" to everyone waiting in line to place their orders. The gunman then commanded everyone in the restaurant to lie on the floor, again shouting, "Everybody get down on the floor or I'll kill somebody."[4] However, it was never Huberty's intention to spare anyone in the restaurant. He immediately began roaming among the crowd of screaming children and adults, randomly executing them as they vainly tried to scurry for what little cover they could find. At one point, Huberty screamed, "I killed thousands in Vietnam and I want to kill more."[5]

Huberty's incredible rampage lasted for over ninety minutes, as police SWAT teams assembled outside of the restaurant trying to determine how to end the siege. Several terrified patrons crashed through the large, plate-glass window at the front of the restaurant in an effort to escape the rampaging gunman. A few were able to avoid Huberty by fleeing through the back door of the establishment. However, many never had a chance at survival.

Alternately using the rifle and the handgun, while pausing to reload each weapon several times, Huberty killed twenty-one and wounded another nineteen individuals before he was finally slain by a bullet from a SWAT team sharpshooter who had been posted on the roof of a building across the street from the restaurant. Huberty's youngest victim was only four months old, and most of his victims were children.

Two days after the massacre, Huberty's wife, Etna, provided a four-page statement and an interview in an attempt to explain her husband's motives in murdering so many innocent children. She pointed out that he had lost two jobs and was plagued by voices that commanded him to do evil. She claimed he had been waiting for an appointment at a local mental health clinic to help him with these problems, but the appointment had never occurred because of a clerical error at the clinic. However, on the day he went to McDonald's, Huberty had left the house with a clear purpose in mind, saying to his wife that he was going out "hunting for humans."[6]

According to Etna Huberty, her husband "would never harm a child." In that interview, she stated: "I think he was trying to get back at society. Make them hurt, like he was hurting."[7] She consistently claimed that he was a loving father and husband who was suffering from severe psychological problems and financial hardships. In fact, Huberty never indicated any propensity for abusing his wife or children prior to the murders at McDonald's. However, he did exhibit symptoms of a mental disorder.

On the day of his crimes, Huberty had taken his family to the San Diego Zoo. According to his wife, her husband had seemed a bit nervous that day;

nonetheless, the trip to the zoo was enjoyable for all. When they were leaving the zoo, Huberty complained to one of his daughters about hearing voices. It was something that had been happening to her father for some time, and the young girl did not seem concerned at the time. After the family arrived home, Huberty went upstairs to his bedroom to change clothes. A few moments later, he came to where his wife was resting from the activity of the trip and kissed her goodbye, making his statement about "hunting humans." According to Etna Huberty, she thought he was just kidding and urged him to stay with her. He left without any further conversation and went directly to McDonald's. Later that afternoon, hearing the breaking news story of the siege at McDonald's, Etna Huberty called police during the broadcast, fearing that her husband might somehow be involved.

James Oliver Huberty, the most vicious mass murderer in American history prior to 1995, left no clear motive for his crimes. Certainly, he was a man who had been angry and frustrated for many years. Perhaps he was suffering from a psychological disorder of significant magnitude. If Etna Huberty's statements were accurate, her husband may have exhibited some of the symptoms of paranoid schizophrenia. That he was a collector of weapons, socially isolated, and deeply angry was clear. On the other hand, he was a man who apparently loved his family, and particularly his children. When he finally struck out, in an indescribable act of atrocity, his primary targets were children. Symbolically, he was attacking the future of the country that he had come to despise so vehemently, by attacking the embodiment of its future. So deep was his hatred and need for revenge that Huberty struck out against the most vulnerable members of our society—our children.

Table 8.3: James Oliver Huberty

Perpetrator	A forty-one-year-old, unemployed male who was deeply frustrated, angry, socially isolated, and possibly suffering from a psychological disorder.
Incident date/location	July 18, 1984, at a fast food restaurant in San Ysidro, California
Incident category	Unexplained.
Weapons	A 12mm pump-action shotgun, a 9mm Uzi semiautomatic rifle, a 9mm Browning semiautomatic pistol, and several hundred rounds of ammunition
Deaths/Injuries	Twenty-one killed, nineteen injured (mostly children).
Motivation	Unknown.
Disposition	Huberty was killed at the scene by police personnel.

We are left with only speculation about the crimes of James Oliver Huberty. In the final analysis, we do not know why he committed such a horrible crime or why he targeted the most vulnerable population that he could find. If this was a crime of revenge against society in general, whether or not carried out by a madman, why did he choose the location and the time that he did to strike? If it was his intention to murder children, as it seems in retrospect, was this an insane act of symbolic retribution against the future of our country or was he so deeply obsessed and severely ill that his victims were merely random innocents who were brought unwittingly into the path of a murderer who cared nothing for any life? It was obvious that his crime was planned and that he was prepared and determined to kill. Why and how he selected his victims, however, will never be known (see Table 8.3).

AN INTENT TO MURDER

Laurie Wasserman Dann was not a mass murderer by the classic definition of the term. She killed only one person during her single day of violence. However, by her intent and efforts, Dann was clearly a potential mass murderer of heinous proportions. On a single day in 1988, Laurie Dann shot six children, one adult, poisoned at least another six individuals, and ended her day of murderous intent by committing suicide. One of the children she shot, an eight-year-old boy, died of his massive wounds. It was clear from her actions that Dann intended to murder many more victims than even those she managed to injure.

May 20, 1988, was a day of incredible violence in the life of Laurie Dann. For some time previous to this day, Dann had been making preparations for revenge. In her apartment in Madison, Wisconsin, she had carefully assembled a list of people who were to die at her hand. Each was to receive a package of food or drink that had been poisoned—laced with arsenic and other fatal chemicals. Thankfully, as police and health officials would later learn, Dann had significantly miscalculated the dosage of arsenic necessary to cause death to her intended victims. In the end, she only managed to make them very sick.

Dann's list of intended victims included both adults and children; her packages had been carefully prepared to personally appeal to each of her intended targets. Some of the packages were disguised as free food samples that were meant for delivery to at least six suburban Illinois homes and two fraternity houses on the campus of Northwestern University. The packages intended for her younger victims contained fruit juice and a Rice Krispie treat. One of the packages was to be delivered to the children for whom Dann was the family babysitter for several years. In her own hand, she had written a note on the package that read: "Love your little sister. Enjoy."[8]

By 7 A.M. that morning, Dann was out of her apartment and delivering the poison packages that she had prepared. In the trunk of her car, she also carried a container of gasoline, several weapons, and ammunition. After delivering at least six packages to various homes in and around the affluent suburb of Winnetka, Illinois, she drove to the home of Padraig and Marian Rushe. The Rushe family had employed her for several years to baby-sit their small children. She gathered two of the Rushe children—the two youngest boys—and told their mother that she had planned to take them to a carnival in the nearby town of Evanston. Mrs. Rushe had no reason to doubt Dann's story. She had always seemed quite fond of the Rushe children and had proven to be a reliable baby-sitter.

Rather than taking the children to Evanston, Dann drove to an elementary school in nearby Highland Park. With the Rushe children waiting in her car, Dann prepared a Molotov cocktail from items that she had previously stored in the trunk of her car. She threw the lighted device against the wall of the school in an attempt to burn it down with the children inside. Dann then jumped back into her car and sped from the scene. Teachers at the school quickly found the fire and were able to extinguish it before any significant damage occurred. Because of their fast action, no one at the school was injured.

Close to the elementary school that she had tried to fire bomb was a day care center and nursery. Dann drove up to the front of the building and tried to enter the nursery, while carrying a container of gasoline, in order to set it ablaze. She was confronted by employees of the nursery and forcefully turned away. Dann now jumped back in her car and headed for the campus of Northwestern University, with the Rushe children still at her side, where she delivered at least two tainted packages of food. Finally returning to the Rushe home, Dann left the bewildered young children with their mother and quickly sped away.

At 10:45 A.M., Dann arrived at the Hubbard Woods Elementary School, which was located just a few blocks from the Rushe residence. When she entered the school, she was armed with three handguns—a .357-magnum, a .32-caliber Smith & Wesson revolver, and a .22-caliber Beretta. This time, she would not be turned away from her passion for revenge.

Dann followed a six-year-old into the boy's bathroom and shot him with the .357-magnum handgun. Although the young boy was shot in the chest and critically wounded, he would survive the attack. She then burst into a second-grade classroom, waving her weapons in the air and shouting at the terrified children that the guns she carried were real and she was "going to teach [them] something about guns."[9] As the class teacher moved to restrain Dann, she began to fire her weapons randomly at the screaming children. An eight-year-old boy was struck by one of the rounds and killed instantly. Four other children in the classroom were seriously injured but would survive their wounds.

Running from the classroom, Dann retreated to her car and sped down a nearby dead-end street. She was forced to abandon the vehicle, and fled on foot through a wooded area until she came upon the home of the Andrew family. By this time, police were in hot pursuit of Dann and she was running out of options. Philip Andrew, a twenty-year-old student at the University of Illinois, confronted the intruder and tried to convince her to give up her weapons. Dann ignored his pleas and insisted on using the telephone to place a call to her mother.

After making the call, Laurie Dann and Philip Andrew began to struggle for the weapon. During the fight, the other members of the Andrew family were able to escape from the home and join the police, who had already begun to surround the home. However, Philip was not so lucky; Dann managed to shoot him in the chest with the .22-caliber handgun. Seriously wounded, but not ready to give up the struggle, Andrew managed to get the gun away from Dann and flee the house. The Andrew home was now completely surrounded by law enforcement personnel, and Laurie Dann was inside, alone.

The standoff outside the Andrew home lasted until 7 o'clock that evening. Police tried to communicate with Dann by using the telephone and bullhorns, but to no avail. In the afternoon, they brought Dann's parents to the scene, hoping that she would respond to them and surrender herself. Finally, receiving no response to any of their attempts to end the standoff, police entered the residence. Once inside, they found Dann's body in a second-floor room. She had shot herself in the head with the .32-caliber pistol. Dann was thirty years old on the day that she died.

Table 8.4: Laurie Wasserman Dann

Perpetrator	A thirty-year-old woman who targeted multiple victims in multiple locations. Dann indicated no history of violence but may have suffered from a mental illness.
Incident date/location	May 20, 1988, at various locations in Illinois.
Incident category	Unexplained.
Weapons	Poison, Molotov cocktail, gasoline, a .357-magnum handgun, a .32-caliber handgun, and a .22-caliber handgun.
Deaths/Injuries	One killed, seven wounded by shooting, and at least six injured by poison.
Motivation	Uncertain. Dann went on a rampage targeting children and adults but left no lucid explanation for her actions or the selection of her victims.
Disposition	Dann committed suicide during a standoff with police.

Laurie Wasserman Dann had no history of violence, although there were indications that she may have been a woman with some psychological problems. At the time of her rampage, Dann was under investigation by local authorities and the Federal Bureau of Investigation (FBI) for making threatening telephone calls to her ex-husband and a former boyfriend. Dann had been divorced in 1986 and, since then, had lived alternately alone in her Wisconsin apartment or with her parents in Glencoe, a Chicago suburb, from where she could easily drive to her baby-sitting job. Dann was also scheduled for trial later in 1988, on charges of shoplifting. According to one of her acquaintances, Dann had a "Jekyll and Hyde" personality. However, there was no history of hospitalization for mental illness and no significant criminal record in her background.

Clearly, however, Dann was at least potentially violent. Between May 1986 and December 1987, she had purchased the three handguns that she later used in the Hubbard Woods school shooting rampage. She had also carefully planned her attempts to poison a number of victims, including their identification by name on a target list. Some of her intended victims were carefully chosen, while others (the children) seemed to be symbolic. In any event, it does not seem likely that Laurie Wasserman Dann simply "went crazy" on the day she tried to murder so many adults and young children. This was an intended murder rampage that had been planned in advance.

Law enforcement officials were unable to pinpoint a precise motive for Dann's incredible actions on May 20, 1988. It was suggested that she may have been upset because the family who provided her with regular employment as a baby-sitter was planning to move from the area. No one could explain why she had targeted so many people for death by poisoning. Dann was obviously deeply angry and resentful, having carefully prepared both a list of victims and the means of their intended death, well before the day that she struck out against them. She also targeted children of a very young age in a particularly gruesome manner, attempting to set fire to at least two organizations that housed young children before her lethal attack on the Hubbard Woods school. For reasons that can never be known to a certainty, her final, fatal onslaught was one that also targeted very young children.

Laurie Wasserman Dann was, by her intent, a potential mass murderer of notorious proportions (see Table 8.4). Thankfully, only one child succumbed to her day of brutal violence. However, one can only imagine how terrible the death toll might have been on May 20, 1988, had Dann not been stopped by a combination of quick intervention by a number of individuals and sheer good fortune.

NOTES

1. Clifford J. Levy, "Former Montclair Post Worker Charged with Killings in Robbery," *New York Times*, 23 March 1995, A1.

2. "A Troubled Man with Many Guns," *Philadelphia Inquirer Online* (Internet edition), 20 July 1984, A02.

3. Ibid.

4. "Clues to a Massacre Motive," *Philadelphia Inquirer Online* (Internet edition), 20 July 1984, A01.

5. "20 Are Slain in Gunfire at McDonald's," *Philadelphia Inquirer Online* (Internet edition), 19 July 1984, A02.

6. "Clues to a Massacre Motive."

7. Ibid.

8. Andrew Cassel, "Woman in Illinois Rampage Suspected in Poisonings," *Philadelphia Inquirer Online* (Internet edition), 22 May 1988, A01.

9. Andrew Cassel, "Woman Kills Pupil, Wounds 6," *Philadelphia Inquirer Online* (Internet edition), 21 May 1988, A01.

CHAPTER 9

Inside the Mind of a Mass Murderer

Is there no way out of the mind?

Sylvia Plath
Apprehensions

What transpires in the mind of a mass murderer that can be so horrendous as to impel him to the inevitable and incredibly vicious finale of his crime? How can he so devalue life—that of others and often his own—that the act of murder becomes, not only an acceptable alternative, but a fundamental and necessary resolution to the problems that he must confront? Why do these men—and, rarely, women—kill in such a particularly heinous and brutal manner?

Even though the crime of mass murder seems to be only a moment of spontaneous ferocity that results in an apparently mindless and incomprehensible loss of life, this is not the nature of the act. This crime is not a simple or straightforward act of brutality, as it is often portrayed in the media. Regardless of its indiscriminate nature, the flash point of mass murder is typically the culmination of a continuum of experiences, perceptions, beliefs, frustrations, disappointments, hostile fantasy, and (perhaps) pathology, which may have been spawned years or decades before lethal violence erupts. The mythology of mass murder that is relentlessly perpetuated in the press is that this ultimate act of killing is a sudden and inexplicable explosion of viciousness that erupts without warning and claims its victims without reason or clear motive. In fact, however, there is nothing about this crime that could be further from the truth.

With few exceptions—those incidents in which the murderer is clearly insane—the act of mass murder is a crime that is often well planned, carefully considered, and, in the mind of the killer, both necessary and inevitable. The consideration and thought that are given to the crime are often in the form of unrelenting and hostile fantasies that are usually of a long-standing nature—fantasies that are richly detailed and frequently organized in surprisingly minute detail. Mass murder is a crime of revenge, retribution, domination, and control—all elements that require, and thrive, in an environment of obsession and dark fantasy. In turn, this obsession is spawned in vague and diffuse thoughts of anger and revenge that eventually develop into a pathological obsession replete with deeply considered details of planning—planning that is directed at a final act of domination through annihilation. In some incidents, such as those involving the murder of family members, the period of fantasy, obsession, and planning may be highly victim-specific, solely targeting particular individuals for death. Other incidents of mass murder are preceded by similar periods of pathological fantasy and planning, but the compulsion for revenge and retribution centers around a more symbolic target, such as a corporation, organization, or group of individuals who represent a feared or hated work, religious, or political belief system. For example, mass murder perpetrated against a background of racial hatred or fear is one of the most common, disturbing, and insidious aspects of the highly symbolic form of this crime.

Whether the victims of the mass murderer are specifically targeted, are symbolic, or both, the fundamental process of an evolving obsession that leads to violence appears to be a relatively predictable aspect of the crime. In fact, for many perpetrators, this process of evolutionary violence may begin very early in life. It seems clear that most perpetrators of mass murder are unable to deal with the vicissitudes and challenges of life that are common to virtually all members of our society. Their inability to cope with the frustrations and disappointments that they must inevitably encounter is often evidenced early in their lives by a failure to deal with their own negative emotions in an effective manner. Perhaps the individual exhibits inappropriate or exaggerated outbursts of hostility; or, alternatively, withdraws emotionally from painful and challenging life situations in a pathological manner. In whatever form it may take, there may be an apparent and painful inability to relate in a positive manner to others. Sometimes this failure is accompanied by a mosaic of early pathological beliefs that the individual is persistently victimized and subjected to unfair and unwarranted domination by others, and is therefore unrecognized for his true worth and uniqueness.

Compounding this growing cancer of self-perception as a victim there may emerge a compensatory sense of inflated self-worth that is designed to ameliorate the pain of rejection, frustration, and disappointment. The individual may begin to falsely perceive himself as especially unique and fundamentally superior to others, yet still unable to achieve the control of his own life that he so desperately needs and deserves. Those around him are perceived as obstacles to this need to compete effectively or to control the exigencies of a life that has proven to be more than can be managed. Whereas the vast majority of well-adjusted individuals face such challenges directly, instinctively trying to move ahead and surmount the obstacles of living that are common to most members of our society, the potential mass murderer perceives only the inequities and unfairness of these obstacles, which he views as inherently unjust and directed specifically against him. These are not mere life challenges that he must face; they are complex, unwarranted, and targeted attacks that are designed to destroy him finally and fully. Since he has never learned to deal effectively with negative emotions, and in order to support his ever-developing, compensatory sense of uniqueness and importance, the potential mass murderer may easily slip into a pathological belief that he has been unfairly engaged in a battle for survival in which he must become the eventual victor, regardless of the consequences to others. In many incidents of mass murder, this need for control, domination, and retribution has become so all-encompassing that, not only have the lives of his victims become meaningless, but the murderer's own life has become secondary to a pervasive drive to control and dominate.

Unlike the perpetrators of crimes such as sexual homicide, who murder in a highly brutal, yet deeply personalized, way, the mass murderer typically depersonalizes his victims at the moment of his attack. The overwhelming weapon of choice for the mass murderer is a gun—a weapon that supports and enhances the perpetrator's need to depersonalize his victims at the crucial moment of his attack. For the mass murderer, victims are often a by-product of the need to control and dominate, not the purpose of the crime itself. In the past decade, the availability of high-powered weapons with immense killing potential have made them especially favored by the mass murderer. These weapons are not only incredibly lethal, they support and enhance the perpetrator's obsession with dominance and depersonalization. Paramilitary weapons, such as the AK-47 assault rifle and the TEC-9 semiautomatic gun, are immensely frightening and intensely destructive. They support the perpetrator's need to depersonalize his victims to every extent possible while dominating an attack scenario with intense fear and intimidation. Such weapons are designed solely for the purpose of killing humans in the most efficient manner. They are the unfortunate, but near-perfect, tools of the trade for the mass murderer, who must express a final, unanswerable need for control, domination, and annihilation, regardless of the cost.

Although the vast majority of mass murderers have an intense need to depersonalize their victims, it is not necessarily true that they have devalued their own life to the point where it has also become meaningless. Many mass murderers do not survive their crimes; however, many others do. Those murderers who survive their crimes do so because they have every intention of benefiting from the fruits of their actions. An individual who murders his family may be responding to a sense of perverted love in which he has decided that they must not suffer the pain of a life that has become meaningless and doomed. However, he may have also planned his crime in response to his own egocentric need to be rid of those individuals whom he perceives to have contributed to his own failures. He may act out of love or, just as likely, out of greed, revenge, or retribution. Many mass murderers who plan and carry out their crimes for political purposes or from a sense of racial or group hatred have no intention of dying in concert with their victims. They have depersonalized their victims to the point where they are deemed to have no right to survive; but, in no way does this dictate a sense of futility and worthlessness for the perpetrator. Rather, this mass murderer has a pathologically heightened sense of importance that demands the death of others, solely because he has deemed them unworthy to live. It has become his mission to rid the world of these individuals who in his mind have become less than human and are representative of failures that are both personal and societal in nature.

In many instances of mass murder, there are elements of the crime that indicate a depersonalization of some victims combined with a high degree of selectivity, or personalization, against others. The embittered, frustrated worker or ex-worker who acts out a compulsion for revenge in the workplace has become a contemporary example of these mixed elements. A common scenario for mass murder in recent years is the crime perpetrated by the worker who has been terminated from his job or has faced other, significant setbacks in the workplace and who sets himself upon a lethal course of retribution. He may attack the workplace and seek out one or more specific supervisors or coworkers against whom he seeks revenge, and then embark on a course of lethal destruction that is clearly indiscriminate and intensely chaotic. In effect, he will not only try to murder those individuals whom he holds responsible for his plight, but he will also attempt to annihilate the entire organization as the symbolic cause of his frustrations, disappointments, and failures. In such incidents, the murderer may be highly selective, and target only supervisors or hated coworkers before ending his rampage; or, at the other extreme, he may slay individuals with whom he has worked for decades and with whom he has formed significant relationships. Many recent incidents of mass murder in the workplace indicate that not only is the perpetrator often willing to kill indiscriminately and symbolically, but he has also decided to forfeit his own life in the process, thereby providing no motivation to spare anyone unfortunate enough to be in his line of sight once the rampage has begun.

Although much of what has been said applies to the majority of mass murderers, it is not a profile of all perpetrators of this crime. Mass murder is sometimes committed in the course of another crime or by individuals who are patently incapable of understanding their own actions; it sometimes occurs for reasons that are inexplicable and devoid of any apparent underlying motivation. Mass murder is not a simple crime that can be explained by a limited collection of fundamental principles, benchmarks, or theories. It is a relatively rare crime that is committed by individuals who do not share consistent experiences or backgrounds. Although it has been historically accurate to say that the typical mass murderer may be male, over the age of twenty-five, and employed, none of this is inherently reliable or accurate. In fact, such a profile may prove to be completely misleading when this crime is examined by a future generation. There simply is no profile of the mass murderer that can be considered trustworthy. Similarly, it is often impossible to pinpoint the absolute and fundamental motivations of the perpetrator or what (in his mind) impelled him to such an inordinate act of violence. For a variety of complex reasons, there are many elements of this crime that may never be understood. However, there is a growing body of tantalizing evidence that indicates possible recognizable patterns of experience and behavior among many mass murderers.

At this point in our limited understanding of the issue, we simply do not know enough about the crime of mass murder, or its perpetrator, to make any definitive statements. Although the emerging patterns of similarity inherent in many of these crimes can be irresistible, they can also prove to be very misleading. It must always be remembered that mass murder is a relatively rare event in this country. We simply do not know enough about the crime or its perpetrator to do more than make some educated guesses about such aspects as motivation, predisposition, and behavioral warning signs; hopefully, these educated guesses, in some instances, may enhance the opportunity for intervention or the prevention of a violent outcome. Compounding our lack of knowledge is the fact that many mass murderers simply choose to not survive their crime, either by their own hand or by an act of suicide-by-proxy.

WHAT CAN WE KNOW?

What can we know about the mind of the mass murderer? What are the motivations and the fundamental processes that drive this heinous crime? Regardless of how unclear the deep motivations for mass murder may be, we know that the fundamental imperatives of revenge and retribution are almost always in strong evidence. At the moment when the perpetrator launches his deadly rampage, his overwhelming compulsion is to destroy life and assert his complete domination over others. This compulsion may be blatantly apparent in his words, if any, and his actions. The murderer's actions are usually clear and unmistakable; his statements may help to shed some light on the dark state of mind that precedes his vicious outburst.

For example, a few moments prior to his incredible rampage at a fast food restaurant in which he indiscriminately targeted both children and adults for death, James Oliver Huberty said to his wife: "I'm going to kiss you goodbye. I'm going hunting for humans."[1] Huberty meant exactly what he said, and he followed through on his statement in the most brutal fashion imaginable. In retrospect, his final statement to his wife was a telling one, in both what he said and how he said it. This was the casual statement of a hunter pursuing game. The cold, ominous phrase, "hunting humans," meant not only that he had made the decision to kill, but also that he had already completely depersonalized his potential victims. In his troubled mind, Huberty was not on a mission to cruelly murder the innocent and unlucky; rather, he was merely going hunting, and his prey happened to be his own kind—in other words, any human would do. Huberty's decision was presented to his wife in an understated, matter-of-fact, off-handed manner—which reduced the significance of his actions to something almost routine or preordained.

When he arrived at the crowded restaurant, seconds prior to randomly executing the unsuspecting, (generally) young patrons, Huberty shouted, "I killed thousands in Vietnam and I want to kill more."[2] Again, the murderer made it clear that the act of killing another human being was not only acceptable but inevitable and almost insignificant. Huberty made it obvious that killing more humans was not something that troubled him. After all, he had done it before—thousands of times. Now, it is obvious that Huberty had not killed thousands of individuals in Vietnam; that simply never happened. However, in his mind, the number of victims simply did not matter, so long as his rampage could be as brutal as possible—so long as his final act of domination could be as complete as he could make it. The age, sex, or condition of his victims was of no consequence, so long as he was able to control, dominate, and annihilate as many victims as possible. He had successfully depersonalized all those around him. In his mind, he was simply "hunting humans" in an effort to compensate for a life of failure, frustration, and disappointment. Huberty's statement prior to his rampage demonstrated the element of victim depersonalization so often associated with brutal acts of indiscriminate mass murder. For Huberty, the act of killing had been transformed into a symbolic and magical deed of retribution in which many victims meant more than one, and no single victim could be granted the precious value of life.

Mass murder that is motivated by racial or group hatred or for political purposes is a crime that should be inconceivable in our society; however, it remains a dark and troubling undercurrent of Americanism that simply will not go away. Murders motivated by these factors are not simple crimes with simple explanations. The pervasive and long-term hatred that eventually explodes into a flash point of mass murder bespeaks years or decades of unsettling and unremitting prejudice that may extend into the early youth or childhood of many perpetrators. That such hatred should erupt into the ultimate form of violence is an obvious indication of a deeply troubled individual who wheels out of control in a final effort to take charge of a life that must, by definition, be clearly out of control. When Kenneth Junior French went on a murder rampage in a family-owned Italian restaurant, he did not target any one individual (or even a specific group of individuals) whom he thought would be at the restaurant that night. The statement that he made just before firing indiscriminately at the owners and patrons of the restaurant was bizarre and completely out-of-context, yet revealing: "I'll show you, Clinton. You think I'm not going to do this. I'll show you about gays in the military."[3]

French had no idea if any of his victims were gay. In reality, they were simply innocent individuals, in the wrong place at the wrong time, who were confronted by a man who had been set on a maniacal course of revenge and retribution. French wanted to show the president of the United States that he was a man who was committed to his own, twisted sense of morality; but the President was not at Luigi's Restaurant that night, and the murderer had no expectations of finding him there. Whatever it was that French wanted to make known to the President and the world, it was not to be found among his victims that night. The hatred and anger that he had carried so deeply and for so long was expunged in a moment of chaos and brutality that had meaning only to the murderer. French proved, once again, that the face of hatred and prejudice can never be logical or explicable; at its root, it must always be twisted, horrible, and unforgiving.

Unlike Kenneth French, who murdered completely without regard to his victims, other mass murderers target their victims with great specificity and carry out their crimes with an apparent regard for innocent individuals who may be unwittingly at the crime scene. When Kenneth Tornes went hunting for those who had made his life unbearable, he targeted only his work supervisors. During his rampage, when confronted by a frightened woman who was trying to flee the scene of the ongoing murders, Tornes warned his potential victim, "Lady, get back, I'm going to blow this place up!"[4] He brushed passed the terrified woman and continued searching for only those supervisors who he had previously decided should die. When his rampage was finished, Tornes had only attacked those he had specifically targeted for death; no others were injured. Tornes was a mass murderer who had focused his anger and pathological need for retribution on a very specific group of individuals—his work supervisors—who had become the living representation of the failures in his life. They, and only they, were to be held accountable, in an ultimate sense—only they should pay the full and final price for his disappointments and frustrations.

A few mass murderers were clearly incapable of understanding the viciousness of their crimes at the moment when they lashed out against their victims. Sylvia Seegrist, who was referred to in the press as the "Female Rambo," could only give a disjointed and incoherent explanation of her actions moments after gunning down innocent victims in a shopping center: "I'm a woman and I have family problems and I have seizures."[5] Trying to further explain her motives to those who were detaining her after the shooting, Seegrist added, "My family makes me nervous. I didn't mean to do it."[6] At her trial, Seegrist was presented as a woman with a long history of debilitating mental illness that had never been ameliorated by any treatment program. However, she was subsequently determined to be legally culpable of her crimes. Although often verbally abusive and violent, it appears that Seegrist had never fully experienced the period of planning that is so frequently associated with sane mass murderers. In fact, the hours preceding Seegrist's murderous rampage were filled with innocuous and mundane activities that belied what was to transpire in the shopping mall later that day. That Seegrist suffered from severe psychological problems was obvious; nonetheless, she was found legally responsible for her crime.

John Frazier was a young man who was clearly psychotic and diagnosed as suffering from paranoid schizophrenia. He claimed to receive messages from God and often told anyone who would listen that his mission in life was to protect the environment at any cost. Living in squalor, in a valley below the impressive home of an eminently successful doctor and his family, Frazier became obsessed with the symbolic luxury that he saw daily at the Ohta residence. Although Frazier was apparently not capable of sustained periods of logical thought and planning, he must have been plagued by dark and vengeful fantasies about his God-given mission. He was clearly obsessed with the ever-present opulence of the Ohta residence, and must have been significantly frustrated by his own oppressive and deteriorating life. Within the twisted maze of his psychotic fantasies, Frazier determined that the Ohta family had become symbolic of the evil that was destroying the environment—which was his sacred destiny to protect. Frazier decided that it was his mandate from God that the entire Ohta family should be annihilated. After murdering four members of the family and the doctor's secretary, Frazier left a rambling and disjointed note on the windshield of the family car, ostensibly written by "the free people of the universe." In this statement, Frazier made esoteric references to tarot symbolism, noted the fast-approaching advent of World War III, and rambled about the destruction of the world's environment that had been caused by the encroachment of man. Frazier's statement was clearly that of a madman, and the Ohta family had become the unfortunate target for his psychotic obsession.

Some incidents of mass murder leave us wondering and unsure about the sanity of the perpetrator; they accentuate the historical dichotomy between the legal definition of sanity and the medical view of culpability. The case of Colin Ferguson, who killed six individuals and wounded another nineteen on a New York City commuter train, is an example of an incident of mass murder that raises far more questions about sanity and culpability than it answers. Ferguson harbored a deep, long-standing hatred of Caucasians and several other ethnic groups. During his rampage, he obviously targeted victims from these hated ethnic groups, despite the fact that he knew none of them personally. In the early stages of the investigation, law enforcement officials were convinced that Ferguson had acted out of racial hatred in a planned crime of revenge. Later, when Ferguson was appointed counsel, his attorneys considered offering a defense of "black rage" in order to make the case that their client had murdered out of a sense of injustice against African-Americans—an injustice that had been pervasive since the foundation of this country. At first, this defense tactic appealed to Ferguson, and he eventually used portions of it in his own courtroom strategy. However, he eventually rejected this line of defense, as well as a possible secondary defense based on insanity. In the end, Ferguson demanded to be allowed to represent himself in court, and he did so in a manner that was both unique and unsettling.

Although articulate, intelligent, and apparently well-versed in the law, Ferguson represented himself in such a way as to create serious doubts about his sanity in the minds of some, while convincing others that he was a man who was talented at the manipulation of all who were in his presence. At one point during the trial, Ferguson tried to convince the jury that an unidentified Caucasian male had actually committed the murders, despite the dozens of witnesses who were able to identify the defendant himself as the shooter. Later in the trial, Ferguson took the line of defense that he, himself, had been a victim of another, unidentified murderer. Addressing the jury about himself in the third person, the defendant said: "Mr. Ferguson did not fire a gun. He simply is the victim of a shooting on a train, like any other victim."[7] Several of Ferguson's statements made during the trial, along with his shifting and sometimes incoherent line of defense, left many doubts in the minds of those observing the proceedings. The question of who did the shooting was never in doubt; however, what about the shooter's state of mind, his motivations, and the meaning of his actions?

Many observers of the trial came to the conclusion that Ferguson suffered from an obvious and debilitating psychological disorder; others thought that the intelligent defendant was play-acting for the court. However, at the end of the trial the jury was convinced that Ferguson was sane at the time of the crime. To what extent was Colin Ferguson responsible for his actions? In a legal sense, he was fully responsible—he was the shooter, he was clearly sane, and he was aware of the import of his actions. On the other hand, from a psychological perspective, we simply do not know.

The question of a mass murderer's decision to survive or not survive his rampage is difficult and troubling. Why do some murderers carefully plan their own deaths while others take extreme measures to survive their crime, even though they may make no plans to escape the legal consequences of their actions? There can be little doubt that the question of surviving their crime is an aspect in the planning of mass murder that is carefully considered by the sane perpetrator. Although many mass murderers make an obvious decision to die with their victims and plan their crimes to account for this final act of violence, there are any number of incidents that make it evident that the killer had every intention of surviving his crime.

Ronald Gene Simmons went to extraordinary lengths to plan his murderous rampage. Over several days that had been carefully selected well in advance of the crime, Simmons brutally murdered sixteen individuals who were mostly members of his own family. After attacking his last victim in a local business near where he lived, Simmons calmly surrendered his weapon and asked a stunned worker, who had witnessed the finale to his three-day murder spree, to call law enforcement officials. The statement that he made at that moment was unbelievably calm and ironic: "I've done what I wanted to do."[8] At his trial, Simmons offered virtually no defense for the brutal killings of so many individuals and added nothing that would shed light on his motivation. Simmons had planned his rampage with extraordinary care; he had carried it

out with deliberation and patience. However, once he had finished with his
heinous crime, Simmons simply waited for the judicial system to take its
course. He had clearly decided to survive his crimes; however, in the end, he
took no action to prolong his own life.

Gian Luigi Ferri, like Simmons, took great care in planning his attack on
a San Francisco law firm. He had carefully preselected approximately forty
victims; he had even prepared a written list of their names, and in some
instances, had recorded the reasons why he had targeted them for death.
Finally, Ferri had carefully prepared a cover sheet for his death list, captioned
with the phrase, "To the families of the victims."

However, when Ferri finally struck, none of the individuals who appeared
on his prepared list were victimized. Rather, eight completely innocent
individuals were murdered and another six wounded, in what turned out to be a
symbolic act of indiscriminate mass murder. Ferri, who was cornered by
arriving police personnel and caught between floors in a high-rise office
building under siege, committed suicide at the crime scene. It was never
determined if suicide was an aspect of Ferri's original planning; however, it
was an option that he openly embraced when confronted with the chaotic
situation that he had created. His planning, like that of Ronald Gene Simmons,
was careful and deadly. However, unlike Simmons, he apparently gave little
consideration to his own survival at the moment of his attack.

In the final analysis, we may never understand what transpires in the
mind of a mass murderer. The dark, unspeakable violence that we know as
mass murder is terrifying and foreign to the vast majority of Americans. What
little we do know is often confusing and deeply troubling. Our base of
knowledge of this crime and its perpetrator is derived from incidents that are
seldom well-documented; we must frequently rely on a history of the murderer
that is largely uncertain. Despite these shortcomings, there are a number of
factors that can be identified with the crime of mass murder and its
perpetrators; there are familiar patterns that appear again and again in many
incidents of mass murder. Whether these elements constitute reliable points of
similarity and understanding is uncertain; however, many of these factors
present intriguing possibilities for a better comprehension of this crime and the
perpetrator:

1. The background of many mass murderers, to the degree that it is known,
frequently indicates that the individual has had a lengthy history of failing to
deal appropriately with negative emotions and experiences, such as anger,
frustration, and disappointment. Rejection and social isolation may be very
prevalent in the perpetrator's background, often extending into early childhood.
The failure to integrate successfully with peer groups or other important social
elements, even when quite young, appears with regularity in the background of
many mass murderers. Early feelings of inferiority, an overt inability to
successfully compete with other children or adolescents, obvious and painful
experiences of rejection, and the absence of a nurturing parental environment

seem to be common themes in the murderer's background. It is not unusual to discover a significantly negative familial environment, early trauma from physical, sexual, or psychological abuse, or other consequential disruptions in the early years of many mass murderers. However, it must be emphasized that such childhood trauma, in and of itself, cannot be identified as the causal factor for murder. Millions of children in this country are subjected to such negative experiences in their formative years yet as adults never turn to a life of crime, or even a single act of violence. The most that can be said of childhood experiences dominated by rejection, isolation, or abuse is that these factors are often found among those few individuals who later go on to commit mass murder.

2. For many perpetrators, these early experiences of rejection, disappointment, and social isolation set the stage for a growing belief that personal failures are attributable to others. The individual develops an ever-increasing, powerful, pathological belief system that is based on a wariness of others, a sense that he is being persistently victimized by those around him, and an assumption that he has been unfairly treated on all fronts, despite the fact that he *should* be a fulfilled, happy, and successful individual.

3. As the individual matures, compensatory belief systems evolve that tend to further isolate him socially. His developing beliefs present many opportunities to bolster a personal credo to the effect that the successes he is clearly entitled to are continually and cruelly ripped from his hands by the actions of those around him. The individual may view others as deliberately threatening and overtly dangerous to his continued well being, and concurrently, he may develop a pathological compensatory belief in his own superiority and righteousness. It is not unusual for the perpetrator to develop a belief system that places him in the unique position of being continually victimized by any number of individuals or groups who, in his mind, are responsible for his personal failures and disappointments.

4. With sufficient periods of failure and disappointment, and the inability to deal with personal setbacks in a positive manner, the perpetrator may turn to dark and unrelenting fantasies of revenge and retribution. Convinced that all positive options are meaningless and ineffectual, the individual becomes obsessed with balancing the scales through an ultimate act of retribution. Those individuals, groups, or organizations responsible for the perpetrator's failures must be annihilated and no longer allowed to pursue their course of deliberate destruction. To the perpetrator, revenge becomes the sole acceptable option, since anything less would condone the continuation of destruction that has led to the unacceptable situation in which he finds himself.

5. As the period of fantasized retribution becomes obsessive and all-encompassing, the perpetrator will evolve a plan of attack that is often surprisingly comprehensive. During this period, the perpetrator may consider the questions of his own survival and who must be specifically targeted for death. The intended victims may be identified precisely or they may symbolic, or a combination of both. The perpetrator may view his own survival as critical, in which case he will carefully plan the crime to ensure his own survival. On the other hand, he may view his planned rampage as a final solution for both his intended victims and himself, in which case he will give consideration to his own death, either by suicide or by the actions of others whom he will incite.

6. Throughout the period of fantasy and planning, the perpetrator will take the appropriate actions that are needed to ensure the success of his rampage. He will obtain the weapons that he requires, consider the location and timing of his attack, and, if appropriate, consider the remnants of his own life. Many perpetrators become severely socially isolated at this point and minimize communications with even their closest loved ones. The protracted process of fantasy and planning, combined with a history of frustration, disappointment, and rejection, has, by this time, resulted in the depersonalization of the intended victims in the mind of the perpetrator. His targets are no longer viewed as human within the context of his pathological thinking. Rather, they are viewed as insurmountable impediments responsible for the failure of his life. In effect, their annihilation has been transformed from a criminal act into an act of justice—the ultimate reestablishment of the control that he so long ago lost, for reasons that he cannot understand, condone, or accept.

7. With the planning of his crime complete, the perpetrator has now fulfilled all the elements needed for his final, lethal actions. The precise moment in which he strikes may be known, or in some instances, the perpetrator will wait for an appropriate opportunity to strike. In some cases, the murderer may delay for a short period, waiting in subconscious anticipation of a final, compelling triggering event that will finalize his decision and provide the impetus for his rampage. However, in many instances the perpetrator has already decided on where, when, and how to strike. If this is the case, he will typically waste little time in pursuing his final act of revenge.

At the moment the mass murderer strikes, he will often act in a methodical, surprisingly concentrated manner. His attack has been designed to dominate, control, and annihilate those whom he has so carefully targeted. Even though he may not know any of his victims personally, and even though his attack may be a purely symbolic effort to annihilate a hated group or organization, his rampage will often be quite controlled from the perpetrator's point of view. In the event that the perpetrator has decided to end his own life in concert with his victims, he will typically wait until he has satisfied his pathological need for retribution before committing suicide or inducing others at the scene to stop him by force. In some instances, such as family mass murders, the finale to the perpetrator's crime may be his own successful escape from the crime scene as his flees to a carefully planned life designed to avoid capture. In other cases, however, he may end it all by his own hand.

NOTES

1. Murray Dubin, "Clues to a Massacre Motive," *Philadelphia Inquirer Online* (Internet edition), 20 July 1984, A01.

2. "20 Are Slain in Gunfire at McDonald's," *Philadelphia Inquirer Online* (Internet edition), 19 July 1984, A01.

3. Martha Waggoner, "Gunman Kills 4 in Restaurant Rampage," *Philadelphia Inquirer Online* (Internet edition), 8 August 1993, A03.

4. "Firefighter Gunman: He Was a Time Bomb Waiting to Go Off," *Associated Press* (Internet), 25 April, 1996, 1.

5. Russell E. Eshleman Jr., and Steve Stecklow, "Step by Step: The Shootings at Springfield Mail," *Philadelphia Inquirer Online* (Internet edition), 25 April 1985, A01.

6. Ibid.

7. "Massacre Trial a Surreal Show," *Reuters News Service* (Internet edition), 30 January 1995, B2.

8. James Alan Fox and Jack Levin, *Overkill: Mass Murder and Serial Killing Exposed* (New York: Plenum, 1994), 153.

CHAPTER 10

Tomorrow's Mass Murderer

Even though the annual victim count has not significantly increased in the past ten years, the crime of mass murder in America is evolving and taking shape in new and foreboding ways.[XII] A few decades ago, it was a generally accepted belief that most mass murderers were demented or insane. Of course, there were those few, exceptional murderers who killed in a planned crime spree and with a motive that was precise, calculating, and criminal. These were the sane mass murderers who were considered to be extreme and exceptional. The majority of mass murderers were typically considered to be insane—their incomprehensible actions made this obvious; or, so we thought. When Howard Unruh, a hero of World War II, murdered thirteen individuals on a public street in his hometown, he was generally considered to be insane. No one questioned this assumption; to the generation that judged his actions, it was obvious.

One of the most notorious mass murderers of his time, Charles Whitman, whose actions were deemed "the crime of the century" when they occurred in 1966, was found to be suffering from a brain tumor after an autopsy was performed following his crime (see Table 10.1). Ironically, Whitman had his own suspicions about the state of his mental health and had requested the autopsy himself in a suicide note that he had prepared the day before his rampage. The results of this medical examination led to a widely accepted assumption that Charles Whitman was deranged when he shot and killed twelve persons and wounded another thirty from a university clock tower in Austin, Texas, the morning after he brutally murdered his mother and wife. Few individuals questioned this assumption about Whitman's state of mind in

---

XII. This is true only if one discounts such vicious acts of terrorism as occurred in the Oklahoma City bombing of 1995.

the 1960s; he simply *had* to be insane to commit such a horrendous crime. Within the boundaries of our limited understanding of mass murder three decades ago, no sane person could possibly have committed such a brutal, senseless crime.

What we have learned in recent years about the mass murderer paints a much different and darker portrait of this perpetrator and his state of mind. Today, the mass murderer is rarely considered to be insane. Rather, he is frequently recognized as a murderer who plans his crime quite carefully, knows precisely what he wants to accomplish, and has predetermined who is to die. He is not often subject to the debilitating delusions and insidious psychotic fantasies of the paranoid schizophrenic. Rather, he is typically a man obsessed with thoughts of revenge, filled beyond measure with the intensity of hate, despairing, frustrated, isolated, desperate, and devoid of hope; however, he is rarely insane, in either the legal or ethical senses of the term.

Table 10.1: Charles Joseph Whitman

Perpetrator	A twenty-five-year-old engineering student who went on an indiscriminate murder rampage the day after killing his wife and mother.
Incident date/location	August 1, 1966, at the University of Austin, Austin, Texas.
Incident category	Unexplained.
Weapons	Multiple high-powered rifles, handguns, and ammunition.
Deaths/Injuries	Twelve were killed and another thirty injured in the sniping attack. Whitman had murdered his wife and mother the previous day.
Motivation	Uncertain. Whitman had some life failures and a somewhat troubled childhood. He was discharged from the military after being certified as a sharpshooter.
Disposition	Whitman was shot and killed by an officer responding to the crime scene.

Since 1986, the year in which Patrick Sherrill murdered fourteen of his coworkers in an Oklahoma post office, the lethal employee has become recognized as a new and formidable mass murderer. In many ways, he is the epitome of the late-twentieth-century mass murderer. The lethal employee typically murders those against whom he harbors a vehement and unrelenting obsession for revenge; however, he may also slay those against whom he holds no grudge or even those with whom he has shared a bond of trust. In many instances, this is a murderer who is driven to destroy an entire organization—to symbolically annihilate the financial benefactor who has somehow been transformed into a hated enemy and the overwhelming emblem of a failed life.

Even though Patrick Sherrill was not the first employee to commit mass murder in the workplace, his crime garnered significant national attention in the media and among several government agencies, such as the National Institute of Occupational Safety and Health (NIOSH), the Centers for Disease Control (CDC), and the Occupational Safety and Heath Administration (OSHA). His actions marked the first widespread, public recognition of the potential for massive and lethal violence in the workplace. Since 1986, the American workplace has been besieged by a continuing series of mass murders carried out by employees or ex-employees who harbored a deep sense of revenge against their employers. The perpetrators of these crimes continue to act out their compulsion for retribution in both the public and private sectors of our economy. These murderers come from the ranks of poorly paid workers, highly compensated managers, skilled employees, and (in one instance) even a professor at a renown university.

In many cases, these lethal employees are motivated to violence by the changing nature of the workplace itself. Recurring periods of downsizing, layoffs, and rapidly changing work environments present frustrations and disappointments so severe, that to a few employees, they cannot be tolerated and must be avenged with violence. It is likely that the lethal employee will become even more threatening tomorrow than he is today simply because the complexities in our society that drive him to his brutal crimes will continue to escalate. Despite these imperatives for violence, the lethal employee who commits mass murder in the workplace is usually quite rational.

Historically, terrorism has been viewed as a crime that rarely occurred on American soil. It has been traditionally considered a horror reserved for elsewhere, and not for this country. We live in an open society, which until recently, assumed itself to be safe from acts of terrorism directed against our citizenry or organized political revenge designed to collapse our national government. Certainly, there were periods in our history that were replete with crimes of limited internal political terrorism. The 1960s spawned a decade or more of these crimes. However, even these acts were not considered as serious terrorist threats to our national security; by contemporary standards, they were not generally viewed as egregious attacks against the American citizenry. In fact, it was generally understood that the targets of these early terrorist activities were never intended to be our own citizens. Rather, the intended targets were symbolic and institutional—they were selected because they were representative of the distrust and disdain for the national government that was popularized among the postwar generation of the 1960s. Today, however, political terrorism has taken on a new and vicious presence that directly and specifically targets our citizens.

Like the American workplace, which was once assumed to be a sanctuary of opportunity and a place of relative safety, our society is no longer exempt from acts of terrorism wrought upon American citizens by American citizens. The bombing of a government building at the peak hour of a workday, or an attack launched against a heavily populated center of private enterprise represents a category of crime that now threatens our country in a very real way. The targets of these criminals are no longer merely symbolic—now they are also human. Today, if successful, crimes of terrorism are often clear acts of intentional mass murder. They are designed to shock our society and our government, through fear and intimidation, by attacking and killing civilians engaged in the business of America. To the minds of the perpetrators of this kind of mass murder, the number of victims determines the relative success of their crime. The motivation behind these crimes is no longer focused on a desire to merely induce a change of policy by our government—the motivation is often to eliminate it entirely, perhaps in favor of something else.

Crimes of hate are not new to America; however, they are also evolving in ominous ways. The bombing of a church meeting attended by African-American youngsters, carried out in the name of racial integrity by Southern extremists, is no longer a parochial, localized, and isolated issue; rather, it has become a nearly institutionalized underground movement that is carried forward in the name of racial supremacy as an emerging and ominous, nationwide philosophy. Radical, right-wing, paramilitary groups that espouse a political agenda based on racial hatred, ethnicity, economics, or anarchy are no longer uncommon in America; nor are they peculiar to any geographical location. Such crimes have developed into a virtual national tradition and are now pervasive in many American locations.

Today, splinter groups that are founded on fear and hatred are numerous, often well funded, and frequently armed with an arsenal of military-style weapons that make them a formidable opponent for any law enforcement agency. Neo-Nazi movements and allied organizations, whose very existence relies on hatred as a unifying principle, have become increasingly popular with many American adolescents and young adults. Increasingly, the youthful members of these organizations have found more reason to distrust and fear diverse ethnic groups than to trust and befriend them. Our national landscape is now peppered with any number of these enclaves—loose-knit organizations that obsessively train in paramilitary war games and engage in a range of violent behavior that can lead to organized mass murder with little warning.

The contemporary mass murderer possess weapons of incredible destruction and brutality, the like of which was publicly unknown in this country prior to the Vietnam War. Automatic or semiautomatic handguns, rifles, and military style weapons predominate the crimes of the contemporary mass murderer. The perpetrators of these crimes are often equipped with more powerful and sophisticated weapons than the law enforcement personnel who are charged with stopping their crimes. It is now common for the mass murderer to bring several weapons to the scene of his crime and to carry lethal ammunition more than sufficient to quickly and easily kill his targets in great numbers. His weapons are capable of inflicting massive and fatal wounds, even in the hands of a relatively inexperience shooter. These are weapons that have been designed to kill humans and do nothing else. The mass murderer is usually quite familiar with these incredibly powerful weapons; he is often a trained expert in their use. He has access to all that he needs to murder people quickly and easily, and in large numbers.

The weapons that the mass murderer requires are readily available throughout this country—even to youthful offenders. Despite the fact that there is some movement at the federal level of government to begin withdrawing the easy access to such brutal weapons, the vast number of these guns currently in circulation in America provides ample opportunity for anyone contemplating mass murder. To worsen matters, this is a situation that does not seem likely to change significantly in the immediate future.

Most forms of American entertainment enthrone violence, grossly misrepresent its real impact, and revel in its outcome. Television programming and the motion picture industry reap enormous financial benefits from the portrayal of violence, in an endless array of manifestations, to all age groups in this country. Whether the entertainment form be children's television cartoons (in which it is estimated that a violent act is portrayed once every 90 seconds to any child old enough to operate the on/off switch) to the most popular, multimillion dollar box office hit, acts of aggression, mayhem, and murder are the mainstay of much of our leisure time. We have become a nation comprised of individuals who accept violence into our own homes as a form of entertainment. In fact, we demand it and pay for the privilege of inviting it into our homes. Incredibly, we often wonder why our children emulate the aggressive actions that have become a staple of their youth. It is a tragic and frightening irony that we cannot truly grasp what we doing to our own children. Gone are the days when the most violent act that was allowed into our home were the easily dismissed, generally harmless pranks of comics like the Three Stooges or Laurel and Hardy. We now must try to deal with the very real aggressions and murderous behavior of characters such as Rambo, the Terminator, and Judge Dredd, whose unacceptably violent conduct is enhanced by the impact of such advanced technology that it is difficult to know what is real and what is fantasy, or who dies and who only seems to die. These are the role models that we have bequeathed to our children; they teach an entire generation that violence is acceptable, rewarded, appropriate, thrilling, and survivable. The legacy that we have granted to our children by this acceptance of violence has destroyed the potential that could otherwise have helped them to be the non-violent, compassionate beings that we so desperately need in order to set things right in this country.

Contrary to one of the strongest myths surrounding the crime of mass murder, the contemporary perpetrator is not a deranged individual whose actions are bizarre and exceptional. On the contrary, he is often a common man who is not unusual in his ability to function in society. Although he may be overwhelmed by the frustrations, disappointments, and anger of a life that seems (to him) to be out of control, he is not crazy. If anything, he is deeply resentful and obsessively angry, with an overpowering compulsion for revenge. The contemporary mass murderer is a man who is unable to cope with the unsettling challenges of his life, unable to find any option but violence, and unable or unwilling to find the support that he desperately needs to stabilize his existence. For whatever reasons—and often they are numerous—this is a man who cannot move ahead and who, in his mind, has already failed. For all practical purposes, this is a man who may already consider himself to be as good as dead. He has lost the ability to perceive any value in life, whether it be his own or others. He is all these things—or he is truly insane.

There is no doubt that the mass murderer of tomorrow will continue to evolve; his crimes will take on new and more lethal forms. Moreover, his motives will become more complex and covert as he himself continues to evolve. Today, he is frequently the lethal employee or the political dissident. Tomorrow, he may be the religious zealot or the right-wing extremist. He may become the alleged defender of all that is held to be good; or he may become the home-grown "Great Satan" who is often identified with Americans by those who have come to hate this country from afar. We do not know who he will be; however, we can be sure that he will be among us tomorrow.

Our nation continues to evolve in ways that are sometimes unpredictable and frightening. The social, political, and economic strain on Americans has increased significantly since the end of World War II, and these stressors will only become more intense and pervasive in the coming decades. In such an unpredictable environment, with its relentless demands for competitive success, our children will inherit a society in which violence will not be diminished but rather, in all likelihood, will become even more pervasive and virulent than it is today. The mass murderer of tomorrow will be equipped with even more lethal weapons than he has today; and he will be quite capable of using them with the greatest impact that he can muster. His opportunities for mayhem will be increased as we increase in our numbers. His opportunities to view his life as a failure will multiply as we, in our ceaseless drive for more, leave behind an ever-growing segment of American society. Tomorrow there will be hate, as there is today. There will always be those who cannot resolve the issues that they must inevitably confront without a gun in their hand and revenge in their heart.

Tomorrow, there will be another mass murder.

CHAPTER 11

A Survey of American Mass Murderers

The mass murderer has been active in America for many decades. However, in recent years, he has become more lethal and his crimes more gruesome. Table 11.1 presents an overview of a few of the most notorious mass murderers whose crimes have been investigated and at least somewhat understood.

This is not a complete list of American mass murderers. It is merely a representative sample of their crimes and possible motivations. All the perpetrators were male unless otherwise noted.

Table 11.1: Overview of American Mass Murderers

Perpetrator	Year	Slain	Possible Motivation	Details
M. Barbieri	1996	4	perverted love	In an apparent family murder/suicide, this mother of three young children drove her automobile into a high voltage electrical transmission tower, killing the children and herself. Barbieri was under treatment for depression at the time of the incident.

N. Yazzie	1996	4	perverted love	Unemployed and addicted to alcohol, Yazzie shot five of his children and then set the family trailer on fire.
K. Tornes	1996	5	lethal employee	After murdering his wife, Tornes went to the fire station where he worked and killed four supervisors, wounding another two.
C. McCree	1996	5	lethal employee	Murdered supervisors and coworkers a year after being fired from his job.
J. Avanesian	1996	7	perverted love/revenge	Murdered his entire family by burning down their apartment.
H. Randolph	1996	4	perverted love	Murdered his wife and children, then committed suicide.
B. Loukaitas	1996	3	revenge	A fourteen-year-old boy who brought a rifle to school and murdered two students and a teacher against whom he held a grudge.
Unknown	1996	230	politics/hate (uncertain)	TWA flight 800 exploded in flight moments after leaving New York for Paris. It has not yet been determined whether this was due to mechanical failure or an act of terrorism.
M. Mendoza-Garcia	1996	3	unexplained	Murdered several members of his family. Possible revenge motivation.
M. Clark	1995	4	perverted love	Murdered family and committed suicide by means of a car bomb hidden in the glove compartment of the family automobile.

J. Simpson	1995	5	lethal employee	Murdered supervisors and coworkers after losing his job.
E. Dehaney	1995	3	perverted love/revenge	Murdered his wife and two children after an argument.
W. Woods	1995	4	lethal employee	Murdered his supervisors because he believed he was to be terminated from his job.
C. Green	1995	4	unexplained	Murdered his former coworkers and customers unknown to him without explanation.
D. Whitson	1995	4	perverted love	Murdered his family by shooting.
J. Hessler	1995	4	lethal employee	Murdered his former coworkers at multiple locations after losing his job.
B. Alvarez	1995	5	unexplained	Bludgeoned and stabbed members of a family whose house he was painting.
J. Davis	1995	3	lethal employee	Murdered his coworkers after being fired from his job.
A. Petrosky	1995	3	perverted love/revenge	Murdered his wife and two bystanders after marital difficulties.
M. Vernon	1995	5	revenge	Shot individuals randomly in a retail store after arguing with an employee.
L. Morita	1995	5	crime	Murdered his family by setting the home ablaze in order to collect an insurance settlement.
R. Smith	1995	8	hate revenge	Shot employees and customers of a clothing store and then set the building on fire.

Unknown	1995	5	mass execution	Five individuals in a bar were murdered during the course of a robbery.
G. Clemons	1995	3	lethal employee	Murdered his supervisor and coworkers after being terminated from his job.
T. Blackwell	1995	3	perverted love/revenge	Murdered his pregnant wife, her fetus, and her friend at an annulment hearing.
T. McVeigh T. Nichols	1995	168	politics/hate	Destroyed a federal building in Oklahoma City with a homemade truck bomb.[XIII]
B. Lawson	1994	4	revenge	Stormed a police station and shot individuals at random.
D. Buenrostro	1994	3	perverted love	Murdered her children. Possibly psychotic, although deemed legally sane.
A. Winterbone	1993	4	politics hate	Murdered state employees and others because he was unemployed and could not find work.
L. Jasion	1993	4	lethal employee	Murdered coworkers with whom he had disputes. Angry about working conditions.
P. Calden	1993	3	lethal employee	Murdered his supervisors and coworkers a year after being terminated from his job.
M. Kansi	1993	2	politics/hate revenge	Shot randomly at CIA employees as they reported to work.
K. French	1993	4	politics/hate revenge	Randomly shot patrons in a restaurant, in protest of President Clinton's policy regarding homosexuals in the military.

XIII. Perpetrators charged but not yet tried.

C. Ferguson	1993	6	hate revenge	Randomly shot commuters on a train. Possible motivation of racial hatred.
G. Ferri	1993	8	revenge	Randomly shot employees and clients of a law firm against which he held a grudge.
Unknown	1993	7	crime (?)	Employees and owners of a restaurant were murdered execution style in a possible robbery.
Several foreign nationals	1993	6	politics/hate	Bombing of the World Trade Center in New York by terrorists. Domestic connections with the perpetrators remain uncertain.
J. Miller	1992	4	revenge	Angered by employees of a public service agency, returned to the office and murdered those employees on duty.
V. Fabrikant	1992	4	lethal employee	University professor who murdered coworkers in their offices.
G. Lu	1991	5	revenge	Angered because he did not receive an academic award, killed professors and a rival student.
J. Harris	1991	4	lethal employee	Fired employee who murdered former supervisor and coworkers.
T. McIlvane	1991	4	lethal employee	Fired employee who returned to murder supervisors and former coworkers.
A. Garcia J. Doody	1991	9	crime	Robbed, then executed, nine Buddhist monks and a nun. Perpetrators were both teenagers at the time.
G. Hennard	1991	23	unexplained	Crashed his truck through storefront of a cafeteria and began executing patrons randomly.

J. Gonzalez	1990	87	perverted love	Set the social club on fire in which his ex-girlfriend was employed.
H. Elizalde	1990	6	perverted love	Burned his children to death while they slept after losing their custody and his job.
C. Brown	1990	8	revenge	Angry at a shop owner, Brown returned to the store and randomly shot employees and customers. He was subsequently murdered by angry witnesses to his crime.
J. Pough	1990	10	revenge	Shot employees and customers at a loan office after his automobile was repossessed.
P. Purdy	1989	5	politics/hate revenge	Shot randomly at elementary school children as revenge against Asian-Americans.
R. Salcido	1989	7	perverted love/lethal employee	Murdered his entire family and boss as revenge for an impending divorce and workplace difficulties.
J. Taylor	1989	3	lethal employee	Murdered his wife while she slept, then went to work and murdered coworkers.
J. Wesbecker	1989	7	lethal employee	Shot supervisors and employees after being placed on disability leave from his job.
M. Lepine	1989	14	politics/hate revenge	Shot women in a rampage while searching for persons he believed to be "feminists."[XIV]
D. Brown	1988	4	perverted love	Murdered family members with an ax.
M. Hayes	1988	4	unexplained	Shot four neighbors without explanation.

XIV. This crime took place in Canada.

R. Farley	1988	7	perverted love	Obsessed with a coworker, Farley went on a shooting rampage at her place of work.
J. Schnick	1987	7	perverted love	Murdered his entire family.
W. Cruse	1987	6	unexplained	Randomly murdered individuals without explanation.
D. Burke	1987	43	lethal employee	Following the termination from his job, on board an airliner in flight, shot and killed his former supervisor and the flight crew, causing the airliner to crash.
R. Dreesman	1987	7	perverted love	Shot his entire family in a murder-suicide rampage.
D. Lynam	1987	8	perverted love	Murdered his entire family.
R. Simmons	1987	16	perverted love	Murdered his entire family and others after his wife threatened divorce.
P. Sherrill	1986	14	lethal employee	Postal employee who murdered his coworkers.
S. Seegrist	1985	3	sane/insane	Female. Randomly murdered individuals in a local shopping center and later ruled insane.
B. McNamara	1985	4	perverted love	Suffering delusions, murdered his family.
J. Huberty	1984	21	unexplained revenge	Murdered randomly, primarily children, at a McDonald's restaurant.
G. Banks	1983	13	perverted love/revenge	Murdered his family and others after a dispute.
H. De La Torre	1982	25	revenge	After a dispute with a relative, set an apartment complex on fire.
A. King	1980	6	unexplained hate (?)	Murdered church members randomly while attending a service.
F. Cowan	1977	6	lethal employee	Shot six coworkers.

W. Bishop	1976	5	perverted love	Beat his entire family to death, buried them in a shallow grave, then disappeared.
E. Allaway	1976	7	unexplained sane/insane	Randomly shot individuals in a library. Found not guilty be reason of insanity.
J. Ruppert	1975	11	perverted love	Killed his entire family at an Easter dinner party.
R. DeFeo	1974	6	perverted love	Murdered his family while they slept. Claimed he was possessed by Satan.
M. Essex	1973	7	hate revenge	An African-American, Essex went to a nearby hotel and shot at white employees and customers.
J. List	1972	5	perverted love	Murdered his entire family and evaded capture for seventeen years before his arrest.
J. Frazier	1970	5	sane/insane	Murdered a family unknown to him. Frazier was a delusional paranoid schizophrenic.
D. Nelson	1970	8	sexual homicide	Sodomized and murdered women and children of wife's relatives and their neighbors.[XV]
L. Held	1967	6	revenge	Systematically murdered those against whom he held a grudge.
R. Smith	1966	5	sexual homicide	Shot women in a beauty salon.
R. Speck	1966	8 4	sexual homicide	Murdered eight nurses who were roommates after sexually assaulting them. Believed to have murdered four other women previously.

XV. This crime took place in Canada.

C. Whitman	1966	18	unexplained	Sniper killings at the University of Texas clock tower. Suffered from a brain tumor.
J. Graham	1955	44	revenge	Planted a bomb on that airliner that was carrying his mother, causing it to crash.
W. Cook	1950	6	crime spree	Shot hostages after forcing a ride in their automobile. Repeated the crime.
H. Unruh	1949	13	sane/insane	Shot individuals at random on the street of his home town.
Unknown	1929	7	mass execution	St. Valentine's Day massacre in which seven members of a gang were executed by a rival gang.

Appendix 1: A Survey of Some Notorious American Serial Killers

This is a survey of some of the most notorious American serial killers—it is certainly not a complete list of such criminals. However, it does provide a representative sample of the crime of serial killing and its perpetrator in summary form. Each of these murderers claimed at least ten victims during the course of their crimes:

Richard Angelo murdered at least ten individuals by injecting them with fatal drugs while working in the emergency room of the Good Samaritan Hospital in Long Island, New York. It is believed that Angelo may have murdered as many as twenty-five patients, although he was only legally linked to ten deaths.

Kenneth Bianchi and *Angelo Buono*, known in California as the *Hillside Strangler(s)*, murdered at least ten women beginning in 1977. The cousins would impersonate law enforcement officers and lure young prostitutes to their deaths, subsequently positioning their bodies on the hillsides near Hollywood.

William Bonin was known as the *Freeway Killer* in California. In the 1970s, Bonin murdered at least fourteen young male hitchhikers whom he picked up while driving his truck along highways in the southern part of the state. Bonin confessed to at least twenty-one murders but was eventually convicted of only fourteen of the crimes. On February 23, 1996, Bonin became the first inmate in the history of California to die by lethal injection.

Eugene V. Britt confessed to the murder of eleven individuals in November 1995. Law enforcement officials located three bodies and are presently investigating the other elements of Britt's confession.

Theodore (Ted) Bundy murdered at least twenty-two young women (many of college age) across a number of states. Luring his victims to their deaths through a combination of ruse and charm, Bundy targeted women who generally bore similar physical characteristics to each other.

Juan Rodriguez Chavez was charged with six murders in October 1995, and subsequently confessed to a total of eleven killings. Chavez apparently selected his victims at random and murdered all of them between March and July 1995.

Joseph Christopher was a psychologically disturbed white racist who murdered thirteen African-American men in New York in less than a year.

The *Cleveland Torso Murderer* claimed as least twelve victims between 1935 and 1938. The perpetrator was never identified or apprehended and could have been responsible for as many as forty similar murders.

Dean Corll, known as the *Candy Man*, was responsible for the mutilation and murder of twenty-seven boys and adolescents in Texas. Corll, with the help of a local teenager, would lure the boys into his home, where he would subsequently torture and murder them. He was shot and killed by his teenage companion, Elmer Wayne Henley, in 1973. Investigating officers found at least seventeen bodies secreted under Corll's boathouse, along with a number of body parts from other victims.

Juan Corona murdered twenty-five men in California by hacking them to death and burying their bodies in an orchard. Corona's murders were considered to be homosexual assaults.

Antone Costa murdered at least twenty women in various locations across the nation. Costa was heavily involved in drug use and would target women who would participate in "getting high" with him. After his arrest, Costa was diagnosed as schizophrenic; he committed suicide in his prison cell in 1974.

Jeffrey Dahmer was probably the most notorious serial killer in modern American history. Responsible for the murder of seventeen boys and young men, Dahmer would lure his victims to his home, where he would kill them and subsequently mutilate their corpses. Dahmer was convicted for his crimes and subsequently murdered by another inmate (Christopher Scarver) while in prison.

Albert DeSalvo, who became infamous as the *Boston Strangler*, murdered thirteen women by strangulation and became nationally known through the publication of a best-selling novel and a feature movie.

Donald Leroy Evans confessed to the murder of a ten-year-old girl in Louisiana in 1991. He subsequently confessed to the murder of more than eighty other individuals in a ten-year period. Law enforcement officials believe that he was responsible for at least fourteen murders.

Larry Eyler murdered nineteen men with whom he had been involved in homosexual relationships. Eyler was tried once for murder but was not convicted due to the inadmissibility of key evidence. He was subsequently tried again after several other murders. Eyler was convicted at his second trial and sentenced to death.

Joseph Franklin was a lifelong racist and former Ku Klux Klan member who primarily murdered African-Americans and, in at least one instance, a

Caucasian (the friend of an African-American man). Franklin murdered fifteen individuals, mostly in sniping attacks.

John Wayne Gacy was a contractor who often dressed as a clown to entertain children. Over several years, Gacy lured young boys and men into his home, where he would torture and murder them. Thirty of thirty-three of Gacy's victims were buried in the crawl space underneath his home before he was apprehended.

The *Green River Killer* has never been identified or apprehended. Between 1982 and 1984 he is believed to have murdered forty-eight women, mostly young prostitutes and missing adolescents, in the Seattle-Tacoma area of Washington. In the late 1980s, San Diego experienced ten additional serial murders that matched the pattern of the Washington crimes. It was never determined if the crimes were related; however, law enforcement officials believe them to be connected.

Vaughn Greenwood murdered eleven homeless indigent men in Los Angeles in the 1970s. His murders were ritualistic in nature.

Robert Hansen was responsible for the murder of seventeen young women over a ten-year period from 1973 until 1983 in Alaska. Until his capture and arrest, Hansen was considered by many to be a model family man and father to his children.

Donald Harvey was a nurse who murdered at least thirty-four patients in what he described as "mercy killings."

Patrick W. Kearney was responsible for the murders of at least twenty-eight individuals in California. Striking repeatedly between 1975 and 1977, Kearney would slay his victims, dismember them, and place their remains in trash bags along various highways in Southern California.

Edmund Kemper, known as the *Coed Killer*, murdered ten women (mostly of college age) in Northern California. After murdering his victims, Kemper would decapitate them and, in some cases, engage in cannibalism. Kemper confessed to his crimes in 1973, while traveling in Colorado.

Paul John Knowles selected most of his female victims at random by entering their homes and holding them hostage at gunpoint. After attempting to rape his victims, Knowles would rob and strangle them. He was eventually shot and killed by agents of the Federal Bureau of Investigation (FBI) in Georgia.

Randy Kraft, known in California as the *Scorecard Killer*, murdered at least sixteen young men who he would lure with drugs and subsequently kill by strangulation. Kraft kept coded, detailed notes about each of the murders that he committed.

Leonard Lake and *Charles Ng* are believed to be responsible for the murder of at least twenty-five victims, both men and women, in California. Lake committed suicide in 1985, after he was arrested for shoplifting. Ng was later arrested in Canada and subsequently extradited to California to stand trial in 1991.

Henry Lee Lucas and *Ottis Toole* are believed to have murdered more than 200 individuals over the course of decades. Together, the two confessed to over 500 homicides; however, law enforcement officials discount many of the confessions. It is uncertain how many individuals fell victim to Lucas and Toole.

Richard Ramirez, known as the *Night Stalker*, murdered at least sixteen individuals in Southern California by breaking into their homes, raping, torturing, and finally slaying his victims.

Joel Rifkin murdered at least seventeen young prostitutes in the New York area. Rifkin was stopped by a police officer for a minor traffic violation and found to be transporting the body of one of his victims.

John Gerard Schaefer was convicted of two mutilation murders in 1973. However, Schaefer is also believed to be responsible for thirty or more murders that occurred in Florida prior to his conviction. It is believed that Schaefer would lure young, single women from their cars by using his police identification and then mutilate and murder them by the roadside.

Arthur Shawcross murdered eleven women and two children; the women were all murdered in a period of less than two years. Shawcross engaged in cannibalism and considered himself possessed by an ancient spirit that commanded him to kill.

Gerald Stano murdered forty-one women, none of whom he sexually molested. Stano expressed a deep and pathological hatred for women throughout his life.

William Lester Suff was arrested in California in 1993, after a routine traffic stop. He is believed to have murdered at least thirteen young women, mostly prostitutes, between 1984 and the date of his arrest.

The *Twin Cities Killer* has never been identified or apprehended. The cities of St. Paul and Minneapolis, Minnesota, experienced at least thirty-four murders between 1986 and 1994. Most of the victims were young prostitutes who were mutilated and dismembered in a similar fashion. Law enforcement officials are uncertain if these crimes were the responsibility of one or more serial killers.

Wayne Williams was suspected of being the *Atlanta Child Murderer* and responsible for the deaths of twenty-eight African-American children and young adults, whose bodies were generally dumped in the Chattahoochee River. Although never formally charged with these serial murders, Williams was subsequently convicted of another capital crime. After Williams's arrest, the serial killing of Atlanta's children came to an immediate end.

Randall Woodfield, an ex-football player, was known as the *I-5 Bandit* in Oregon for his relentless crime sprees along the interstate highway of the same name. He was arrested in 1981 on murder charges and believed to be responsible for the murder of at least thirteen individuals.

Appendix 2: Organized and Disorganized Serial Killers

In their landmark book, *Sexual Homicide: Patterns and Motives*, authors Robert K. Ressler, Ann W. Burgess, and John E. Douglas outlined the categorization of serial killers into two typologies: *organized* and *disorganized*. This categorization scheme provided for two characteristics of each type of murderer—*profile characteristics* and *crime scene characteristics*—by which the murderer could be profiled and his crime better understood. An understanding of this categorization scheme aids in the ability to profile an unknown offender and thereby enhances the ability of law enforcement personnel to eliminate certain suspects and focus more diligently on those individuals who most closely match the profile of the murderer.

According to the authors, the organized offender tends to exhibit the following profile characteristics:

1. good intelligence;
2. significant social competency;
3. generally employed in a skilled trade or other stable employment;
4. sexually functional and competent;
5. is of a high birth order status, often being the firstborn son;
6. father indicates a history of stable employment;
7. exhibits a childhood history indicating inconsistent or variable discipline;
8. is capable of controlling his mood, emotions, and reactions during the commission of the crime;
9. may use alcohol in conjunction with the commission of the crime;
10. may have experienced a situational stressor that precipitated the commission of the crime;
11. is probably living with a partner;
12. is mobile and owns an automobile that is well maintained;
13. will tend to follow the reports of his crime in the news media; and,

14. may change his employment or living situation after the commission of the crime.[1]

The crime scene attributable to the organized offender will exhibit the following characteristics:

1. evidence that the crime was well planned;
2. evidence that the victim was unknown to the perpetrator;
3. a high degree of personalization of the victim will be apparent;
4. indications that a controlled conversation took place with the victim;
5. an overall crime scene appearance indicating that the perpetrator was in control of the situation during the commission of the crime;
6. indications that the perpetrator demanded the submission of his victim;
7. evidence of the use of restraints on the victim;
8. indications of aggressive criminal acts against the victim prior to his or her death;
9. will probably attempt to hide the body in some manner;
10. will leave minimal or no evidence of a weapon (or other significant evidence); and, will probably transport the victim's body in some manner.[2]

As can be seen from the personal characteristics and crime scene evidence of the organized killer, this individual is able to maintain control of himself and the situation into which he lures his victim. There is evidence of careful planning, a high level of interest in his own role in the crime, and an abiding interest to succeed in evading apprehension. On the other hand, the characteristics attributed to the disorganized killer indicate a quite different personality and methodology. Here are the profile characteristics of the disorganized murderer:

1. average intelligence;
2. underdeveloped or immature social skills;
3. poor or erratic employment history;
4. sexually dysfunctional or incompetent;
5. is of a low birth order status;
6. father experienced an erratic or unstable employment history;
7. may have experienced harsh and erratic discipline in his childhood;
8. is anxious during the commission of the crime and may be unable to control his mood or emotional state;
9. tends not to use alcohol in conjunction with the commission of the crime;
10. does not demonstrate a situational stressor related to the commission of the crime;
11. is probably living alone;
12. will probably live and/or work near the crime scene;
13. will demonstrate minimal or no interest in following the reports of his crime in the news media; and,
14. will exhibit little or no change in lifestyle after the commission of the crime.[3]

The crime scene attributable to the disorganized offender will exhibit the following characteristics:

1. evidence that the crime was spontaneous and unplanned;

2. evidence that the victim was known to the perpetrator;
3. a high degree of depersonalization of the victim will be apparent;
4. indications that minimal conversation took place with the victim;
5. a crime scene that generally indicates a lack of control and exhibits elements of randomness;
6. indications that the perpetrator attacked his victim in a sudden and violent manner;
7. minimal or no evidence of the use of restraints on the victim;
8. may indicate sexual activity after the death of the victim;
9. will not attempt to hide the body;
10. will leave evidence of a weapon or other significant evidence at the crime scene; and,
11. will probably leave the victim's body at the crime scene.[4]

NOTES

1. Robert K. Ressler, Ann W. Burgess, and John E. Douglas, *Sexual Homicide: Patterns and Motives* (New York: Lexington, 1988), 122.
2. Ibid.
3. Ibid.
4. Ibid.

Appendix 3: Chronology of Patrick Purdy

The following events and incidents in the background of mass murderer Patrick Purdy were first published in a report to the attorney general of the state of California dated October 1989. This report was prepared by Nelson Kempsky, chief deputy attorney general of the state of California, and was reprinted in the May 1990 issue of *Field and Stream* magazine.[1] These events clearly indicate that Patrick Purdy was a man who favored violence and lawlessness throughout his life. However, they do not explain the pathological racism that was the genesis of his incredible crimes against children:

April 1977- suspect in an assault incident (not arrested).

*December 1978-*arrested for possession of a dangerous weapon and stolen property.

*March 1979-*arrested for possession of a dangerous weapon.

*July 1979-*arrested for possession of a dangerous weapon and extortion.

*August 1979-*accepted for treatment into a program for alcoholism.

*August 1980-*arrested and convicted for prostitution.

*August 1982-*arrested for cultivation, possession, and sale of marijuana.

*October 1982-*arrested for vandalism.

*February 1983-*arrested for public drunkenness.

*February 1983-*arrested for possession of a dangerous weapon.

*September 1983-*suspected of vandalism, but no charges were filed.

*April 1984-*purchased a .25-caliber handgun.

*October 1984-*arrested for attempted robbery.

*October 1984-*convicted of being an accessory to a felony.

*November 1984-*diagnosed as suffering from a substance-induced personality disorder.

July 1986-purchased a .22-caliber pistol.

October 1986-purchased a 9mm pistol.

April 1987-arrested for a variety of offenses, including assault.

August 1987-purchased an MAC-10, 9mm pistol.

August 1988-purchased a semiautomatic rifle.

December 1988-purchased a 9mm pistol.

January 1989-committed mass murder in a Stockton, California, schoolyard.

NOTES

1. Reprinted in "The Patrick Purdy Rap Sheet." Internet (http://www.almond.srv.cs.cmu.edu/patrick_purdy.rapsheet), 2 August 1996.

Appendix 4: The Five Most Deadly U.S. Mass Murders

The five most deadly crimes of mass murder in U.S. history are listed below. In one of these incidents, the perpetrator is unknown; in a second, the perpetrators have been charged but not yet convicted. In all other incidents, the perpetrator has been identified. Crimes of mass murder that occurred outside of the U.S. national boundaries are excluded:

1. The downing of TWA Flight 800 on July 17, 1996, in which 230 passengers and crew were killed (perpetrators, if any, are unknown). This incident has not yet been proven to be a criminal act (see Chapter 3, Table 3.2).
2. The bombing of the federal building in Oklahoma City, Oklahoma, on April 19, 1995, in which 168 individuals were killed (perpetrators charged but not convicted; see Chapter 1, Table 1.12).
3. The arson murder of patrons of the Happy Land social club in the Bronx on March 6, 1990, in which eighty-seven individuals were killed (Julio Gonzalez, see Chapter 2, Table 2.8).
4. The bombing of a United Airlines flight on November 1, 1955, in which forty-four passengers and crew were killed (John Gilbert Graham, see Chapter 11, Table 11.1).
5. The downing of a Pacific Southwest Airlines flight on December 7, 1987, in which forty-three passengers and crew were killed (David Burke, see Chapter 4, Table 4.4).

Appendix 5: Timeline of the Oklahoma City Bombing

On August 10, 1995, an indictment was filed in the U.S. District Court for the Western District of Oklahoma. This indictment charged Timothy McVeigh and Terry Nichols with the bombing of the Alfred P. Murrah Federal Building on April 19, 1995, in which 168 individuals died and over 400 were injured. The document also outlined a series of events leading up to the bombing that provide a timeline of the activities of McVeigh and Nichols. All dates specified in this timeline are approximate.

September 22, 1994. McVeigh rented a storage unit in Herington, Kansas, under the fictitious name of "Shawn Rivers."

September 30, 1994. McVeigh and Nichols purchased some 2,000 pounds of ammonium nitrate in McPherson, Kansas. This was the same material used in the truck bomb that demolished the federal building in Oklahoma City. The ammonium nitrate was purchased in forty separate bags weighing fifty pounds each, under the fictitious name of "Mike Havens."

September 1994: Late in the month, McVeigh made a series of telephone calls in an attempt to purchase detonation cord and racing fuel to complete the homemade bomb.

October 1, 1994: McVeigh and Nichols stole explosives from a storage magazine in Marion, Kansas.

October 3-4, 1994: McVeigh and Nichols moved the stolen explosives to Kingman, Arizona, and, on October 4, rented a storage unit to house the explosives.

October 16, 1994: Nichols registered at a motel in Salina, Kansas, under the fictitious name of "Terry Havens."

October 17, 1994: Nichols rented a storage unit in Council Grove, Kansas, under the fictitious name of "Joe Kyle."

October 18, 1994: McVeigh and Nichols purchased an additional 2,000 pounds of ammonium nitrate in McPherson, Kansas, under the fictitious name of "Mike Havens." They were now in possession of 4,000 pounds of ammonium nitrate.

October 1994 (dates uncertain): McVeigh and Nichols planned to rob a firearms dealer in Arkansas to finance their criminal activities.

November 5, 1994: McVeigh and Nichols stole firearms, ammunition, cash, and precious metals from a firearms dealer in Arkansas.

November 7, 1994: Nichols rented a storage unit in Council Grove, Kansas, under the fictitious name of "Ted Parker." This unit was used to conceal the property stolen on November 5, 1994.

November 16, 1994: Nichols rented a storage unit in Las Vegas, Nevada.

November 21, 1994: Nichols wrote a letter to McVeigh, to be delivered only in the event of Nichol's death, discussing the storage units in Council Grove, Kansas, and giving instructions about how to deal with them. Nichols then left the United States for the Philippines.

December 16, 1994: McVeigh drove to the Alfred P. Murrah Federal Building in Oklahoma City, to become familiar with the area while traveling to Kansas to take possession of the firearms stolen on November 5, 1994.

Early 1995 (dates uncertain): Nichols (now back from the Philippines), McVeigh, and Michael Fortier received cash from the sale of the firearms stolen on November 5, 1994.

February 9, 1995: Nichols paid the rent due on storage unit No. 40 in Council Grove, Kansas.

March 1995 (date uncertain): McVeigh obtained a driver's license under the fictitious name of "Robert Kling" with a date of birth of April 19, 1972. The date of the bombing of the federal building in Oklahoma City was April 19, 1995.

April 14, 1995: McVeigh paid cash for a 1977 Mercury Marquis in Junction City, Kansas. On that same day, he telephoned Nichols at his residence in Herington, Kansas. He then telephoned a business in Junction City, and, using the fictitious name "Bob Kling," inquired about renting a truck that was capable of transporting 5,000 pounds of cargo. Finally, McVeigh rented a motel room in Junction City.

April 15, 1995: McVeigh placed a cash deposit for a truck rental using the fictitious name "Bob Kling."

April 17, 1995: McVeigh took possession of a twenty-foot rental truck in Junction City, Kansas.

April 18, 1995: McVeigh and Nichols constructed the truck bomb at Geary Lake State Park in Kansas. It was comprised of barrels filled with a mixture of ammonium nitrate, fuel, and other explosives. The explosives were loaded into the rental truck.

April 19, 1995: McVeigh parked the truck bomb directly outside the Alfred P. Murrah Federal Building in Oklahoma City and caused the truck bomb to explode. The federal building was nearly destroyed; 168 individuals were killed and over 400 others were injured in the explosion.

Selected Bibliography

American Psychiatric Association (APA), *Diagnostic and Statistical Manual of Mental Disorders (DSM IV)* 4th edition, Washington, DC: APA, 1994.

Boxer, P. A. "Assessment of Potential Violence in the Paranoid Worker." *Journal of Occupational Medicine*, 2 (1993): 127.

Cassel, Andrew. "Woman in Illinois Rampage Suspected in Poisonings." *Philadelphia Inquirer Online* (Internet edition), 22 May 1988, A01.

Cassel, Andrew. "Woman Kills Pupil, Wounds 6." *Philadelphia Inquirer Online* (Internet edition), 21 May 1988, A01.

Croft, Adrian. "California Gunman Sought Revenge, Officials Say." *San Francisco Examiner Online* (Internet edition), 3 July 1993, A03.

Dubin, Murray. "Clues to a Massacre Motive." *Philadelphia Inquirer Online* (Internet edition), 20 July 1984, A01.

Eshleman, Russell E., Jr. "Step by Step: The Shootings at Springfield Mall." *Philadelphia Inquirer Online* (Internet edition), 25 April 1985, A01.

Forrest, Susan and Nagourney, Eric. "Insanity Defense Is Possibility." *Philadelphia Inquirer Online* (Internet edition), 11 December 1993, A04.

Fox, James Alan, and Levin, Jack. *Mass Murder: America's Growing Menace*. New York: Plenum, 1985.

Fox, James Alan, and Levin, Jack. *Overkill: Mass Murder and Serial Killing Exposed*. New York: Plenum, 1994.

Gaute, J. H. H. H. *Murderers Who's Who*. New York: Methuen, 1979.

Goldman, H. H., ed. *Review of General Psychiatry*. Norwalk, VA: Appleton and Lange, 1988.

Hays, Tom. "Police ID Harlem Man Who Killed 7, Himself." *San Francisco Examiner Online* (Internet edition), 11 December 1995, 1.

Hamilton, William. "Familiar Echoes of Rage." *Philadelphia Inquirer Online* (Internet edition), 12 December 1993, A01.

Hawkins, Stephen. "Mississippi Firefighter Kills Wife and Four Colleagues, Police Say." *Philadelphia Inquirer Online* (Internet edition), 25 April 1996, A01.

Holmes, Ronald M. *Profiling Violent Crimes: An Investigative Tool.* Newbury Park, CA: Sage, 1990.

Holtzman, Phyllis. "Seegrist Gets 3 Life Terms in Mall Spree." *Philadelphia Inquirer Online* (Internet edition), 1 November 1986, A01.

Kanaley, Reid. "Her Demons Stilled, Seegrist Hopes for Freedom." *Philadelphia Inquirer Online* (Internet edition), 18 March 1991, B01.

Kelleher, Michael D. *New Arenas for Violence: Occupational Homicide in the American Business Community.* Westport, CT: Greenwood/Praeger, 1996.

Kelleher, Michael D. *Profiling the Lethal Employee: Case Studies in Workplace Violence.* Westport, CT: Greenwood/Praeger, 1996.

Kennedy, J. Michael. "Missouri Slayings: Doubts, a Probe, Then a Confession." *Los Angeles Times* (Internet edition), 12 October 1987, 1.

Kozel Multimedia, Inc. *Mind of a Killer.* CD-ROM. Chatsworth, CA: Cambrix, 1995.

Kurtis, Bill. "Long Island Railroad Massacre." In Bill Kurtis, *American Justice.* Television series available in video. Arts and Entertainment Network, televised 25 April 1996.

Kurtis, Bill. "Mass Murder: An American Tragedy." *American Justice.* Television series available in video. Arts and Entertainment Network, televised 4 August 1996.

Levine, Susan, and Matza, Michael. "Rage at Women Set Off Massacre." *Philadelphia Inquirer Online* (Internet edition), 8 December 1989, A01.

Lunde, Donald T. *Murder and Madness.* San Francisco: San Francisco Book Company, 1976.

Mantell, M. *Ticking Bombs—Defusing Violence in the Workplace.* New York: Irwin, 1994.

Microsoft. *Encarta 96 Encyclopedia.* MS-Windows 95 (computer software). 1996 Edition. Redmond, WA: Microsoft, 1995.

Microsoft. *Microsoft Bookshelf.* MS-Windows 95 (computer software). 1995 ed. Redmond, WA: Microsoft, 1995.

Milton, Pat. "Suspect In Attack on NY is Indicted on 93 Counts." *Reuters News Service* (Internet edition), 19 January 1994, A16.

Peterson, Bill. "Relief Felt as Farm Boy Is Absolved." *Washington Post* (Internet edition), 7 October 1987, 1.

Ressler, Robert K., Burgess, Ann W., and Douglas, John E. *Sexual Homicide: Patterns and Motives.* New York: Lexington, 1988.

Samuel, Terrence. "NY Gunman Got Pistol Legally." *Philadelphia Inquirer Online* (Internet edition), 9 December 1993, A01.

Samuel, Terrence. "Jury Deliberates 10 Hours, Finds Ferguson Guilty in Train Killings." *Philadelphia Inquirer Online* (Internet edition), 18 February 1995, A01.

Seery, Tom. "Friends Think Iowa Killing Suspect Was Jealous of Kin." *Philadelphia Inquirer Online* (Internet edition), 1 January 1988, A04.

Spencer, Hal. "Scary Man Charged in Shooting Spree." *Philadelphia Inquirer Online* (Internet edition), 27 March 1993, A05.

Van Biema, David. "A Fool for a Client." *Time Domestic* (Internet edition), 145, no. 6, 6 February 1995.

Waggoner, Martha. "Gunman Kills 4 in Restaurant Rampage." *Philadelphia Inquirer Online* (Internet edition), 8 August 1993, A03.

Wheeler, E. D., and Baron, S. A. *Violence in Our Schools, Hospitals and Public Places*. Ventura, CA: Pathfinder, 1994.

Woestendiek, John. "Tranquil Lives Shattered by Gunfire." *Philadelphia Inquirer Online* (Internet edition), 12 August 1991, A01.

Index

About the Author

MICHAEL D. KELLEHER specializes in strategic management, human resource management, staff education, threat assessment, and management crisis resolution for organizations in the private and public sectors. He has written *Profiling the Lethal Employee* (1997) and *New Arenas for Violence* (1996), both published by Praeger.

ISBN 0-275-95925-2

EAN

9 780275 959258

HARDCOVER BAR CODE